Oliver Kozlarek, Jörn Rüsen, Ernst Wolff (eds.)

Shaping a Humane World

Being Human: Caught in the Web of Cultures
Humanism in the Age of Globalization

Volume 15

Editorial

Globalization demands for setting up new cultural orientations. Different traditions and forms of life struggle for recognition throughout the world and have to meet the necessity of values and norms with universal validity. Similarities and differences in understanding the world have to be analyzed and recognized which requires a new reflection on what it means to be a human being concerning its anthropological universality, but also its diverseness and changeability.

The books of the series **Being Human: Caught in the Web of Cultures – Humanism in the Age of Globalization** are committed to a new Humanism, which not only highlights humaneness in its cultural and historical varieties but also presents it as a transculturally valid principle of human interaction in all cultural life-forms.

Oliver Kozlarek, Jörn Rüsen, Ernst Wolff (eds.)

Shaping a Humane World

Civilizations – Axial Times – Modernities – Humanisms

[transcript]

In Cooperation with the Institute for Advanced Study in the Humanities, Essen, the Institute for Advanced Studies in Humanities and Social Sciences, National Taiwan University, the Faculty of Humanities of the University Duisburg/Essen

Humanism in the Era of Globalization –
An Intercultural Dialogue on Humanity, Culture, and Value
sponsored by Stiftung Mercator

Bibliographic information published by the Deutsche Nationalbibliothek
The Deutsche Nationalbibliothek lists this publication in the Deutsche Nationalbibliografie; detailed bibliographic data are available in the Internet at http://dnb.d-nb.de

Cover concept: Kordula Röckenhaus, Bielefeld
Proofread and typeset by Angelika Wulff
Printed by Majuskel Medienproduktion GmbH, Wetzlar
ISBN 978-3-8376-1941-6

Global distribution outside Germany, Austria and Switzerland:

Transaction Publishers
New Brunswick (U.S.A.) and London (U.K.)

Transaction Publishers
Rutgers University
35 Berrue Circle
Piscataway, NJ 08854

Tel.: (732) 445-2280
Fax: (732) 445-3138
for orders (U.S. only):
toll free 888-999-6778

Content

Foreword

OLIVER KOZLAREK/JÖRN RÜSEN/ERNST WOLFF

This book is the product of a joint project on »Humanism in the Era of Globalization – An Intercultural Dialogue on Humanity, Culture, and Values«, which took place between 2006 and 2009. It was sponsored by the Stiftung Mercator and organized by the Kulturwissenschaftliches Institut in Essen (Institute for Advanced Studies in the Humanities in Essen, Germany). Among the activities of this project were conferences which were meant to bring together scholars from different countries interested in discussing the issue of »humanism« from the specific perspective of intercultural encounter, comparison, and exchange. The starting point of and common ground for this discussion was a common interest in finding transculturally valid ideas and principles of cultural orientation, so that the challenges of the growing one-world in the globalization process can be met. This process has brought along the danger of uniformization and uniformity, thus denying the rich variety and difference of traditions and experiences which have proved so important and effective in making sense of the contingent, highly conflictual, and thus entangled ways of growing together. Therefore the transcultural perspective asks to be shaped by the recognition of these differences.

Humanism may be an idea capable of bringing together different traditions in, and experiences of, global modernity in order to reach agreement on a comprehensive idea of humanity as an intellectual answer to globalization. At the same time it may serve as the framework for articulating cultural differences on the common ground that being a human being endows man with inbuilt dignity, which demands respect and recognition. This encounter is impossible without dealing with and working through the tensions and negative historical experiences of domination and suppression in cultural interaction. Therefore mutual criticism can become an effective means to examine humanistic traditions and their chances for further development. But this criticism should be pursued as an entrance to discussion, deeper understanding and a chance for recognition.

This intercultural encounter needs a historical framework. To find an outline for such a framework was the main intention of the conference on »Civilizations, Axial times, Humanisms«. This conference was organized in cooperation with the Centre for Comparative Studies on World Civilizations of the Chinese Academy of the Social Sciences in Beijing as its »Third International Conference of the International Forum on World Civilizations«. It took place at Iserlohn over 8–10 September 2007. This book took some important inspiration from the conference, but it is not a publication of the conference papers. Some papers are included in revised form, while others were acquired later on. Not all aspects of a historical framework for intercultural humanism could be covered. Rather, the conference was intended to shape some essential elements of the structure of such a universal historical perspective. In doing so, the authors and the editors wish to promote the outline of this future-directed intercultural humanism.We want to thank the Chinese Academy of the Social Sciences in Beijing and the Institute for Advanced Study in the Humanities in Essen for their engagement in planning and pursuing the conference, the Mexican Consejo Nacional de Ciencia y Tecnología (CONACyT) for their support of the book project, and, of course, our authors for their contributions. Additionally, we want to thank Angelika Wulff, Aslı Aymaz, and Iain Sinclair for their work in copyediting the manuscripts and brushing up the English.

Bochum, Morelia, and Pretoria in autumn 2011
Oliver Kozlarek, Jörn Rüsen, Ernst Wolff

Introduction

Towards a Humane World of Many Worlds

OLIVER KOZLAREK/JÖRN RÜSEN/ERNST WOLFF

We are living today in a world that is shared by all human beings. »One world, one humanity« is no longer an empty, abstract slogan; it has become a reality. However, we are also still living in a world in which the opportunities to participate in this single world are very unevenly distributed. This is true in many ways: politically, economically, socially and culturally. But it is also true for the ways in which human beings are trying to make sense of this common world.

Sense generation is important for all human beings. It is one of the conditions for living a full and humanly dignified life. Or to put it differently: lack of sense is dehumanizing. Sense generation is a core aspect of the construction of the world. Human beings are not merely living *in a* world to which they simply adapt more or less successfully. They also have to reconfigure their worlds constantly anew[1] as something meaningful for them. Creating the world as a cosmos of sense and meaning that human beings exist in is a primary precondition for acting and thinking meaningfully.

The world in which we are living today is less and less limited by local, national, regional, ethnic or cultural constraints. We are *all* living more and more in a world that spans the whole planet. This is true not only for wealthy jet-setters but also for migrant labourers, landless peasants and everyone in between.[2] However, the means to make sense of this common world of all human beings are still produced in very

1 Dux, Günter: *Historisch-genetische Theorie der Kultur*, Weilerswist 2005.

2 Castells, Manuel: *End of Millennium*, Oxford 1998, especially chapter 2.

few places which are concentrated in the ›Global North‹ – mainly Europe and North America. It is here where the languages that bring the common world of all human beings into the picture have been invented. These languages are not separable from the historical circumstances that created them. One of the most important sets of historical processes in this context is colonialism. Wolfgang Reinhard wrote: »[Colonialism] can indeed claim to have merged the many worlds of humanity into one world, the one we live in today«.[3] Although this does not provide a full picture of factors of globalization, it does highlight the brutal injustice weaved into the very fabric of the globalized world.

An important task for the creation of a world that is ultimately going to be a world in which all human beings feel at home, *i.e.* a world in which all human beings find the means to make sense of their lives in this global setting of human affairs, would be to challenge the conventional languages. What is needed, ultimately, is a language that reflects all of our different experiences in and within global modernity.

It would be a mistake, however, to think that these languages have to be invented from scratch. In this book we would like to discuss *three* concepts that have been particularly important for the sense generation of a world in which we are living: ›civilization‹, ›modernity‹, and ›humanism‹. These concepts can be seen as gateways for the imagination of a world that encompasses all worlds without reducing their differences. All three of them represent visions of a growing together of all of humanity. However, in many of the usages that were given to these words, it was also implied that civilization, modernity and even humanism were still privileges granted to Western societies and cultures, while the ›Rest‹ of humanity was not yet ready for them. This supposed singularity of Western civilization was also the key to many discourses that legitimized the tutelage of the West over colonized or formerly colonized peoples.

But it would be a much too narrow perspective to see the West only as the perpetrator of colonialism and imperialism and the others only as victims. We should not overlook the fact that the West itself has brought forth principles for criticizing domination and has insisted time and again on the need to limit domination through the law, which

3 Reinhard, Wolfgang: *Kleine Geschichte des Kolonialismus*, Stuttgart 2008, p. 375.

has been used to push back illegitimate suppression outside and within its territories. Human and civil rights have to be mentioned in this context. Additionally, some basic principles of understanding cultural difference have been developed in the academic disciplines of the humanities which originated in the West and are still valid – even in the turn to indigenous traditions in the scholarly work of non-Western countries. The hermeneutic nature of understanding and the practices of intercultural translation are deeply rooted in the human mind and the humanities and social sciences have ceaselessly striven to reflect this fact in their methodological forms. Despite all their shortcomings and pitfalls it cannot and should not be overlooked that they advanced an important vocabulary that helps us to understand and imagine a world comprised of all human beings.

Nevertheless, there are grounds for many intellectuals and scholars to want to erase the key words of civilization, modernity and humanism from the vocabularies of the cultural and social sciences. They think that these words convey Eurocentrism, and that they consequently foster the uneven distribution of linguistic and conceptual means to address this common world of all humans, reproducing even a colonial or post-colonial grammar of domination and exploitation. But instead of proposing alternatives, they are leaving a dangerous void which in some cases leads to suspicion against any attempt to think beyond the limits of a particular culture, nation or one's own religion. The cultivation of new forms of provincialism and ethnocentrism are the consequence. Most criticism of the West and mainly of its ethnocentric marginalization of the other civilizations reproduces ethnocentrism by negating it. Many scholars and intellectuals of the non-Western world seek an understanding of today's world which has pushed away the cultural dominance of the West. But in doing so, they dialectically remain dependent upon it.

Additionally, one cannot overlook the fact that criticism of the West very often uses criteria of humanness and autonomy which can be found in the Western tradition, or may even stem from it. Therefore it appears to be not very promising to play off Western and non-Western traditions and ways of thinking against each other. It is much more promising to look for elements in all traditions, world-views and modes of thinking which can serve as starting points of an intercultural communication about valid principles of understanding the world today and to solve the urgent problems humankind is sharing.

One of these problems is the unsolved question of how the power of cultural difference can be mediated through the transcultural commonality of dominant features of modernity which all human beings are exposed to. Is there any chance to think about and conceptualize humankind as a comprehensive dimension of the lives of all people and as a manifestation of peculiarities in all forms and procedures of identity formation today? And at the same time, can fundamental and universal values be derived from this interrelationship between difference and commonality in being a human being? These questions lead to the necessity of thinking again about what civilization is with respect to different human life forms, what humankind means with respect to the shared cultural nature of human beings, what modernization has brought about in these life forms and in the idea of a comprehensive humankind, and whether humanism can be identified as a common denominator of those principles, rules and values of intercultural communication – which, if so, could prevent the bitter continuation of ethnocentrism and ›clash of civilizations‹ and change it into cultural features of critical recognition of differences in the name of a common humanity.

In this book we would like to advance the thought that civilization, humanism and modernity still provide important orientations in our current world. They were always thought to overcome parochialism and provincialism; ›Civilization‹ may facilitate efforts to reflect on the universality of human affairs without, however, negating the importance of cultural particularities. ›Humanism‹ responds to the need to understand *all human beings* as such. And ›modernity‹ helps us to envision a world that – for the first time in human history, for better or worse – is materially capable of and destined to be a world for all human beings.

In addition to these justifications, discourses in non-Western or formerly colonized societies make us understand that ›civilization‹, ›humanism‹, and ›modernity‹ are concepts that intellectuals and academics of these societies have appropriated in a very creative manner (see for instance the chapter on humanism in China by Stefan Schmidt). In other words, ›civilization‹, ›humanism‹, and ›modernity‹ are no longer solely Western concepts. They have long been an integral part of critical discourses in the colonial and post-colonial world. Instead of inventing new and incommensurable languages, we propose an intercultural renegotiation on a semantic and conceptual level. What meaning do ›civilization‹, ›humanism‹ and ›modernity‹ convey in Africa, Asia and Latin America? How do these concepts help to orient post-colonial cultures to install themselves in the common world of all human beings? And how do these concepts support the criticism of eurocentrism or any other kind of ethnocentrism?

An answer to these questions can only be found and steps in the direction of a new way of intercultural communication can only be taken if the present-day situation of the growing together of the world and its different traditions and fraught relationships between people are put into historical perspective. Only then can we hope to identify the dynamics of change and its factors, which we have to analyze thoroughly in order to find the solution to our topical problems of cultural orientation in the globalizing world. New ideas for a universal history are needed in order to understand our complex and all encompassing situation today.

More than 60 years ago the philosopher Karl Jaspers published a remarkable book. In *The Origin and Goal of History* (first German edition: 1949) he laid out a fascinating theory according to which some two and a half thousand years ago different civilizations in Asia and Europe independently developed very similar ways of conceiving the world and the human being. One of the most important consequences of this civilizational break was the belief in the universality of the human being. This breaking point in human history is called the ›axial age‹ (*Achsenzeit*) – the *fourth* concept that we think should be connected to that of ›civilization‹, ›humanism‹, and ›modernity‹. One of the undeniable merits of Jaspers' ›axial age‹ theory is that it rejected a reading of human history as centered in the excellence of European cultural development, and thus paved the way towards a mindset that takes into consideration the whole of humanity – and that it does so not in mere abstract terms, but through the comparison of diverse particular civilizations. However, Jaspers himself did not succeed in completing this project. His study of ›axial age‹ civilizations remains weak on Islam, South America or Africa, a weakness which is not easy to remedy and which leaves human societies outside of the axial turn in an uncomfortable position with respect to the universalist breakthrough (see Stauth's contribution on ›axial ages‹ and Islam, below). It is precisely here that modernity imposes itself upon our reflections.

One of the consequences of modernity is that humanity is increasingly united into a network of interaction. This does not mean that the globalisation of modernity entails a positive normative universality – quite the contrary: through the unjust differentiation by which it tends to integrate all different people into a common network of human interaction and the consequences thereof, it actually imposes on us the question of the normative coordination of people in the global order. Never before has the unity of humanity been more evident in our practical, day-to-day lives. But at the same time we witness violent splits and fragmentations of humanity – brought about by the same practices – that perhaps have never been more overwhelming or obvious.

It is for this very reason that we contend that our contemporary global modernity is a second ›axial age‹. An important difference from the first one is that we now have not only the opportunity but also the obligation to prove the universality of all human beings in the face of the conspicuous violation of this universality. This is basically a task for the cultural and social sciences. But our second ›axial age‹ also poses another task. While communication between the ›axial age‹-civilizations about which Jaspers was concerned remained quite restricted, in modernity, understood as a second ›axial age‹, communication and dialogue among civilizations became imperative. Our common world has yet to be constructed. But this will only be possible if as many voices as possible participate in this effort. Such a confrontation of different perspectives and experiences may be called a »dialogue«, not in the sense that humanity is presented as a chat room or conference hall, but in so far as this notion reflects the will to allow for the interplay of the peaceful resources of different traditions, instead of a coercive free-for-all. Precisely by recognizing the fact that interaction between peoples (intercultural exchange) simply does not happen in most cases in the form of a dialogue on values, but simply in the context of day-to-day commerce, the need for dialogue can be appreciated (see the chapter by Wolff in this regard). The violent, monological alternatives to the recognition of human plurality tarnish the beginning of the twenty-first century, just as it mars most of human history.

Such a dialogue on the different perspectives on human universality requires a number of efforts. First, since humanity as a whole is at stake, the different perspectives of different peoples (of which the current book is but a limited sample) – in other words, the vision of different traditions to understand what a humanly dignified life means, as well as different experiences with and within global modernity –

should be taken into account. Second, in order to appreciate the ›axial age‹ and ›modernity‹ as an ›axial age‹, it needs to be placed in the perspective of the long development of civilizations (*i.e.* the history of all of humanity). Only thus could the horizon be drawn in which to perceive a common future which is to a great extent technically and economically already here, but politically, symbolically, and ethically still to come. Third, in adopting this universal historical perspective, two misconceptions need to be avoided. On the one hand, the temptation of idealizing a future consensus on the ideal of humanity, a homogenous civilization, or a template for modernity needs to be discarded and the pluralities of *humanisms*, *civilizations* and *modernities* have to be made to bear on each other. On the other hand, a universal historical perspective departs from equating one particular historical path (European industrial modernization or rationalization) with moral development, since this simply boils down to reiterating an ideology of paternalism by which colonial violence was justified in a bygone era. Rather, discourses and practices standing outside of a (narrow conception of) Western rationality should be allowed full participation in the necessary dialogue on humanity. At the same time, representatives of marginal or marginalized cultural, linguistic or religious expressions should be called upon to recognize their *de facto* belonging to a world in which they participate and to which they contribute ideas and visions on its future correspondingly. Cultural chauvinism and cultural autism are equally inappropriate responses to the world in which we live and the future one we will have to build.

Humanisms, civilizations and modernities are thus still important conceptual tools that remind us of the need to think humanity as a whole. But they will only be effective building blocks for a common world of all human beings if we take into account how they are understood by other cultures and civilizations. This book wishes to take a step in this direction and this ambition is reflected in the three sections of which the book is composed. In the first section, a long view of human history and civilization is adopted under the title »The shape of history«. Whereas the concern in this section is to contribute to general anthropological considerations that come to light in a universal historical and civilizational perspective, the second section focuses on epochal turns in human history. This section is entitled »The breakthrough of axial ages and modernities«. Since the notion of epochal turns already implies cultural plurality, the second section also prepares considerations regarding the »Challenges and paradigms of humanity«, thematized in section three.

A short overview of the respective chapters may be helpful to get an initial grasp on the book:

Opening the section on »The shape of history«, ERNST WOLFF adopts the long historical perspective on humanity in order to examine the significance of human technicity for our understanding of civilizational change and inter-cultural dialogue. Hominization is the collection of civilizing processes by which people of different cultures in different times and places are formed. This happens through the changing combination of human nature with the three interdependent anthropogenetic components – society, signs and technics. In this chapter, an outline is given of the manner in which the third of these components is constitutive of all cultural events. Human technicity consists of three interdependent elements: habitus (technical disposition), instruments (the system of technical objects) and worldliness (the understanding interaction with the technical system). The changing interrelation of these elements through a structural sequence of prefiguration, configuration and refiguration describes a hermeneutics of technicity, comparable to the hermeneutic structure of narrativity demonstrated by Paul Ricoeur. As such, technics is an aspect of all civilizing processes: not only is all culture dependent on the technical means of its existence, but all technical events, by virtue of their instrumentality, carry meaning, transmit, and humanize. Consequently, any inter-cultural dialogue – as an intervention in the processes of civilization – presupposes and depends on technical means of existence that have to be taken into account if the dialogic process is to remain self-reflective and in touch with the problem of symbolic efficiency. This means that to render the transmission of ideas efficient is also to interfere with the ideas that are conveyed.

JÖRN RÜSEN presents a philosophy of history which is centered around the idea of an intercultural humanism. This idea takes up the challenges of globalization, which call for new modes of cultural identity formation. Since modern Western humanism – as it has come about at the end of the eighteenth and the beginning of the 19th century – has been critically reviewed and misjudged, it is reinterpreted and presented as a paradigm for a humanistic concept of cultural identity. This concept is based on a temporalized idea of humanity, which emphasizes a synthesis of transculturally valid values of humanity and the variety and differences of human life forms. Its strength lies in the fact that here universalism and pluralism are mediated and amalgamated into an idea of a universal history. This, however, is ruled by anthropological universals, which shape all human life forms and move their temporal dynamics from archaic times to the present. Here three main ensuing periods can be distinguished: In the first, the cultural quality of being a human being is limited to one's own group. The second is characterized by the idea of an ›axial age‹, which has developed the idea of humanity as universal so that all members of the human race are included. The third progresses with a new step in this universalization: when thematizing humanity, there is a movement from exclusion to inclusion with regard to cultural pluralism. Thus a normative idea of humanism, the plurality of civilizations with universal value systems, and the unity of humankind in a universal historical perspective are interwoven. This historical image of humankind is characterized by unity and can be used to solve basic problems of identity formation today.

The complexity of civilizations is reflected in the diversity of approaches and perspectives on it and in the fact that there is no consensus on the proper definition for »civilization«. Such is the point of departure of the chapter by ZHANG JIE. Taking as a working circumscription of civilization »the cultural achievement accumulated over the course of social evolution of mankind«, Jie argues for diachronic and synchronic perspectives on civilization. The historical or diachronic perspective on civilization is the dominant approach to civilizations, and examines the origin, genesis and metamorphoses of civilizations. Here one has to complement the history of the rise and demise of civilizations with the (in principle) infinitely continuing interpretation thereof. The latter is a source of nourishment for subsequent civilizations and, one could add, for other contemporary civilizations. As synchronic approaches to civilizations, Jie highlights literary criticism (which occupies itself through the texts with the world as it appears in the light of the texts and by so doing reveals the unfolding of a civilization) and the study of language (where the exploration of the linguistic mediation between people and the world reveals the linguistic support of civilization at any given stage). Having considered the merits of these divergent approaches, Jie makes a plea for the co-existence of multiple, complementary and interdependent perspectives on civilization, which alone would otherwise simply succumb to their own partiality. The chapter concludes with a reminder that reflection on civilization is itself a civilization-forming activity: the confusing questions in which we are entangled by civilization studies also fertilizes our contribution to civilization.

Shifting the focus from the universal historical view of humanity to »The breakthrough of axial ages and modernities« (section two), BERNARD GIESEN's paper raises an important question: Why do we need the demarcation of historical epochs like that of an axial age or modernity? Two common answers to this question are: The idea of historical epochs follows simply »a logic of human narration«. The second common answer is: modernity likes to think in epochs because it defines itself first of all as being a new era that simply by being new has already important advantages over former historical eras. Giesen, however, challenges these explanations. He emphasizes that the way in which epochs are marked is itself subject to historical transitions. The important turning point is for Giesen the ›axial age‹, when »concepts of synthesis and transcendence« started to define epochs rather than more primitive categories like »we and others« which Giesen understands as deeply »ethnocentric«. Concepts of synthesis and transcendence opened the possibility to think beyond the limits of geographically constraints of social and cultural entities. For Giesen our contemporary modern world, precisely because of its decentralized and polyphonic character, needs languages that allow us to think and imagine the whole.

GEORG STAUTH follows two intertwined questions: 1. What is the place of Islam in ›axial age‹ theory? 2. How far can ›axial age‹ theory inform our contemporary modernity, in which the conflict between Islam and the West has become preeminent? In order to answer these questions, Stauth delves deep into Jaspers's original version of ›axial age‹ theory. He underlines the humanist conviction that motivates Jaspers's project. It is the idea of thinking of »humanity as a whole« that Jaspers enthusiastically embraces after World War Two. But Stauth also emphasizes another aspect of the intellectual revolution that occurs during the ›axial age‹ simultaneously in many unconnected civilizations: the idea that through this revolution communication became the foundational principle of the new »world culture« in the making. If this is so, the question about the significance that ›axial age‹ theory could have with respect to Islam would be in how far it explains the potential for communication between Islam and other civilizations, particularly the West. The difficulty in answering this question has to do with the fact that Jaspers himself never discussed Islam directly. Another problem is, according to Stauth, that certain presuppositions of universal communicability do not apply in the case of Islam.

GEORG ESSEN explores the content of the axial-age breakthrough from a theological perspective in order to demarcate the role of religion in dialogue about the values of a plural, modern world. If the axial differentiation between a transcendent and a worldly order can find expression in such divergent views as the individualization of the human being with respect to the world (as in the great monotheisms) or as participating holistically in the world (as in Eastern religions), would it not be possible to rediscover the axial-cultural common ground behind this diversity, and with which the divergent religious views would be compatible? Likewise, both religion and secular philosophy could be shown to have been engendered by the axial-age breakthrough. As contemporary inheritors of these plural fruits of the axial age and, besides, of the multipolarity of the globalised world, the need for intercultural dialogue is urgent. As the centre from which the plurality of axial value systems emerged, religion has to be heard in the dialogue of cultures; but at the same time, on the basis of this plural axial origin of its own value, religion can recognize the plural manifestations of axial universality. »By turning the cultural plurality of the world into its own immanent problem«, Essen claims, »Christianity mainly contradicts fundamentalist drives to associate with anti-globalist tendencies of re-particularisation in the ›Clash of Cultures‹«.

VOLKER H. SCHMIDT's contribution discusses Eisenstadt's multiple modernities approach. He is particularly interested in the question raised by Eisenstadt, namely whether Japanese modernity represents a form of modernity essentially different from that of Western societies. Schmidt's claim is that it does not make much sense to talk about »multiple modernities« since modernization in Japan and in other parts of East Asia clearly follows the same lines that are characteristic of modernization processes in the West. Schmidt's paper maintains a critical distance from classical modernization theories. He is convinced that these theories have lost their credibility. However, he defends the convergence hypothesis of modernization theory, albeit to advocate his own »varieties of modernity« stance. When it comes to the »basic structure of societal organization«, East Asian societies have undertaken in recent decades a very successful effort to modernize without losing their cultural particularities. Schmidt's main point is that today modernity is global reality. It is thus still – or even more than ever before – a concept that could and, according to Schmidt, actually does orient the building of a common world of all human beings without suppressing cultural differences.

Yet such an ambition remains to be pursued, an effort that needs to be guided by insight into the »Challenges and Paradigms of Humanity«. In the first of the series of contributions in this regard, OLIVER KOZLAREK traces the concept of the ›axial age‹ back to Karl Jaspers. By doing so he shows that Jaspers' motivation for the use of this concept did not only stem from the empirical evidence of a convergence of the axial civilizations some 2500 years ago. Rather, it seems that for Jaspers much more important was the »belief« that humanity has a common »origin« and a common »goal«. In the second step of his argumentation, Kozlarek tries to show that in the current use of this concept, especially in the sociological debate about »multiple modernities« for which Shmuel N. Eisenstadt has become an important icon, this humanist conviction is being lost. Another problem that Kozlarek sees in the current use of the ›axial age‹ hypothesis is that it diverts attention from our present global modernity by losing itself more and more in discussions about the ›axial age‹ civilizations that existed 25 centuries ago. With the help of the civilization theory that the Brazilian anthropologist Darcy Ribeiro presented, Kozlarek proposes to focus attention once again on our current modernity. He understands modernity as a »second ›axial age‹« in which all humanity has to build a world in which all human beings can feel at home. However, modernity as a second ›axial age‹ is still an unfulfilled promise. It has yet to come to terms with the multiple experiences that human beings around the world have made in the processes of growing together.

GEORG W. OESTERDIEKHOFF's essay presents a theory of cultural evolution which is valid across cultural differences and emphasizes the structural change of cognitive capacities. It describes the different components of his theory (like Elias' theory of civilization and Piaget's and Kohlberg's developmental psychology) and outlines its importance for understanding universal history. That it can be usefully applied becomes evident when the ideas of humanity and moral principles come to the fore. Moral behaviour has substantially changed in practical life according to a structural change in human cognition – as has already been thematized in developmental psychology. Oesterdiekhoff presents a shocking example of inhumanity considered ›normal‹ in the minds of premodern people: He hints at the gladiator fights in ancient Rome, the cruelty of which is not singular, but typical for human behaviour in the framework of a non-universalistic morality. By looking at this inhumanity and at the attitudes and views in modern societies, Oesterdiekhoff deduces the idea of progress – which, of course, is highly unfashionable today. But the evidence presented in favour of it should not be set aside. So modernity and humanism are given a new face, which remarkably differs from the topical criticism dominating the intellectual discourse about them.

HUBERT CANCIK's paper gives a condensed image of Western humanism from ancient times to the present. It starts with a description of what Europe (or the West) means by referring to antiquity and presents its main features as shaped by and preformed in Homer's poetry. For Cancik, European humanism has not really been shaped by the intellectual movement of the Renaissance and that of later centuries, as has often been repeated, since even the notion of humanism and its specific meaning in intellectual discourse only emerged at the end of the 18th century and the beginning of the 19th century. Cancik vividly emphasizes that »occidental humanism first and fundamentally is an educational movement, rooted in classical tradition«.[4] He gives reasons for this understanding of humanism by analyzing the history of its basic terms (e.g. humanitas). He finally concludes that there is a close relationship between the anthropology of the classical literature regarding Roman Stoic philosophy, on the one hand, and the idea of basic human and civil rights of the European Enlightenment, on the other. It is only in the form of this synthesis that humanism has reached the shape of a universal ethics. Thus it is capable of presenting the peculiarity of historical origins and developments as a basic starting point for universal principles of cultural orientation today.

The representatives of »Contemporary New Confucianism« engaged with Western thought in an attempt to find a modern conceptual expression for the Confucian tradition. Tang Junyi's contribution in this regard – and the theme of STEFAN SCHMIDT's chapter – is centred upon the exploration and advocacy of the Confucian humanism as the essence of Chinese culture. If Confucian humanism is argued by Tang

4 See p. 249.

to be superior to Western humanism, this result is delivered only at the end of a trajectory of critical dialogue with and appropriation of elements of Western philosophy. This humanism is not so much a set of beliefs as an attitude guiding human action. It consists of cultivating a seed that all people carry in them. Three considerations develop and support this point. First, New Confucianism attempts to reveal the primordial normative or moral nature of self-awareness that guides human agency, as well as the applicability of traditional Confucian values to contemporary circumstances. Fellow-humanness, dignity or humaneness is at the core of this self-awareness. Second, the sense of the self that guides action could be epistemological or moral, where the former tends to limit perspective on others to what could be known about them, and the latter consists of transcending individuality through compassion, *i.e.* by a pre-epistemological responsiveness to the other's suffering. Third, taking a page from the book of Buddhism, Tang accordingly distinguishes between the attitudes of clinging to individualism – with the consequence of viewing interpersonal contact primarily as struggle – or of not-clinging, by which the other is given priority in responsible action. Schmidt shows the way for a continued exploration, following in the steps of Tang, through a critique of the latter's unrealistic claims for the saving potential of this New Confucianism in the broader political order.

BIBLIOGRAPHY

Castells, Manuel: *End of Millennium*, Oxford 1998.

Dux, Günter: *Historisch-genetische Theorie der Kultur*, Weilerswist 2005.

Jaspers, Karl: *Vom Ursprung und Ziel der Geschichte*, München 1949 [English: *The Origin and Goal of History*, Westport, Conn 1976].

Reinhard, Wolfgang: *Kleine Geschichte des Kolonialismus*, Stuttgart 2008.

I. The Shape of History

I.1 Habitus – Means – Worldliness

Technics in the Formation of ›Civilizations‹

ERNST WOLFF

> Tools and instruments are so intensely worldly objects that we can classify whole civilizations using them as criteria.
>
> HANNAH ARENDT

1. Introduction: Civilising Processes as Processes of Hominisation

The human being that we are today has not always existed. It came into existence through a double process of hominisation: first through the very long process of biological evolution, which was subsequently overtaken by a shorter and diversifying process of ethological or cultural change.[1] The roots of the latter process or lines of processes,

1 I have formerly used the term »ethological evolution« (»Hominisation and humanisation: a perspective from the sociology of technics«, in: The Journal for transdisciplinary research in Southern Africa 2.2 (2006), p. 233) to refer to the sequence of changes undergone by *homo sapiens* since the completion of the species' biological evolution. For as long as the former term serves only to oppose two forms of progression (i.e. the biological and the ethological) and to insist on the fact that human development has not ended with the end of biological evolution, one could accept the use of the term »ethological evolution«. However, I reject any evolutionary perspective on the subsequent changes of *homo sapiens* that would imply a natural, hierarchical ordering of worth between cultures. The sequence of ethological change of *homo sapiens*, unlike biological evolution, is not ir-

which have filled the earth with a great multiplicity of modes of human existence and their cultural expressions, lie in the times before *homo sapiens*, and the process continues to change modes of existence and their cultural expressions towards open, unknown futures. One might call these processes by which human beings become what they are »processes of hominisation« or »processes of civilization«. To introduce my chapter and to orient it with reference to the book, I shall adopt (and slightly adapt[2]) this latter notion of civilising processes from Norbert Elias.

Although people have often succumbed to the temptation of considering civilization something that is acquired, and in particular, something that is acquired only by some, while others still lack it, it is much more accurate to consider it a process that includes all of humanity,[3] albeit in different forms, in different times and in different places. Civilization is (according to Elias) the complex of processes by which the biological »given« of the individual human being is shaped by learning of societal standards of co-existence, which in turn results in a kind of individual behaviour that could be called civilised or culti-

---

reversible; and it is unjustifiable to hold one culture and its development up as the future of others (cf. Jonas, Hans: *Das Prinzip Verantwortung: Versuch einer Ethik für die technologische Zivilisation*, Frankfurt/Main 1979, pp. 200–203). The progression of hominisation of which I speak is not a unilinear evolutionary progress. This does not, however, mean that the question of evaluating cultural changes and differences should be rejected completely. But it does call for the utmost vigilance with regard to the cultural specificity of the means of evaluation or comparison of cultures. Cf. Anthony Giddens' deconstruction of evolutionist theories of social change in *The constitution of society: Outline of the theory of structuration*, Berkeley/Los Angeles 1984, pp. 227–243.

2 These adaptations are motivated not only by the need to adapt Elias' notion for my own research problem, but also by an attempt to respond to the criticisms formulated against Elias' work. For an overview thereof, see Mennell, Stephen: *Norbert Elias: Civilization and the human self-image*, Oxford/New York 1989, pp. 227–250 and van Krieken, Robert: *Norbert Elias*, London/New York 1998, pp. 118–134. In this regard, see also Giddens: »The constitution of society«, pp. 240–242.

3 Cf. Elias, Norbert: »Zivilisation«, in: Schäfers, Bernard (Ed.): *Grundbegriffe der Soziologie*, Leverkusen 1986, p. 383.

vated, in other words, one more or less adapted for living with other people.[4] But the coming into existence of a particular kind of behaviour in an individual is not the result of a programme, neither his/her own nor that of his/her parents (but not without these either), but first of all the result of the position in which that person grew up in a particular society. Wherever individuals enter the world, they do so by entering into social *figurations* that describe a particular mode of coexistence, a network of interdependency and thus the power relations of a society. A figuration is like a dance:[5] it does not exist independently from the individuals that constitute it, but nor does it depend for its existence strictly on any particular individual. It is therefore only within such figurations that a new human being is *socialised*, but also obtains the means for his/her *individualisation*. And as socialised individuals take the initiative, they in turn influence the process of sociogenesis, that is, the figurations in which they interact, so that the same people could form different figurations, or different people could participate in the same or similar figurations at different times and places. Mostly, the changing of figurations takes place over long periods by means of social processes spanning generations.[6] This happens,

---

4 In what follows I, unlike Elias, shall use the terms »civilization« and »culture« interchangeably, as has become the convention in anthropology (cf. Bollenbeck, G.: »Zivilisation«, in: Ritter, Joachim/Gründer, Karlfried (Eds.): *Historisches Wörterbuch der Philosophie*, vol. 13, Basel 1971–2007, pp. 1365–1379). It should also be stated categorically that I could use the words »civilization« and »culture« only devoid of a prejudice of progress (as was still present in the earlier work of Elias, but from which he too departed later on – on this subject, cf. the commentary of Martucelli, Danilo: *Sociologies de la modernité*, Paris 1999, pp. 258–259) or of cultural superiority. Since »civilization« and »culturing« refer here to the process by which human beings take on a specific form of existing as human beings, i.e. to hominisation, the expression »an uncivilised human being« is a contradiction in terms.

5 As van Krieken explains in: »Norbert Elias«, p. 58.

6 Cf. Elias, Norbert: »Figuration«, in: Schäfers: »Grundbegriffe der Soziologie«, p. 90.

as Elias succinctly states, »[f]rom plans arising, yet unplanned; by purpose moved, yet purposeless«.[7]

Civilization as event (*Zivilisierung*, civilising) is then, on the side of the individual, a process of psychogenesis, namely as »an individual self-regulation of relational impulses that are momentary conditions of desires and emotions or the rechannelling thereof from the primary to the secondary goals and if necessary also the sublimating reshaping thereof«,[8] in other words, a process by which the constraints inherent in a social figuration are interiorised to form personal or self-constraints. This does not mean that all external constraints (*Fremdzwänge*) necessarily lead to the acquisition of personal constraints (*Selbstzwänge*), but in as far as they do (and this is to a great extent), the process takes the form of a process of civilization that results in the enablement of a form of co-existence. Individuals acquire the habit, or rather a stable and durable disposition (in Bourdieu's terms) or second nature – a *habitus*[9] – of acting in certain ways; this gives a personal style to socially acquired forms of acting. As can be seen from the short definition of the process of civilization above, Elias is particularly interested in self-constraint as a process of mastering and sublimating drives (that is, the psychogenetic aspect of sociogenetic processes). Such a *habitus* is not only formed when young individuals enter a social figuration, but it is also formed under the influence of the powers inherent in the gradual change of figurations. To summarise, Elias presents us with a vision of the nature of change of social existence in which human beings are »conceptualized as *interdependent* rather than autonomous, comprising what he called *figurations* rather than social systems or structures, and as characterized by socially and historically specific forms of *habitus*, or personality structure«.[10]

---

7 Elias, Norbert: *The society of Individuals*, Oxford, UK/Cambridge, Mass. 1991, p. 64.

8 »[…] eine individuelle Selbstregulierung momentaner triebe- und affektbedingter Verhaltensimpulse oder deren Umleitung von den primären auf sekundäre Ziele hin und gegebenenfalls auch deren sublimatorische Umgestaltung« (Elias: »Zivilisation«, p. 382).

9 This term will be one of my central notions in the section on technics in this chapter. For Pierre Bourdieu's definition of the term, see *Le sens pratique*, Paris 1980, pp. 88–89.

10 van Krieken: »Norbert Elias«, p. 55.

It is this perspective on human beings, namely the description of the processes of the socio-individual formation of human beings, that is of interest to me in Elias' theory of the process of civilization, rather than the thesis that civilising is an attenuation of habits and an augmentation of sympathy due to the double mechanism of a concentration of state power and the concomitant interiorisation thereof as a mastering of the biological urges.[11] Elias provides us with a theory of civilization as a non-monolinear process of hominisation that is without any specific beginning and that remains open-ended. However, whereas Elias concentrates especially on *society* as an anthropogenetic factor, one could engage in the quest for similar theories of the two other anthropogenetic factors, namely *meaning* and *technics*. To put it another way: the process of civilization or hominisation is not only one by which societal processes take shape, but hominisation is also a set of processes by which the creation of meaning and technisisation take place. Society, meaning and technics are interdependent factors of hominisation – none of them exists without the others – and all three share the same double structure of generality and particularity, be it society/individual (in the case of human socialisation), language system/language usage (in the case of human signification) or technical system/technical action (in the case of human technical praxis).

These historical processes by which the nature and interrelation of the biological, the social, the meaningful and the technical in human beings change, are the conditions for anthropogenesis or hominisation, that is, the formation of human beings. Since times immemorial, human beings have reflected on their own human condition – the condition in which these processes leave people – be it through ritual, narration, philosophy or science. They have done so in attempts to intervene in the processes of hominisation. If there is to be a global, intercultural dialogue on intervention in the processes of hominisation, it is obvious that the process of hominisation – the question of what is it to become and be a human being – should be at the centre of the discussion. We ask ourselves, in that dialogue: what is a human being? what can a human being become? what should a human being be? And in order to

11 I am especially uncomfortable with the remnants of a link between civilization and progress that marks Elias' earlier work. For a study of how this idea was gradually attenuated by Elias, see again Martuccelli's chapter on Elias in »Sociologies de la modernité«.

contribute to an answer to these questions, each person draws on his/her particular position in a historically contingent, social, meaningful and technical figuration.

2. HUMAN TECHNICITY AND THE CIVILISING PROCESSES

How does one know what a human being is or could be? Certainly one learns of the human being by being human, by personal experience, but these experiences are mediated, from very early childhood onward, and they are mediated especially by *stories*.[12] I learn what I am, could and should be and what others are through the imaginative variations of actions and manners of being that are transmitted in the stories of my culture. This statement summarises the essence of Paul Ricoeur's theory of narrative hermeneutics. The importance of stories (fictional or scientific) for reflection on civilization and humanity hardly needs to be argued. However, we know that stories are not transmitted in isolation: the stories of early childhood are often accompanied by games (playing out a narrative); many stories are enacted or danced; others stories are recited, accompanied by ritual actions and objects; many stories are learned off by heart in poetic form; others are written down in books and sold or stored in libraries. In short, stories have a *Sitz-im-Leben* that is not made of the same narrative material as the stories themselves; stories are supported, amongst other things by technical support. In fact, by changing slightly the angle from which one views things, one could consider stories as being technically supported by things that form part of a larger technical system (a book, for instance, is part of the education process, the library, the editing and printing processes, etc.).

If this is the case, one can ask oneself whether stories are the only things that are carried by these technical objects and procedures; or to put the question differently: are the technical objects themselves not perhaps telling a »story« of what a human being is or could be? And indeed, it is well known that technics are not only mnemonics or mnemo-technics (support for not forgetting stories); but any technics,

12 What is presented here with reference to stories should, in a more complete theory, be complemented by a parallel theory of games.

to be efficient, presupposes a *history* of its use, and all technical artefacts summarise, while simultaneously hiding, a history of their invention, development, production, wear-and-tear and maintenance. If one concedes that technical objects and procedures »tell stories« (in this metaphorical way), one could well ask whether people do not perhaps know what human beings are, not only through the mediation of socially transmitted constructs of meaning (such as stories), but also from the *means* by which these ideas about humanity are transmitted. And if this is the case, could it not be possible that all technical experiences mediate, albeit implicitly, ideas about what a human being is or could be? This is indeed the *hypothesis* I would like to support: *the process of the acquisition and use of technical objects and technical know-how brings about an intervention or mediation analogous to that of stories in our ideas and lived experience of what it is to be human.* This hypothesis states, in other words, that the technical aspects of the processes of civilization or hominisation are *de facto* processes by which people learn how to be human.

Perhaps the most important objection that one might raise against this hypothesis is that stories are symbolic and even fictional entities, whereas technical objects and procedures are practical entities. I shall use Ricoeur's hermeneutics to problematise this objection and to argue that human interaction with technical means shares with the interaction with stories the element that, in both, the user and the reader are confronted with a world of references that transcend the internal references of either the story text or the technical means – this reference of the story and of technics beyond themselves is called the *world* and the fact of its enactment, *worldliness.*

In order to embark on my project, I need to specify what I mean by »*technics*«. The following demarcation serves a three-fold purpose: first, to accommodate as far as possible the plurality of legitimate, but partial, perspectives provided on technics in the history of philosophy;[13] second, to avoid reducing human technicity from the outset to its instrumental rational aspect; and third, to give a descriptively neutral or general rendering of technicity, in the sense that this rendering would be able to account for both beneficial and malignant aspects of human technicity. Technics, then, is a complex consisting of three in-

13 As pleaded for by Lenk, Hans: *Zur Sozialphilosophie der Technik*, Frankfurt/Main 1982, pp. 21–22.

terdependent aspects: *habitus* (the technical disposition of the technical agent), instruments or *means* (the system of technical objects and accompanying human procedures) and *worldliness* (the understanding interaction of the technical agent with the technical system).

Human technicity as a whole, the nature of each of these three elements, as well as the nature of their interaction, are always *changing.* They change, first, whenever an individual child acquires skills that he/she did not have as a new born-baby and throughout his/her life in the acquisition of new skills or in the gradual loss of it. They change, second, »naturally« across an entire cultural group during the process of civilization (albeit sometimes at a slow transgenerational pace). But, third, technicity also changes in smaller or larger interventions in the »normal« flow of events – nowadays this is what happens most often when we speak of »development« or of »transfer of technology«. Technical change, but also the everyday technical use of technics, will therefore be considered here as analogous to the transmission of stories.

3. TECHNICS AND NARRATIVITY

Using the transmission of narration as an analogy, I would like to adapt Ricoeur's transcultural theory of narrativity[14] to develop an outline of a hermeneutics of technical change – in other words, the general anthropological pattern of changing human technicity that is an element of the formation of all civilizations.[15] Ricoeur presents his

---

14 Cf. Ricoeur, Paul: *Temps et Récit 1: L'intrigue et le récit historique,* Paris 1983. (henceforth TRI), p. 105. In doing so, for the explorative purposes of this chapter, I limit myself to TRI pp. 105–162; what I say here and later on about narrativity depends on this text (and some others) by Ricoeur. The adaptation of Ricoeur's theory of time and narrative has been facilitated by his own adaptation of this theory to space in architecture, in his article »Architecture et narrativité«, in: Urbanisme 303 (1998), pp. 44–53. I have previously explored the possibility of appropriating Ricoeur's general hermeneutics of texts in »Transmettre et interpréter«, in: Médium 6 (2006), pp. 30–47.

15 By doing so, I answer (amongst others) to the challenge of Lenk when he stated: »Wenn die Sozialwissenschaft solche im Alltag wirksamen ver-

hermeneutics of narrativity in three phases: (1) a pre-understanding of narrativity embedded in everyday life, (2) text/writing and (3) reading. These phases are also called (1) the prefiguration, (2) the configuration and (3) the refiguration of understanding respectively. In passing through these three phases, human beings change the manner of their understanding, not only of the stories and histories transmitted to them, but also of their understanding of themselves. My basic hypothesis, as formulated above, is that a similar hermeneutic circle of prefiguration, configuration and refiguration structures changes of human technicity,[16] and consequently, over long periods, of the processes of civiliza-

---

steckten Selbstverständlichkeiten, Einstellungen und Vorfixierungen ans Licht bringen, ›aufklären‹ kann, so gewinnt dies für eine vernünftig abwägende Theorie des Technischen und der Technik und auch für eine Technikphilosophie umso mehr an Bedeutsamkeit, als technische und systemtechnologische Zusammenhänge immer stärker unsere weitgehend künstlich gewordene Umwelt und auch unser soziales Zusammenleben beeinflussen«. (Lenk: »Zur Sozialphilosophie der Technik«, p. 23). My blueprint of a hermeneutics of human technicity should serve, *inter alia*, as a general theory for the manner in which the forces of everyday existence affect technical events.

The following hermeneutics of technics is, however, not the same thing as the sociology of (everyday) technics that Lenk (together with Günther Ropohl) pleads for (in: Lenk: »Zur Sozialphilosophie der Technik«, chapter 2). Whereas the former takes the participant perspective as its point of departure and fits the observer perspective within this perspective, the latter would do the inverse. Be that as it may, it should be clear from a comparison between what I shall present here and the outline for a sociology of technics that the findings of the two modes of research are very compatible and mutually supportive.

16 Such a threefold perspective on technics is not entirely new. It is already suggested by Benjamin in »Das Kunstwerk im Zeitalter seiner technischen Reproduzierbarkeit« [zweite Fassung], in: Tiedemann, Rolf/Schweppenhäuser, Hermann (Eds.): *Walter Benjamin: Gesammelte Schriften*, vol. I.2, Frankfurt/Main 1971–1989, p. 500–501 (n. 26), where Benjamin explains that every form of art is situated at the point of interference of three developmental lines – that of the transmitted effort or quest of which it is the provisional end-point, that of its technical support, and that of its changing reception. Similarly, Hegel, in his Jena lectures, analysed three dialectical

tion that are responsible for the formation of diverse forms of human life.

3.1 Prefiguration

Understanding narrations about actions, and coming to a new understanding of oneself as an agent through the experience of understanding a narration, can occur only on the basis of a non-explicit pre-understanding of action. According to Ricoeur, this pre-understanding of action is situated in a threefold familiarity:

(1) a familiarity with the semantics of action – that is, a person's capability to use a network of notions by which human actions are distinguished from general physical movements; they are notions denoting the »who«, »how«, »why«, »with whom«, etc. of actions.
(2) familiarity with the symbolics of action – people act in a regular way, and this regularity forms an implicit symbolics that makes it possible for other people to understand what they are doing and why they are doing it.[17] This readability of action testifies to its social setting and production, and to its conformity with social norms that give action its rule-like character.
(3) familiarity of the agent with his/her own temporality – the fact that the agent is himself/herself time, or temporal, means that the agent knows temporality as something different from a succession of

---

relations between the subject and the object, namely patterns of speech, utensils and the family (cf. Habermas, Jürgen: *Technik und Wissenschaft als »Ideologie«*, Frankfurt/Main 1969, pp. 9–47, in particular pp. 9–10.) However, these suggestions are completely reworked here within the framework of a phenomenological hermeneutics.

17 Ricoeur situates this notion of symbolicity, widely used in anthropology, between two other notions of symbolicity, namely that of simple notation and the symbolics of double meaning inherent in metaphors (TRI 113). In this regard, it is useful to consult Geertz, Clifford: »Thick description. Toward an interpretive theory of culture«, in: *The interpretation of cultures: selected essays*, New York [1973] 2000, pp. 3–30, and also the very lucid essay by Taylor, Charles: »To follow a rule ...«, in: Shusterman, Richard (Ed.): *Bourdieu: A critical reader*, Oxford/Malden 1999, pp. 29–44.

»now's«; one could say that the agent is himself/herself like a »plot« that unfolds without being narrated.

If it is true that human beings live every day in a narrative way, that their experience of living is structured in a pre-narrative manner[18] (in the sense of a lived-through pre-comprehension of action), is it perhaps also true that they live in a technical way, that living is structured in a pre-technical manner (in the sense of a lived-through pre-comprehension of technicity)? Is technical action not just a particular form of action, and is pre-technicity therefore a subspecies of pre-narrativity (in other words, is one's implicit or latent understanding of technics just a form of implicit or latent understanding of human action in general)? Since all three of the above elements of pre-comprehension apply to the understanding of the agent of technical action, the technical procedure and the technical objects, human technicity is subject to the process of interpretation that is described by Ricoeur's theory of narrativity. But in a hermeneutics of technical change, the emphasis is different:

(1) although human pre-technicity is informed by a semantics of action, the hermeneutics of technical change moves the means of action and of that semantics to the centre of its concern; there is a »vocabulary« of possible actions (i.e. not words) over which every agent disposes;
(2) although technical action is just as symbolic as other actions, *as* technical action the concern is the normativity (i.e. the compatibility with other actions and events) and the practicability of that action; even though action is symbolic, it is not reducible to its symbolicity; and
(3) temporality is as much part of narrativity as of technicity, but the emphasis in the latter case is more on functionality than on plot.[19]

---

18 »structure pré-narrative de l'expérience« (TRI 141).

19 In his presentation of temporality of pre-understanding, Ricoeur borrows from the »in-structure« of »within-time-ness« at the end of Heidegger's *Sein und Zeit*; without in the least degree taking away from this temporality, the exploration of the in-character of understanding in technicity would take as its first point of reference the in-character of being-in-the-world as introduced by Heidegger in his small phenomenology of instrumentality:

> At the level of prefiguration, the human being's temporality is (as will be discussed below) the condition of »I can«.
> Not only is the emphasis different; in considering the pre-technical experience of living in this manner, one notices that all three of Ricoeur's elements of narrativity relied on, or presupposed, a technicity.[20] What draws together this three-fold technical pre-comprehension is the phenomenon of habitus. Habitus is the essence of the human pre-comprehending of technicity (and equally of the pre-comprehending of sociality and signification); it is the technical second nature.

But what does this mean in more concrete terms for changing human technicity? We know that a human infant that is not stimulated by games, dances and stories will not develop repeatable, (at least partially) reliable means of doing things. These culturally specific forms of social interaction not only socialise a young human being and initiate him/her into the world of meaning of the particular cultural group he/she is born into (just as was explained in the processes of civilization described in the introduction), but infants also learn how to use something *as* something, be it those initially alien masses of human flesh that are used as a means of perambulation, be it teeth that are used as a means to bite, be it crayons used to express innate artistic genius on the lounge walls. Young human beings acquire the capability to use their bodies with and against the forces of nature (gravitation, the impulses of their own bodies, the brute biological given of the speech equipment, etc.), with and against objects, with and against other people. This continual process of stimulation and learning from earliest childhood on results in the formation and transformation of a habitus.[21] As will become clear, the habitus is always already taken up

---

using something as something, that unfolds the basic pre-predicative understanding or hermeneutic mode of existence.

20 What Ricoeur presents here as the three elements of pre-narrativity already depends on and is entwined with its own technicity; similarly, all technical actions, even if it is only the practice of a bodily technics, has a narrative quality that gives meaning to it, even if it is only episodically. Thus, I do not claim that either technicity or narrativity is more original than the other.

21 The technicity of the habitus has been thoroughly described under the name »bodily technics« since Marcel Mauss' 1934 essay, »Les techniques

in a hermeneutic spiral of interaction with technical events that transform it.[22]

The habitus is then a name for the growing and changing range of capabilities incorporated in the body of the developing child, and later in the developing adult, by means of cultural forms of implicit or explicit learning. It is a set of durable dispositions that do not predetermine action, but that predispose an agent to embark on a certain kind of action – the habitus is the name of its possibility (it is the »I can this or that«). It is like a feeling for the game(s) that one plays (*le sens du jeu* – Bourdieu), whatever that »game« or situation of life that might be. The *habitus* is the bodily, pre-reflective, pre-predicative mode of existence of »I can« (Merleau-Ponty). *I can* is the way in which the body is familiar with the *world* – familiarity in a non-intellectual, non-consciousness-centred way, but without excluding the consciousness; *I can* means having to do with matters in such a way that a horizon of familiarity takes form, not only in my consciousness, but in my action. The metaphor used in phenomenology to describe this acquaintedness by my very being in the world is dwelling. The *dwelling* metaphor helps me to illustrate what this technical prefiguration or pre-understanding is like: it is familiarity or socially and symbolically (culturally) formed know-how. For example, my acquaintedness with my shower (with opening the tap, locating the soap, standing without slipping, etc.) is just one element out of a whole bodily »vocabulary« or »semantics« of the kind of action that would be possible for me as agent.

In all of this, the symbolic and social (and biological) aspects of the habitus, of the technical prefiguration, are explicitly affirmed; the anthropogenetic triad of society, meaning and technicity is maintained.

---

du corps«, in: *Sociologie et anthropologie*, Paris [1934] 1950, pp. 365–386; see also especially the work of Leroi-Gourhan, André: *Evolution et techniques*, vol. 1: *L'homme et la matière*, Paris 1943 and that of Haudricourt, André-George: *La technologie science humaine: Recherches d'histoire et d'ethnologie des techniques,* Paris 1987.

22 The point here is not to reduce the experience of bodily efficiency to a form of instrumentality at all; I simply want to highlight that even if one were to claim that »I don't have a body, I am a body«, this bodiliness has a specific technicity associated with it, namely as habitus.

3.2 Configuration

People's lives and events might have a pre-narrative structure, but narratives exist only when they are told or written down or filmed. And it is by this process of formation of a narrative that one enters the domain of the »as if« (TRI 125). »As if« does not necessarily mean that narration is fictional; the domain of »as if« covers fiction as well as historiography. In fact, Ricoeur prefers the notion of »as if« to that of »fiction« to refer to the most general category of the process by which one takes a step away from the events »themselves« in order to represent them narratively. According to Ricoeur, the process by which a narrative is formed (that is, a set of events is represented) consists of

(1) an intrigue or plot – drawing a configuration from a succession of events that simply follow each other, i.e. putting into a plot or relating events;
(2) a syntax of action – putting together heterogeneous elements such as agents, interactions, circumstances, means, goals, unexpected turns, etc. This is where the transition is made from a semantics of action to a syntax of action, there is a telling of the fact that someone did something when...; and
(3) followability – at the same time, the creation of a plot that configures heterogeneous elements brings about a temporal line that could be followed or understood.

In this three-fold process, there is an imaginative schematisation of events at work along traditional lines, implying that at the same time there are movements of a *sedimentation of forms* and *innovation* at work in the creation of a narrative.

In this form, the configured narration mediates between the prefiguration of the lived pre-narrativity and what follows, namely the audition or reading of the narrative, that is, the application or appropriation of the narrative to the lived narrativity. Thus, if we want to follow this analogy, we would have to ask if there is such a mediation in technicity. I would wager that this mediation is realised by the technical system (by the set of artefacts and procedures that could exist independently from any specific individual technician, if not from human technicians as such).

I do not wish to embark on a detailed analysis of technical artefacts or instruments here. It would be impossible in any case, since here we find ourselves in the domain in which competence regarding the internal coherence of the technical system is not the speciality of philosophers, but rather of carpenters and chemists, engineers and artisans. I would rather pursue the analogy between technicity and narrativity by indicating, firstly, one similarity between the narrative and the artefact, and then two dissimilarities.

(1) Autonomy – The most general term that can be used to name the commonality between narrative and the technical system is *autonomy*, or at least the potential of autonomy.[23] »Writing« (or »text«) is the typical form of autonomy of any narration or discourse: it is autonomous in respect of, or decontextualised from, the intention of the author, from the socio-cultural conditions of its production and from the original addressee.[24] Practically all technical artefacts

23 The notion of autonomy is not drawn from my guiding text (TRI), but from the anthology *Du texte à l'action: Essais d'hérméneutique II*, Paris 1986. Whereas the anthology was published after TRI, all but two of the essays in it predate *Temps et récit*. This is true also for my references to the notion of autonomy that had been written when Ricoeur wrote *Temps et récit*. I suspect that the reason why Ricoeur does not use the notion of autonomy here (in TRI) in his theory of narrative, as he did in his more general theory of textual hermeneutics, is that he associates autonomy very closely with the textual form of discourse, i.e. with writing, and not with oral discourse, i.e. with speech. I have argued elsewhere that what he describes as the autonomous state of discourse characterises speech (or does so at least in principle) as much it does writing – see my »Transmettre et interpreter«, pp. 34–36.
Bruno Latour also deploys the metaphor of text or script (see »Where are the missing masses? The sociology of a few mundane artefacts«, in: Bijker, W. E./Law, J.: *Shaping Technology/Building society*, Cambridge, Mass. 1992, pp. 225–258), but he does so to describe the agency of technical objects, whereas I refer this issue to the facilitation structure of the autonomous socio-technical system. Since his manner of exploring this analogy, as well as his aims in doing so, differ considerably from mine, the complex comparison between his approach and my Ricoeurian one will have to be elaborated on in further research.

24 Cf. Ricoeur: »Du texte à l'action«, p. 404.

and procedures are stamped by this writing-like character, or are at least partially constructed of elements that are like writing in this sense. Everything in the technical life of humanity that has durability or existence that in one way or another transcends the life of the individual technician should draw our attention here. It is easy to name tools and machines, toys and means of transport, processes and the channelling of sources of energy; less evident perhaps are alphabets and grammars, the bodily technics as social heritage and divisions, institutions, procedures and programmes of work. What all of them share is that they could be decontextualised and recontextualised, very often due to the training and information that accompany the selling, learning and/or transmission of technical procedures and instruments; the decontextualisation maintains or safeguards a practical essence of the instrument. Just like a written story keeps in stock the »what it is about«, so the instrument keeps in stock the »what it is for«. (But as shall be seen later, this does not mean in the least that the reading of what is written means simply taking over the stock – reading always implies an element of transformation.)

It is this aspect of technics especially that technical specialists learn about in their textbooks. Explaining how things work, how to maintain their working, how to use them, is made possible by the *technical* knowledge of technics (whereas I incorporate that kind of knowledge here into a *hermeneutic* interpretation of technics). Just as there is a science that studies the constitution of narratives – narratology – so too there are sciences explaining the constitution of technical things. An umbrella science of the socio-technical system is called a technology.[25]

(2) Usability – thus far for the similarity. At the beginning of the discussion of configuration it was said that the narrative configuration is the domain of the »as if«. Now it would be no use denying that technical artefacts are capable of supporting »as ifs«: my mobile phone, for instance, is not only a means of mobile communication, it is also a status symbol; it is a means by which I introduce myself into a symbolic or even fictional space of social esteem, that is, a

25 Günther Ropohl gives an excellent analysis of the socio-technical system in its autonomy in chapter 3 of his *Allgemeine Technologie: Eine Systemtheorie der Technik*, (second edition), Munich/Vienna 1999.

space of »as if«. This secondary or external reference of technical objects transcends the internal or technical reference of the parts of the technical system and is an integral part of technics (as such, this phenomenon will reappear in the discussion of refiguration below). But as an autonomous technical configuration it has its own mode of existence that I would like to call the »usability«. One discovers usability as the mode of existence of technical means when the »as if« thereof is lost from sight and the conditions for its functionality highlighted. The autonomous technical system does not, like a narrative, represent something, it does not stand for something; it organises things, namely objects, sources of energy, institutions, agents. It channels power; it divides actions; it synchronises or sequentialises procedures. The usability which characterises instruments is especially made up of a normativity, the tendency to form networks and a traditionality and historicity that have the same dialectics of improvisation and sedimentation of form as narration has.[26] In short, whereas the story is created when a syntax of action forms a plot, the creation of a technical artefact coordinates or configures heterogeneous elements together in specific manners in order to form a usable means.

(3) Facilitation – On the basis of its usability the technical instrument, procedure, institution or source of energy is an implicit proposition of what could be done or how something could be done. The technical means makes one kind of action possible, stronger, finer, smaller, quicker, etc. and makes others impossible or difficult (both with greater or smaller side effects).[27] However (as will become clear in Section 3.3 below), this does not determine or exhaust its practical application. The »could be« suggested by the technical means is very often accompanied by a social means of instruction that opens up the »could be« by teaching how to use something and what to use it for. Just as the storyline of a narrative creates a followability to the heterogeneous elements that are con-

26 As Jean-Pierre Séris describes the threefold essence of the technical phenomenon *La technique*, Paris 1994, pp. 45–105.

27 For analyses on the amplification/reduction effect of technical events, see Ihde, Don: *Technics and Praxis*, Dortrecht/Boston/London 1979, pp. 38, 48 and *Technology and the lifeworld: From garden to earth*, Bloomington/Indianapolis 1990, p. 78.

figured together, so the technical instrument facilitates certain usages (while making others more difficult or impossible).

The formation of typical technical actions and instruments are amongst the most visible traits of cultures and civilizations; and it is one of the senses of the words by Arendt cited in the epigraph to this chapter, that »Tools and instruments are so intensely worldly objects that we can classify whole civilizations using them as criteria«.[28] Wherever there are processes of civilization, processes of the transformation and transmission of culture, technics is involved. In the next section more is said about the manner in which technics contributes to hominisation. However, it is perhaps important already to note here that the metaphor of writing invites us to consider a whole series of critical questions pertaining to the transfer of technics. These involve particularly the interests that are carried over during the transfer of technics, the prejudices sedimented in technics and the effects of particular technical conditions on the users. When one puts it this way, it soon becomes clear that as long as one limits one's reflection to the level of *technical* knowledge of technics and ignores its social and symbolic implications and the appropriation of technics in the use of it, a vast domain of critical questions concerning technics is simply lost. A full criticism of technics can only be done if the recontextualisation of autonomous technics is considered. That is why technics is not only a matter of concern for whoever contemplates the processes of the formation of human beings and how they should live together, but also why such a reflection should have a cross-cultural dimension.

3.3 Refiguration

Thus far, I have isolated, in turn, the first two elements of the technical whole: first the habitus or technical pre-understanding (that is, the *I can* that dwells in the world), and then the configuration of technical means. In order to present the third aspect of technicity (namely worldliness), and by so doing to present the third aspect of technical change (namely refiguration), the interaction of all three aspects of human technicity should now be considered. The guiding metaphor for the process of refiguration is *reading*.

28 Arendt, Hannah: *The Human Condition*, Chicago 1958, p. 144.

In this context, reading is, of course, a metaphor drawn from textual practices, like the reading of stories. In reading, the pre-narrative disposition (or habitus) is confronted with a configured narrative. This confrontation of the reader's expectation or pre-judice with the followability of the text elicits a response to the followability of the text, in that it reactualises the plot or story line which the configured narrative invites its reader to follow. This reactualisation of the narrative in the reading event entails an application or understanding of the narrative – either to accept or to reject it. Of course, the reader never reads as a simple individual, but rather reads as a member of a community of readers[29] that invests its members with a specific type of reading culture; it accompanies the reading with the know-how of reading over which the reader disposes (which is not to say that there is no singularisation of interpretation in reading, but only that all reading is socially mediated to some extent). Furthermore, one reads within a particular context, a horizon, that gives further meaning to the reading event. Thus the socially and contextually influenced reader enters into a fusion of horizons (Gadamer) between his/her own horizon of understanding and the horizon of understanding offered by the »as if« of the story. Thus, in reading, something is offered that goes beyond the text, namely a world. The world, says Ricoeur, »is the whole of references that are opened up by all kinds of descriptive or poetical texts that I have read, interpreted and loved«[30] and it should be added that »what is interpreted in a text is the proposal of a world in which I could dwell and in which I could project my very own abilities«.[31] Thus, one's preconfigured, pre-narrative existence is reconfigured through reading.

It is much the same in human interaction with technical means. In the same sense that there is no story if the book is not read, no music if

---

29 Cf. Ricoeur, Paul: *Le conflit des interprétations. Essais d'herméneutique I*, Paris 1970, p. 7: »toute lecture de texte, aussi liée soit-elle au *quid*, au 'ce en vue de quoi' il a été écrit, se fait toujours à l'intérieur d'une communauté, d'une tradition, ou d'un courant de pensée vivante, qui développent des présupposés et des exigences«.

30 »Le monde est l'ensemble de references ouvertes par toutes les sortes de texts descriptifs ou poétiques que j'ai lus, interprétés et aimés«. (TRI 151)

31 »ce qui est interprété dans un texte, c'est la proposition d'un monde que je pourrais habiter et dans lequel je pourrais projeter mes pouvoirs les plus propres«. (TRI 152)

the score is not played, there is no technicity without the *use* of technics, be it by the handling of tools, maintenance of processes, administration of institutions or any other technical artefact. Reading, as a metaphor applied to human technicity, refers to the confrontation of the agent's technical pre-understanding or habitus with the technical configuration of an object (and the manner in which it is embedded in the technical system). In this event, the agent responds to the »could be« that is facilitated by the technical object, by reactualising it or by reactivating it as a means to do something. What was, a mere instant ago, still a lifeless object, is now used *as* a saw, *as* a table, *as* an oven. By using the technical configuration, the agent suspends the configuration's autonomy and inserts it into the context in which it is used with or in coordination with other things in order to attain a certain goal. It is this »using something as« (what Heidegger called the »hermeneutic as«[32]) that opens up the world of technics. In the use of a technical object, the technical agent makes use of a technical object and thus recontextualises the facilitation offered by the technical object; the range of technical possibilities open to the technical agent when using an object depends on the complexity of the technical pre-understanding of the agent. At the same time, in using technical means, the agent is *disciplined* into how to use it and thus his/her technical habitus is refigured. In this sense, this two-way »dialogue« between a human being and the technical means could be considered a fusion of horizons.[33] One could also say that when engaging in technical activity, the agent is confronted by a proposal of ways to do things and at the same moment his/her *I can* is refigured. In learning how to use and mastering the use of certain objects in certain ways, the way in which one dwells in the world is transformed.

---

32 Heidegger, Martin: *Sein und Zeit*, 17th ed. Tübingen [1927] 1993, especially §32.

33 This »dialogue« should certainly be taken metaphorically, since a lot of the interaction between human beings and the technical configuration takes place without the technical agent's being conscious or fully conscious of the entire scope of that interaction – hence my introduction of the Foucauldian notion of »discipline«.

Of course, just as is the case with texts, where one does not read alone, one does not use tools alone either.[34] The know-how of technical activity is to a large degree mediated by socially acquired skills (for example, a master craftsman teaches apprentices how to use the tools of the trade). This, again, does not exclude singularizing innovation, which could be seen in the style of an individual, his/her failure to meet the requirements of his/her training or in the excellence of brilliant technicians. Also, the use of technical means, and thus the meaning thereof, depends on the context or project in which it is used. The input from society and the context of the technical procedure co-determine the nature and meaning of that technical event. This situatedness of technics is responsible for the fact that when technics is understood purely *technically*, it is not fully understood. To be precise, technics have a *threefold reference*. First, there is the internal reference of the different elements of the technical object or procedure to one another, due to their technical qualities and design. One might call this the *technical* reference. Second, there is the reference of *usage* that identifies a technical means *as* this or that by using it in the context of a certain project, by using it for this or that. Third, there is the *symbolic* reference by which technics refers to social values of precision, aesthetics, fashion, sophistication, consumability, and so forth. The last two kinds of references constitute the worldliness of technics.[35]

---

34 François Caron's book, *Les deux révolutions industrielles du XXe siècle*, Paris 1997, does not only use the intimate relation between the social and the technical as a grid for his historiography of the more recent developments in the socio-technical system (see pp. 14ff), one could just as well read this book as a justification for the thesis that a technical community accompanies and guides the technico-hermeneutic process.

35 The first of these corresponds to the observer perspective on technical configurations; the second and third depend for their description on a hermeneutics of action. The description of the second or usage reference develops what Merleau-Ponty called concrete actions, whereas the description of the third or symbolic reference develops what he called abstract actions. See Merleau-Ponty, Maurice: *Phénoménologie de la perception*, Paris 1945, pp. 127–130.

4. CONCLUSIONS

I shall allow myself two concluding remarks in order to argue that my sketch of a hermeneutics of technical change should be acknowledged as an indispensable part of an inter-cultural discussion on civilizations.

In the third phase of my presentation of the hermeneutic circle of technics, I have indicated that the interaction between the technical habitus and the configured technical means is characterised by the emergence of worldliness, that is, the threefold reference of technical action. It should have become clear that the meaning of technics is certainly not only determined by the *technical* qualities of the technical objects, but also by the qualities and usage of the technical agent, which are socially formed, and by the context, which includes interaction with the social and symbolic aspects of human life. But this interaction of the diverse factors that shape technical events does not simply happen in a haphazard way – the changing life of technics is *stabilised* by the slowly changing habitus of the technical agent, by the practical given that one's life condition or occupation remains *fairly constant*, by the *stability* of the community that transmits a know-how, by the society that *maintains* certain symbolic values. We see this daily in the fact that children and students spend time acquiring skills and use those skills later on to practise a profession which has a place and status in society. But we also see it in other practices in which an interaction with technics and the acquisition of a habitus is involved, such as the acquisition of social roles, including, for instance, gender roles (for example, knowing how to walk with high-heeled shoes), religious roles (for example, who does what in a particular religious community), age roles (for example, how one walks with a frail body and a cane). One's engagement in the hermeneutic circle of technics is a constitutive element of one's identity, of what one is to oneself and for others. Just as we can be introduced to someone by means of a narrative (»this is Susan; she is the person I met at the conference in Essen«), we could also be introduced to someone by means of a name of the position that he/she takes in the technical system (»this is John, he is a computer programmer«). My point is, of course, not to reduce professions and other social roles to their technical aspect, but to caution that we need to guard against a forgetfulness of that technical aspect. *Human beings typically occupy relatively stable, socially and symboli-*

cally shaped, technical roles.[36] At the core of such a role is the habitus, the second nature, the manner in which one is predisposed to act.

In the introduction I have used Elias' theory to show that civilization is the process by which the habitus as mediation between the social and the individual is accomplished on a cross-generational scale. The habitus is not only formed by culturally specific objects, or by a culturally specific training on how to use them, but also, and at the same time, of the virtues involved in using them. When one learns carpentry, one learns not only how to saw and chisel wood, but also to be patient in doing so – an impatient carpenter is a second-rate carpenter. All technical training involves such virtues, since the excellence of technical executions depends on them (but negligence in this regard is also a form of training about virtues). Think of consistency, fidelity, precision, perseverance, collaboration, patience with oneself, with the instruments and materials and with one's co-workers, parsimony, prudence, etc. It should be clear that with these requirements for technical excellence and the requirement that they all be incorporated in the habitus, we have come very close to the domain of ethics. In fact, in many cases it would be impossible to distinguish whether a virtue is more technical or more ethical. What is certain is that training in the technical virtues of patience, consistency, etc. makes it possible to act with those same virtues outside of our daily professional domain. In fact, I posit that we know what those virtues mean, first of all, not through a theoretical understanding thereof but by an acquisition thereof on the level of our dwelling *I can*. It is practically impossible to teach someone how to become a good artisan, without at the same time offering to that person an entry to the teacher's culture or civilization and thus teaching the apprentice something of what that culture or civilization considers a good human being to be. Thus I come back to my conviction expressed in the introduction that the cycle of technical change constitutes a hominisation – forming someone as a human being and transmitting to that person what a good human being is supposed to be like. We only need to think here of the global discourse

36 One should thus radicalise Jonas' conviction (as developed in *Das Prinzip Verantwortung*) that contemporary technics has changed the range of action and the context of application of action that are susceptible to ethical judgement – the agent himself/herself and the constitution of his/her role in society could be changed by developments in the domain of technics.

and practice of *development* in all its different forms in order to be convinced of the magnitude of this cross-cultural process of civilization and hominisation by means of technical transfer.

My first point is thus to claim that the processes of technical change are processes of civilization that transmit culturally specific elements of ideal human existence and my hermeneutics of technical change proposes a schema for understanding how this happens. My second point focuses on inter-cultural dialogue as an intervention in the processes of civilization and on the technical requirements for its effectiveness in order to indicate aspects of its dependency on its technical means of existence.

From the point of view of technics, the problem of inter-cultural dialogue could be summarised as a problem of symbolic efficiency.[37] It seeks to be a discourse on culture, humanity and values (that is the symbolic aspect) and it wants this discourse to be an intervention in human sociality, symbolics and technicity (the aspect of efficiency). Whatever that intervention might entail, it will of necessity depend on a transmission of the symbolic content thereof. Transmission is the event by which symbols are enabled to cover not only space, but more particularly, time. Transmission consists of a number of stereotypical elements. In my opinion, they follow a trajectory that is very close to the hermeneutic circle of technics that I have developed above. Firstly, the message or the »what it is about« is deposited (inscribed in some or other form of support). By means of this process, the message gains autonomy, made possible by the autonomy of the technical configuration that supports it. From the point of view of the transmission, this autonomy is simultaneously the best and the worst of all possible things: on the one hand, its autonomy makes it susceptible to being uprooted from the situation in which the message was created and to

37 I summarize here the essential characteristics of the mediological theory of transmission as developed by Régis Debray, and with the revisions and qualifications for which I have made the case in two studies on mediology and in particular its relation to hermeneutics, namely »Transmettre et interpréter«, in: Médium 6 (2006), pp. 30–47, and »Mediologie en hermeneutiek«, in: Tydskrif vir Geesteswetenskappe 47.1 (2007), pp. 81–94, where the same argument is developed in more detail. Debray's mediology could be found in his *Cours de médiologie générale*, Paris 2001 and more accessibly in *Introduction à la médiologie*, Paris 2000.

being recontextualised elsewhere at another time; but on the other hand, it is the trajectory that links the decontextualisation with a recontextualisation that exposes the message to transformation. Hence transmission is not only an attempt to safeguard a message against disappearance, but also an attempt to supervise and control the transformation thereof. Subsequently, secondly, transmission consists of mechanisms by which the support of the message is changed into a vehicle (Debray calls this a *vecteur*) that will take charge of the movement of the message through time. This vehicle has a dual character: technical and institutional, or in other words, equipment and organisation.[38] Both of these dimensions change and take shape as part of a broader technical and institutional (and therefore symbolic) milieu. Thirdly, the means of transport mediates its messages, in other words, energises it with its transmissive energy that amplifies the impetus of the message to an extent that the message never had. Inevitably, this mediation constitutes a transformation of the message and aims to accompany the last phase of transmission, the reception or reading. Fourthly, then (an arca unfortunately neglected by Debray), there is the appropriative or rejecting reading of the message under the influence of its very means of transmission. The reception of the message already constitutes a further extension of the life of the message, that is, of the transmission thereof.

For any ideas coming forth from an inter-cultural dialogue which one would wish to support, what is to be concluded from this trajectory of the means by which such ideas would become effective? Any inter-cultural dialogue worthy of the name would also have to include a technics, in the sense that it would have to be structured by a means of transmission that could convert its theory into practice.[39] This is true not only because what will be formulated here in inter-cultural dialogue is to be transmitted, but also because the latter will have to mediate old cultural specific ideas concerning human existence from all the corners of the world, i.e. transmit whilst transforming the ideas left by our respective ancestors.

I would not be surprised to find that what I say about transmission sounds quite obvious here, in Germany. The reason for this is that the very milieu in which we find ourselves (the German university and re-

38 Cf. »Introduction à la médiologie«, p. 126.

39 Cf. »Introduction à la médiologie«, p. 114.

search environment) is to a large degree the fruit of a cultural project that understood itself as an endeavour of transmission and that was very successful in what it did. But the obviousness of this system of transmission is undercut by the nature of this project as an inter-cultural one. In simple terms: whatever agreement could be reached on humanity and values will have to be transmitted to cultural specific locations; but since this is an inter-cultural dialogue, the means of transmission will have to be culturally specific and will thus transform the message in diverse, culturally specific manners; and the original agreement will be in danger of falling apart in practice. Thus the diversity of praxes (and technologies) of transmission threatens the possibility of a coherent and honest inter-cultural dialogue.[40]

Let me rephrase this point. People who are looking for a new manner of co-existence of the great variety of human cultures, and who understand this endeavour as an inter-cultural dialogue, implicitly want their ideas to become practice – if they did not, everybody could just have remained human and humane in his/her own way, in his/her own corner of the world. If one then supposes that the means to reach this goal, for the transmission of the acquisitions of an inter-cultural dialogue, already exists in Europe in the form of schools and universities, libraries and book shops, etc., one will have to consider the question of whether the technologies for the transmission such acquisitions exist elsewhere, for instance, in Africa.[41] Or will it have to be provided – from the outside, as it were? That would imply, at the same time, the

---

40 Cf. Wim van Binsbergen, who observes from a southern hemisphere perspective: »It is the irony of many identity constructions and identity claims outside the North Atlantic today, that in order to succeed, in order to be taken seriously by their actual and potential adherents and by others including national and international governmental bodies, they need to be formulated in the academic and commodified format stipulated (even imposed) under North Atlantic hegemony.« in: Ubuntu and the globalization of Southern African thought and society (http://www.shikanda.net/general/ubuntu.htm, 2002 [last retrieved 23 April 2008]).

41 Or could such an inter-cultural dialogue be invented that it would suit the existing means of transmission in Africa and elsewhere? Debray has recently expressed his own reservations (and hopes) concerning inter-cultural dialogue in *Un mythe contemporain: le dialogue des civilisations*, Paris 2007.

provision of a technics with the concomitant implicit culturally specific civilising force that would change people's culture in the name of making them ready to participate in an inter-cultural dialogue. Or if the means to an inter-cultural dialogue are already present or possible in Africa, is it not perhaps already only on the basis of a universal monocultural technics of transfer that spreads itself over the globe in a very non-dialogical, non-inter-cultural manner?

What I am trying to convey is the idea that any inter-cultural dialogue that is not at the same time a technology (in the sense of an essential reflection on its means of transmission) runs the risk of using and propagating culturally specific means of transmission, which will transform an inter-cultural symbolic invention according to its own homogenising logics in a naïve way. Or to put it positively, a global inter-cultural dialogue would be worthy of this name (on a descriptive level) only if it is effective as a result of a truly inter-cultural dialogic practice in all three of the elements of hominisation: society, signs *and* technics.

BIBLIOGRAPHY

Arendt, Hannah: *The Human Condition*, Chicago 1958.

Benjamin, Walter: »Das Kunstwerk im Zeitalter seiner technischen Reproduzierbarkeit« [zweite Fassung], in: Tiedemann, Rolf/Schweppenhäuser, Hermann (Eds.): *Walter Benjamin: Gesammelte Schriften*, vol. I.2, Frankfurt/Main 1971–1989, pp. 471–508.

Bourdieu, Pierre: *Le sens pratique*, Paris 1980.

Caron, François: *Les deux révolutions industrielles du XXe siècle*, Paris 1997.

Debray, Régis: *Cours de médiologie générale*, Paris 2001.

Debray, Régis: *Introduction à la médiologie*, Paris 2000.

Debray, Régis: *Un mythe contemporain: le dialogue des civilisations*, Paris 2007.

Elias, Norbert: »Zivilisation«, in: Schäfers, Bernard (Ed.): *Grundbegriffe der Soziologie*, Leverkusen 1986, pp. 382–387.

Elias, Norbert: *The society of Individuals*, Oxford, UK/Cambridge, Mass. 1991.

Geertz, Clifford: »Thick description. Toward an interpretive theory of culture«, in: *The interpretation of cultures: selected essays*, New York [1973] 2000, pp. 3–30.

Giddens, Anthony: *The constitution of society: Outline of the theory of structuration*, Berkeley/Los Angeles 1984.

Habermas, Jürgen: *Technik und Wissenschaft als »Ideologie«*, Frankfurt/Main 1969.

Haudricourt, André-George: *La technologie science humaine: Recherches d'histoire et d'ethnologie des techniques,* Paris 1987.

Heidegger, Martin: *Sein und Zeit*, 17th ed., Tübingen [1927] 1993.

Ihde, Don: *Technics and Praxis*, Dortrecht/Boston/London 1979.

Ihde, Don: *Technology and the lifeworld: From garden to* earth, Bloomington/Indianapolis 1990.

Jonas, Hans: *Das Prinzip Verantwortung: Versuch einer Ethik für die technologische Zivilisation*, Frankfurt/Main 1979.

Latour, Bruno: »Where are the missing masses? The sociology of a few mundane artefacts«, in: Bijker, W. E./Law, J.: *Shaping Technology/Building society*, Cambridge, Mass 1992, pp. 225–258.

Lenk, Hans: *Zur Sozialphilosophie der Technik*, Frankfurt/Main 1982.

Leroi-Gourhan, André: *Evolution et techniques*, vol. 1: *L'homme et la matière*, Paris 1943.

Martucelli, Danilo: *Sociologies de la modernité*, Paris 1999.

Mauss, Marcel: »Les techniques du corps«, in: *Sociologie et anthropologie*, Paris [1934] 1950, pp. 365–386.

Mennell, Stephen: *Norbert Elias. Civilization and the human self-image*, Oxford/New York 1989.

Merleau-Ponty, Maurice: *Phénoménologie de la perception*, Paris 1945.

Ricoeur, Paul: »Architecture et narrativité«, in: Urbanisme 303 (1998), pp. 44–53.

Ricoeur, Paul: *Du texte à l'action: Essais d'hérméneutique II*, Paris 1986.

Ricoeur, Paul: *Le conflit des interpretations: Essais d'herméneutique I*, Paris 1970.

Ricoeur, Paul: *Temps et Récit 1. L'intrigue et le récit historique*, Paris 1983.

Ritter, Joachim/Gründer, Karlfried (Eds): *Historisches Wörterbuch der Philosophie*, Basel 1971–2007.

Ropohl, Günther: *Allgemeine Technologie: Eine Systemtheorie der Technik* (zweite Ausgabe), Munich/Vienna 1999.

Séris, Jean-Pierre: *La technique*, Paris 1994.

Taylor, Charles: »To follow a rule …«, in: Shusterman, Richard (Ed.): *Bourdieu: A critical reader*, Oxford/Malden 1999, pp. 29–44.

van Binsbergen, Wim: *Ubuntu and the globalization of Southern African thought and society*, 2002 (http://www.shikanda.net/general/ubuntu.htm [last retrieved 23 April 2008]).

van Krieken, Robert: *Norbert Elias*, London/New York 1998.

Wolff, Ernst: »Hominisation and humanisation: a perspective from the sociology of technics«, in: The Journal for transdisciplinary research in Southern Africa 2.2 (2006), pp. 231–248.

Wolff, Ernst: »Mediologie en hermeneutiek«, in: Tydskrif vir Geesteswetenskappe 47.1 (2007), pp. 81–94.

Wolff, Ernst: »Transmettre et interpréter«, in: Médium 6 (2006), pp. 30–47.

I.2 Humanism

Anthropology – Axial Ages – Modernities

Jörn Rüsen

> »Der Mensch muss … etwas aufsuchen, dem er, als einem letzten Ziele, alles unterordnen, und nach dem er, als nach einem absoluten Maasstab alles beurteilen kann. Dies kann er nicht anders, als in sich selbst finden, da in dem Inbegriff aller Wesen sich nur auf ihn allein alles bezieht; … es kann daher nur in seinem inneren Wert, in seiner höheren Vollkommenheit liegen«.
>
> Wilhelm von Humboldt[1]

1. Cultural Identity and the Quest for Humanism

Humanism is a commandment of our time. Why? Because we need a cultural orientation for our lives, one which covers the full variety of traditions and world views with universal standards and which, at the same time, systematically takes this variety into account. Cultural dif-

1 »Man has to seek something as his highest aim, to which he can subordinate everything and according to which he can judge everything as an absolute parameter. This he can only find within himself, since in the entire concept of all creatures everything is only related to him; […] therefore it can only be situated in his internal value system, in his higher perfection«. Humboldt, Wilhelm von: »Über den Geist der Menschheit«, in: Flitner, Andreas/Giel, Klaus (Ed.): *Werke in fünf Bänden*, vol. 1: *Schriften zur Anthropologie und Geschichte*, Darmstadt 1960, pp. 506–518, cit. S. 507.

ference has always been a challenge, the answer to which is achieving an integration of difference and common ground at the same time.

This is true for every single person as well as for every social formation of human life. All need an integration of different relationships into the context within which they live so that a stable unity of personal or social life can be established. In this unity the differences do not vanish, but rather become organized and interrelated into a coherent structure of the personal and social ›self‹.

One of the most important elements in the cultural constitution of this ›self‹ is to dissociate and distance oneself from others.[2] This is evident for every single person. Subjectivity is organized by a clear self-relationship, a strong awareness of his or her own self and at the same time by a clear distinction of this self from other persons with whom one lives. This togetherness is, of course, very important and essential for human life, but it is always structured by an awareness of the distinction between self and others. These others may have become a part of oneself (or, in the language of psychoanalysis, are introjected into the self) like parents or loved ones, but nevertheless, they are not the same as this individual, but different from it and its fundamental self-relatedness. From the very beginning of human life this self-relatedness is a basic psychic fact. It may be totally abstract or undifferentiated in its beginning and it gets its ›personal‹ characteristics through communication with others, but it is a fundamental form of human life and not only the result of social conditions. On the contrary: it is a necessary condition for the possibility of social life.

The personal and the social self have different structures. Nevertheless, the human social self shares similar elements and the factors of distinction and distance. Without the distinction between people to whom one belongs and people who do not belong, social life in its human form would be impossible. This distinction between self and others is a decisive part of humans' subjectivity and cannot simply be attributed to external life conditions.

The fundamental difference between self and others is realized in a vast variety of life-forms. According to its fundamental logic of difference it is variable, highly changeable in space and time. One of the

---

2 See the special issue on »The Interaction between Self and the Others in the Age of Globalization« of the Taiwan Journal of East Asian Studies 7.2 (2010).

most fundamental activities of the human mind lies in its permanent work in bringing about identity vis-à-vis the complexity of life conditions and their permanent challenge to the stability of the human personal and social self. So it is the outcome of a permanent mental process working out a livable balance between one's own desires and the demands of others. ›Identity‹ is the term which expresses this balance in the personal and social human self-relatedness.[3]

The cultural life of today has to meet specific challenges in this process of constituting the human self in the struggle between internal and external demands and internal and external conditions, limits and opportunities. One of the most important challenges is the encounter of different cultural traditions in shaping the human self. The process of globalization has heavily shaken the deeply-rooted pregiven patterns of belonging to one culture defined in terms of its difference from others. China, India, Africa, Europe, the West, and comparable terms have a clear geographical meaning. But beyond geography they play an important role in forming social identity on the level of cultural sense generation. They denominate world views and life forms and their interrelationship with other forms. They are a product of pregiven and historically deeply-rooted mental structures and have become a second ›nature‹ of human life. At the same time they are issues of controversial debates, struggles and political activities.

For a very long time these different mentalities and life forms could coexist alongside each other at a relative distance. Others were relatively far away, and their being different, their strangeness, did not really bother one's own life. They had their places outside the well-known world of one's home. There have always been some kinds of connection, mainly through trade, but they had not touched the center of one's own world and its mental and spiritual shape.

In a universal historical perspective this juxtaposition has now become a source of growing problems, tensions, and conflicts. Colonialism and imperialism have radically shaken many established concepts of self- and otherness; they have made evident that cultural identity is an issue of permanent struggle within and outside the realm of estab-

3 Friese, Heidrun (Ed.): *Identities – Time, Difference, and Boundaries*, New York 2002 (= Making Sense of History, vol. 2); Straub, Jürgen (Ed.): *Narration, Identity, and Historical Consciousness*, New York 2005 (= Making Sense of History, vol. 3).

lished life forms. Globalization is a specific form of historical change in the interaction of different peoples and cultures.[4] It is characterized by an emergence of transculturally effective elements and forms of human life and their dominance across established differences in the organization of human life in all its dimensions. This is not only true for economic life where the power of capitalism (or a free market economy) is effective. It also applies to the political, social and cultural dimensions of life as well. Today, besides the economy, the environmental consequences of modern industry prove to be the most urgent ›global‹ problem for human survival. It has become an urgent issue to pursue a transcultural common activity of all peoples in the world to confront the dangers of catastrophic developments.

In the cultural dimension of globalization a radical challenge of a different kind is taking place. Here the emergence of global forms of human life confront the necessity of differentiation between self and others in the processes of identity formation, which tackle the deepest level of human subjectivity all over the world. Humankind is emerging as a real dimension of human life in all its manifestations. It unites humans across their cultural differences in a way that excludes keeping up the traditionally pregiven concepts of the self in a relation of difference to others. What will remain in establishing difference in the identity-forming process which, of course, is still necessary for human life?

At first glance, global common ground and cultural difference seem to exclude each other. Yet the contrary is true. Difference is not only evident in political approaches to environmental problems; it has definitely shaped the established forms of capitalistic economy as well. Though capitalism in the US, in Europe, in China and India follow the same rules in bringing about profit, it is performed in clearly distinguishable ways, which even compete with each other.[5] Similar examples can be shown in many other realms of global life forms. Take for example the realm of secularism. Here, in a field of mental activities, which aim at establishing spheres free from religion, and which have

---

4 Osterhammel, Jürgen/Petersson, Niels T.: *Globalization: A Short History*, Princeton 2009.

5 An instructive example of this difference (between Germany and the US) is presented by Abelshauser, Werner: *The dynamics of German industry: Germany's path toward the new Economy and the American Challenge*, New York 2005.

undeniable importance for human life, the dominant presence of difference can be noted. Secularism is a necessary condition for science, and no country can deny the necessity of science and its technological applications in human life today, but the extension, depth and form of secularism in human cognition is a matter of controversy all over the world.

One of the most urgent questions of cultural life in the globalization process is the compatibility of global humanity and identity-forming difference in personal and social life. Modern humanism should be understood as an answer to this question:[6] It refers to the common cultural nature of humans as a source for cultural orientation. And by so doing it crosses all cultural differences by addressing the sameness of being a human being. It understands this anthropological sameness as an opportunity for identifying general and fundamental values valid for all humans despite their cultural differences. One of the most convincing expressions of this normative element in being a human being was formulated by Immanuel Kant. In his philosophy of ethics he attributed dignity to every human being. By dignity Kant meant that he or she always is more than just a means for the purposes of others, but rather is a purpose within him- or herself.[7]

At the same time modern humanism underlines the fact that this common cultural nature of being a human being is only a potential, the realization of which leads to very different forms of life owing to the fact that they are generated by different conditions and in different

6 See Rüsen, Jörn/Laass, Henner (Eds): *Humanism in Intercultural Perspective: Experiences and Expectations*, Bielefeld 2009.

7 »Man as a person, i.e., as the subject of a morally-practical reason, is exalted above all prices. For such a one (homo noumenon) he is not to be valued merely as a means to the ends of other people, or even to his own ends, but is to be prized as an end in himself. This is to say, he possesses a dignity (an absolute inner worth) whereby he exacts the respect of all other rational beings in the world, can measure himself against each member of his species, and can esteem himself on a footing of equality with them.« Kant, Immanuel: »Metaphysik der Sitten«, in: Weischedel, Wilhelm: *Kant. Werke*, vol. 7: *Schriften zur Ethik und Religionsphilosophie*, second part, Darmstadt 1975, pp. 304–643: A 93 (English: http://praxeology.net/kant7.htm).

contexts.[8] In this concept of humankind normative and empirical facts are synthesized. This is performed in such a way that the identity-forming idea of difference no longer contradicts the anthropological sameness of humans and its cultural realization in global forms of human life.

2. Humanism as Philosophy of History

It is the intention of my paper to make such a humanistic idea of humankind plausible by working it out into a new philosophy of history. It picks up the traditional form of modern philosophy of history. This philosophy conceptualizes the human past as a comprehensive temporal totality of humankind. History is now a master narrative of humankind. As such it has offered a pattern of significance and meaning for the experience of the human past. This ›sense in history‹ – which can function as a guideline for all detailed work in representing the past for the purpose of orienting the present – is based on the experience of the past in its temporal dimension, thus giving it a future perspective.

In its classical manifestation of the late 18th and early 19th century, this philosophy integrated the accelerating knowledge of the variety of human life in space and time into an all-encompassing concept of human development. This concept gave meaning to the dynamics of change in the modernization process. It carried the potential for inspir-

---

8 In this respect the philosophy of history by Johann Gottfried Herder, an antagonist of Kant, is paradigmatic: *Ideas for the Philosophy of History of Humanity* (1784–91) (Herder, Johann Gottfried: *Ideen zur Philosophie der Geschichte der Menschheit*, ed. Martin Bollacher, Frankfurt/Main 1989, p. 508): »*Nur Zeiten, nur Örter und Nationalcharaktere, kurz, das ganze Zusammenwirken lebendiger Kräfte in ihrer bestimmtesten Individualität entscheidet, wie über alle Erzeugungen der Natur, so über alle Ereignisse im Menschenreiche. Lasset uns dies herrschende Gesetz der Schöpfung in das Licht stellen, das ihm gebühret*«. [»Only times, only places and national characters – in short: the whole concurrence of vital forces in their most distinctive individuality decides upon all events in the realm of humanity as it decides upon all creatures of nature. Let us put this dominating law of creation into the light which is due to it«.] (Book 12, chapter 6).

ing human activity. It anchored the identity of the people in the core of temporal change. Temporal change was understood as moved by the power of the human mind and spirit. The historical insight into this depth of history reassured the addressees of this master-narrative of their identity as an individual representation of humankind. They could understand their life-form and their identity in and by it as a moment in the general development of humankind.

This humanistic philosophy of history was only an episode in the historical culture of modern (Western) societies. The emerging institution of historical studies as an academic discipline criticized it as missing the methodical rationality of historical research, and the universalistic outlook at the wide fields of historical experience narrowed in favour of a national perspective of historical thinking. The human frame of historical identity received a national feature. And the humanistic values of universal history were limited to the idea of one's own nation as representing humankind. Otherness as a necessary condition for this idea of one's own social self was defined as a lack or aberration of humanity.

Why should we go back to this episode in thematizing the issue of intercultural communication in the process of globalization? What makes it worthwhile to pick up the traditional Western philosophy of history at the brink of modernity? There are four reasons for this return: This philosophy contained

(1) a universalistic approach to historical experience;
(2) a general historization of the idea of humankind;
(3) a general individualization of the idea of humankind;
(4) a general cognizability of history by hermeneutics.

Ad 1: It is evident that historical thinking needs a universalistic perspective in the age of globalization. Its challenging experience requires a globalization of history as well, the most adequate dimension of which is humankind. Humankind is an anthropological fact with normative impacts, and as such it can function as a historical category to define the field of historical experience and to work out perspectives of its interpretation. It covers the whole field of the human past in all its variety. At the same time it is both a value-laden idea, since it addresses not only a simple biological unit, but the cultural nature of humankind, since it defines what makes it specific and different from all other creatures. Since culture is defined by the ability of humans to organize their lives according to norms and values, humankind is a comprehensive and inclusive idea of the normative- and value-systems of human culture.

Ad 2: The variety and multitude of human life-forms can only be brought into a coherent concept of understanding if humankind as a whole becomes fundamentally historized. History prevents any idea of a super-temporal cultural nature as the essence of human life prevailing for once and all below all changes so that all differences might only be understood as variations of the same substance. History endows the ›nature‹ of human culture with the ›substance‹ of temporality, so that change becomes its essential attribute. The ›nature‹ of human culture has the potential of difference in store. But at the same time history combines difference with temporal change. The variety of difference receives a coherent structure through the perspective of an encompassing development. Therefore we can observe in historical narratives a distinctive shape: differences do not vanish in favour of some general features; on the contrary, historical narratives give different life-forms a unique character as single occurrences by stressing their peculiar character within comprehensive trends of temporal change.

Ad 3: This kind of historical thinking bridges the gap between general concepts like humankind on the one hand and single and unique human life forms on the other through the category of *individualization.* Every single human being and every single human life form represents the general mental and spiritual quality of human culture in a unique way. Humankind finds its historical reality in the variety of human life forms and their temporal interconnections. Individuality is a pattern of significance, which prevents any devaluation of peculiarity and difference in favour of generalizations, where the specific historical features of events and structures in the human past are dimmed and disappear.

Ad 4: Cognition is impossible without integrating single facts or information about them into conceptual patterns of meaning where generalizations play an important role. To keep up the individualistic aspect of temporal appearances of human culture it is necessary to develop a specific way of thinking, namely the *hermeneutical* one. Hermeneutics is based on difference in the articulation of the human mind and spirit in its interrelationship with the world. It starts when we experience that there is something strange outside and beside us, something different which moves our minds and states the high importance of difference in the cultural organization of human life. To understand means to dissolve strangeness into difference. Strange articulations of meaning in practical life become recognizable. They can be translated into a familiar form of symbolizing the world. In this form of translation – that is, the essence of hermeneutics – the difference in symbolization will not vanish, but rather finds an articulation.

The concrete way in which these four principles were realized has been met with fundamental criticism. The core of this criticism lay in its quest for a synthesis of commonness and difference in human life. This quest, however, usually stems only from one culture, and when applied to the way of thinking of the otherness of other cultures, features of its own are introduced into the difference. Logically this procedure alienates, if not essentially misses them.

The argument that there is no neutral standpoint in viewing cultural difference is true. According to the logic of individualization and historization there is no starting point of thinking about humankind apart from its different manifestations in space and time. But this does not necessarily lead to relativism. There is always a possibility of reflecting on the peculiarity of one's own life form vis-à-vis other life forms, and there is always a possibility of communicating with the people of these other life forms about their peculiarity and their awareness of one's own culture. One cannot deny the fact that in every communication there are elements of political power which play a role. But this does not prevent insights into difference. Therein might be attempts to dominate others by imposing one's own worldview into the cognitive approaches of understanding other world views and life forms. Yet there is a specifically cognitive (and essentially humanistic) interest in hermeneutics aimed at getting a better insight into the peculiarity of one's own culture by mirroring it in the otherness of others.

This does not mean that the idea of humankind defined along the lines of traditional and modern humanistic thinking is free of any ethnocentric biases and elements. The question is not how to completely overcome them in favour of a ›pure‹ humanism, but how to domesticate, tame or ›humanize‹ them.

In the following argumentation I will attempt a ›humanized and humanizing‹ humanism, which is committed to the tradition of Western Humanism (in full awareness of its limits and failures, especially in respect to the Western attitude of dominating non-Western forms of thought in intercultural communication).[9]

3. Anthropological Foundations

It is not my intention to give a future-directed interpretation of classical modern humanism. I will refer to this tradition in order to give meaning to the term of a ›humanistic‹ approach to a philosophy of history. I will try to indicate its intellectual place in the different approaches to come to terms with the challenges of globalization and to find a ›global‹ cultural orientation, within which identity-forming differences are recognized.

I want to start by indicating and making plausible the taming power of humanism in the struggle over cultural identity. So let me begin my argumentation with an *anthropology of difference in human life*. In order to avoid the widespread methodological mistake of speaking about cultural difference by using the above-mentioned culturally specific pattern of interpretation (mainly that of the West), I would like to start with anthropological universals as a ground for a theory of universal history.[10] Very often the ›universal‹ character of a historical per-

---

9 See Rüsen, Jörn: »Traditionsprobleme eines zukunftsfähigen Humanismus«, in: Vöhler, Martin/Cancik, Hubert (Eds.): *Humanismus und Antikerezeption im 18. Jahrhundert*, vol. 1: *Genese und Profil des europäischen Humanismus*, Heidelberg 2009, pp. 201–216; Rüsen, Jörn: »Humanism in Response to the Holocaust – Destruction or Innovation?«, in: Postcolonial Studies 11.2 (2008), pp. 191–200.

10 I owe Reinhart Koselleck and Christoph Antweiler a lot of inspiration. See Koselleck, Reinhart: »Historik und Hermeneutik«, in: Koselleck, Reinhart/Gadamer, Hans-Georg: *Hermeneutik und Historik*, Heidelberg 1987, pp. 9–28 (= Sitzungsberichte der Heidelberger Akademie der Wissenschaften, Phil.-hist. Klasse, Jg. 1987, Bericht 1); also in: Koselleck, Reinhart: *Zeitschichten*: *Studien zur Historik*, Frankfurt/Main 2000, pp. 97–118; Antweiler, Christoph: *Mensch und Weltkultur: Für einen realistischen Kosmopolitismus im Zeitalter der Globalisierung*, Bielefeld 2011.

spective is not more than a generalized specific perspective, which does not take us any further. So I turned to anthropological universals with their potential to help avoiding this wrong generalization.

I am looking for cultural elements and factors of human life, which have as attributes two preconditions: They have to be shared in all life forms and they have to bear the temporal dynamics of change. The second attribute opens up the possibility of variousness in pursuing human life, whereas the first keeps this multitude and diversity together in one single coherent feature of humankind. It is not sufficient to identify structures and procedures of human life, which remain the same in all of its different manifestations in space and time. Such a concept would lock history in an anthropological standstill, whereas an anthropological foundation of historical change and variation allows a perception of its dynamic power. Human life has to be conceptualized in such a way that allows its basic structures to become visible as remaining the same in all times and spaces. This works when we apply a specific perspective which shows the forces of change – the unrest of time – within them.

The dynamics of time becomes visible on the level of anthropological universals if fundamental antagonisms become explicated in these fundamentals, within which human life is pursued and which permanently challenge the human mind and spirit to come to terms with them. These antagonisms are the basic patterns of human life defining the space where its specific human form takes place.
I would like to list them in the form of a simple enumeration without a distinct systematic order:

Human life always takes place in the following antagonisms or juxtapositions:

- between a position of above and below in social ranking;
- between center and periphery as a position in the special organization of social life;
- between man and woman, defining the realm of gender and its specific communication;
- between old and young, defining intergenerational relationship;
- between the internal and external dimension in forming identity;
- between power and powerlessness in interaction, deciding on the ability to give commands and compel obedience;

- between the necessity to die and the possibility to kill, defining the social space of violence;[11]
- between friend and foe in dimensioning the field of political activity;
- between master and servant, structuring the intersection of social, political and economic life;
- between poor and rich, defining the distribution of economic wealth;
- between individuality and collectivity in dimensioning human subjectivity;
- between conscious and unconscious, structuring the mental life of individuals and social communities;
- between good and evil, defining the moral dimension of human activity and suffering;
- between the innerworldly and the outerwordly dimension of human worldview;
- between the human and non-human dimension in categorizing the understanding of reality.

This list could be easily enlarged (its individual items depend upon the question, the answer to which is demanded by universal historical perspective). But for the purpose of explaining the anthropological basis of philosophy of history it is sufficient. All of these single items are interrelated with each other, so together they are logically structured as a network of universals. The whole field of historical experience can be categorized by this net. It endows the past and its experience in the present with a time-bridging meaning; this meaning is structured by categories which are valid for the experience of the past as well as its historical understanding.

It is the antagonistic and tensional nature of these universals which explains why human life forms permanently change over the course of time. Wherever a person or a group of people is situated in this network of conditions in the human world, they have to refer to them. This reference takes place in two different ways: passively in the mode of suffering, actively in the way of acting; both ways are inseparably interconnected. These structural conditions are pregiven for every human life, but in a principally open way: open to the mental work of sense generation by the people in concern. In the concrete situations of human life these structural conditions are impregnated with sense and meaning. But this pregiven conditioning sense and meaning is never

11 A more general juxtaposition would be between agency and suffering.

totally sufficient for pursuing life, since suffering derived from them is an anthropological universal as well. Pregiven sense has to be actively tackled in order to become effective in the human mind.

Through this tackling of pregiven sense, the pregiven life-form can be accepted or refused, legitimated or changed – in any case, it never simply remains the same after it has been interpreted and practically executed over the course of time and throughout the changes of ages and generations. This is the reason for the historical movement of the human world.

It is this mental activity which defines the historical character of the human world. History is more than only a temporal change in human life which happened in the past. Actually, it is a sense-filled and meaningful interrelation between past and present. Today the prevalent interpretation of this character of sense and meaning has agreed upon that of (only) a construction, of an invention of the present with reference to the past. To me this is not convincing at all, since the sense-generating process of historical thinking always takes place in the context of pregiven, i.e., socially powerful patterns of significance in cultural life. These patterns are the outcome of developments in the past, ending in the life situation of the people of today. They, however, deliberately refer to the past and its experience in order to create an idea of the temporal dimension of present-day lives. Thus one can say that the past has already brought along elements of its meaning into the present. This meaning is effective in the circumstances of the cultural processes of historical sense generation itself. Before it constructs, it has already been constructed.

How does this pregiven sense and meaning come about; how is it generated? It emerges from the cultural processes by which the past generations came to terms with the above-listed tensions of their living conditions. Temporal change always happens in the network of anthropological universals, and it is always impregnated by the meaning with which the people concerned are placed and place themselves within the challenging oppositions in their personal and social lives. With this meaning the change of human life caused by juxtapositions in its conditions of possibility gets a *direction*. The human mind culturally inscribes a temporal direction into the relationship of the people to the network of their tensional life conditions. This direction ontologically *changes temporal change into historical development*. To be precise: ›development‹ as an objective character in the temporal change of human life is not historical in the full meaning of the word, since it can be only applied in the way it is interpreted later on in awareness of what has happened after the events, the historical meaning of which are the matter of concern. They receive their historical character afterwards. By this post-festum interpretation the temporal changes in the past are put into a meaningful interrelation with the present. Only in the framework of such a comprehensive idea of time mediating its three dimensions into a pattern of significance are the changes of human life in the past historically shaped. But this pattern has necessarily integrated the cultural meaning by which people in the past have answered the challenge of their life conditions.

I wouldn't mind calling this integration a ›construction‹ since it is much more than just a repetition of the cultural efforts of the past. Instead, it is a cultural effort of the present brought about when coming to terms with the pregiven structures of sense and meaning manifest in real-life conditions, under which historical thinking takes place.

The consequences of this argument for the philosophy of history are evident: on the level of anthropological universals, basic cultural principles of sense generation have to be identified. These principles must be as universal as the juxtapositions are, which they render livable. Here is not the place to systematically explicate them; here I only can give examples and focus my argumentation on those principles which anthropologically underlie the idea of humanism as an outcome of long-lasting developments in universal history.

All of these principles are ideas of legitimation (including the criticism of pregiven legitimacy). They can take the form of morality and corresponding rules of behavior, the form of justice and its realization by a set of laws, and other forms of interpretation which make human life livable and transform suffering into activity.

Humanism as it has emerged in the formative period of modernity in the West is one of these ideas covering most of the enumerated juxtapositions. It orientates human life

- in the juxtaposition between above and below with the idea of justice brought into the form of basic human and civil rights;
- in the juxtaposition between centre and periphery with the idea of polycentrism, based on the principle of mutual recognition of cultural differences;
- in the juxtaposition between man and woman with the principle of equality;

- in the juxtaposition between young and old with the idea of solicitousness, and especially so with a concept of education and self-cultivation (*Bildung*);
- in the juxtaposition between power and powerlessness with the idea of political equality (so that on principle the dominated can and should dominate as well);
- in the juxtaposition between the necessity of dying and the possibility of killing with the idea of life in its most emphatic sense (of ›humane‹ or ›good‹ life and not only biological survival);
- in the juxtaposition between friend and foe with the idea of peace;
- in the juxtaposition between master and servant with the idea of social equality;
- in the juxtaposition between poor and rich with the idea of sufficiency;
- in the juxtaposition between individuality and collectivity with the idea of mutual recognition;
- in the juxtaposition between conscious and unconscious with an idea of psychic coherence or stability;
- in the juxtaposition of good and evil with principles of universal morality;
- in the juxtaposition between the innerworldly and the otherworldly dimension of the human worldview with the idea of the spiritual quality of human subjectivity;
- and, finally, in the juxtaposition between the human and the non-human dimension in categorizing the understanding of reality with the idea of awe and respect.[12]

This humanism, in its reference to anthropological universals, is a historical peculiarity. In order to make it plausible it is necessary to develop an idea of an encompassing historical development covering societies from archaic to modern and to put it into this development. This idea should bring about two achievements in historical thinking: It should cover the realm of universal history in a twofold way: making visible a general line of change by culturally treating the juxtapositions

---

12 Johann Wolfgang von Goethe has presented this idea as the guiding rule in the »pedagogical province« of his novel »Wilhelm Meisters Wanderjahre« (1829) (Goethe, Johann Wolfgang: »Wilhelm Meisters Wanderjahre«, in: Trunz, Erich (Ed.): *Goethes Werke*, vol. III, Munich 1994). [»Wilhelm Meister's Journeyman Years«]. [Goethe, Johann Wolfgang: *Wilhelm Meister's Travels*, translation of the first Edition by Thomas Carlyle, Columbia, SC 1991].

of human life, and at the same time making visible fundamental cultural differences.

I will try to outline such an idea in three steps of argumentation:

- first by depicting basic similarities in archaic societies,
- secondly by holding up the idea of an evolutionary step of humankind in the so-called axial ages of world civilizations,
- thirdly by interpreting the step of humankind into modernity as a second axial age.

I will not address all juxtapositions in their particular individuality, but will rather concentrate on one of the fundamental principles of orientating human life within the juxtaposition of its social conditions. It is a principle which is simply derived from the elementary fact of being a human being. It is not related to one or two of the stated juxtapositions, but addresses most, if not all of them. Indeed, there is no form of human life in which being a human being does not play a role in the cultural orientation of life. The meaning of this anthropological universal has substantially changed over the course of time, of course. It is this change which may furnish a red thread of historical thinking and be a cue to meet the demands of coming to terms with the globalizing process of today (as I have pointed out at the beginning of my paper).

4. Stages of Development

In all cultures, at all times and places in the world, human life is morally regulated by a clear distinction between good and evil and related principles of human conduct.[13] The ability for such a distinction and its application to human agency presupposes a certain idea of what it means to be a human being:[14] humans are defined as persons; they are

---

13 I mainly refer to Antweiler, Christoph: »Pankulturelle Universalien – Basis für einen inklusiven Humanismus?«, in: Rüsen, Jörn (Ed.): *Perspektiven der Humanität: Menschsein im Diskurs der Disziplinen*, Bielefeld 2010, pp. 93–144.

14 A logical confirmation of this anthropological universal is given by Gethmann, Carl Friedrich: »The Special Status of the Human Being as a Topic of Practical Philosophy«, in: Duncker, H.-R./Prieß, K. (Eds.): *On the Uniqueness of Mankind*, Berlin/Heidelberg 2004, pp. 95–105.

individuals with a physical and psychic continuity. As such they are responsible for what they do or fail to do - at least on the level of everyday life. This responsibility furnishes every human being with the quality of dignity (as we would express it in our modern language). This ›dignity‹ demands respect and recognition in all social contexts of life.[15]

This idea of a substantial moral quality of every human being is based on another anthropologically universal quality of humans, namely, the ability to change one's own perspective of perception and interpretation by taking over the perspectives of others. The humanistic idea or ›dignity‹ of man is anthropologically rooted in the human ability of making decisions in the tension between good and evil and in the ability for empathy. This anthropological quality demands forms of human cooperation which, across all cultural differences, are important for the social organization of human life.

Out of these roots grows the tree of human culture with its numerous branches and leaves. In order to come closer to its multitude and variety some basic temporal differentiations are useful. They are very abstract, but for the concept of universal history, extremely necessary, so that this multitude and variety can be placed in it and get its historical meaning.

(a) Archaic Societies

Archaic societies are the oldest forms of society. In the framework of a humanistic philosophy of history they can be generally characterized by their cultural definition of what a human being is, namely: only the people of one's own community own this quality. The people living beyond one's own sphere of life are not perceived as human; they are lacking essential elements of one's own humanity.[16]

15 Müller, Klaus E.: *Das kleine Dorf und die große Welt – Grundzüge des Humanitätsideals*, in: Rüsen, Jörn (Ed.): *Perspektiven der Humanität: Menschsein im Diskurs der Disziplinen*, Bielefeld 2010, pp. 145–190.

16 Klaus Müller had characterised this excluding particular universality of being a human being in archaic societies with the term »Eigenweltverabsolutierung« (setting one's own world as absolute): Müller, Klaus E.: »Einführung«, in: Müller, Klaus E. (Ed.): *Menschenbilder früher Gesellschaf-*

The cultural rules of this form of life are characterized by the imperative to keep up tradition, to inscribe it into the minds and hearts of one's people and by all means to continue it. Social interrelationship is cultivated according to the principle of reciprocity. Morality is not universal but split into ethical principles of treating one's own people (pre-scribing this reciprocity) on the one side and the exploitation and subjugation of the others. Slavery and cannibalism are eloquent examples.

(b) Axial Time Societies

The term ›axial age‹ implies a fundamental change in human worldview.[17] It goes along with changes in the other dimensions of human life as well, of course. Taking all these developments together one can speak of the new life form of so called ›advanced civilizations‹. They came about at different times in different places (roughly between 600 BC and 600 AD). As life forms they share essential elements, qualities and factors which define their epoch-making historical novelty. For the purpose of my argumentation the most important quality in this change is the *universalization of the idea of humankind.* Now, not only are one's own people human, with their special abilities, but (principally) all other members of the human race are endowed with this quality as well.

This cultural turn of the axial age is characterized by a new way of distinguishing and interrelating the human self, the divine and the sub-human world, or the human, extra-human and super-human sphere of reality. These spheres become more separated, and therefore their new interrelationship develops new forms of cultural activities. For the cultural orientation of practical life the most important change lies in the transformation of the divine world into a new dimension of transcendence and the increase in subjectivity of the human self. In this respect, the universalization of the moral quality of being a human being is at the same time a *subjectivation*

---

ten: *Ethnologische Studien zum Verhältnis von Mensch und Natur*, Frankfurt/Main 1983, p. 15.

17 The following part is mainly based on the work of Shmuel N. Eisenstadt. Eisenstadt, Shmuel N. (Ed.): The *Origins and diversity of axial age civilizations*, Albany 1986; see Arnason, Johann P./Eisenstadt, Shmuel N./Wittrock, Björn (Eds.): *Axial Civilizations and World History*, Leiden 2005.

of the human self. Universalizing humankind is a consequence of the new transcendent character of the divine. God is no longer the God of one people (when others have another God of their own), but the God of every human being. This is evident in the monotheistic religions which emerge in the evolutionary step of axial age. But it applies as well to the previous axial age transformations of archaic societies into advanced civilizations. In Buddhism, Hinduism, Confucianism and Daoism, for instance, the use of the idea of a metaphysical order allows interpretation of the world. This order is not simply evident to the senses, but requires intellectual effort to apply them to human affairs. It is expressed by the use of highly abstract and universal concepts or principles like Dharma, Brahma, Dao, Li, Logos etc. These are evident, true and obligatory for everybody.

The evolutionary step of the axial age has brought about an increase in transcendence and in subjectivity. Both together give humanity a new cultural shape. In the perspective of humanism this shape shows an increase in humanity. The moral quality of being a human becomes humanized. A very eloquent example of this axial age humanism is Confucianism and its moral principle of ›ren‹ (benevolence).[18] Morality bears its own universalism, expressed by the ›golden rule‹. In both, humanity broke the constraints of ethnicity.[19] This is expressed in central statements of the different axial age religions (we call them ›world religions‹). In the Christian relationship between the single individual and God, all differences among men vanish;[20] and it becomes possible to say

---

18 See Huang, Chun-Chieh: *Humanism in East Asian Confucian Contexts*, Bielefeld 2010.

19 It is important to note that ›evolution‹ does not mean that the older forms of cultural orientation dissolve and vanish. They remain in very different manifestation, including vast regions of the subconscious. But they change their place in the framework of culture. Ethnicity in the modern age, for example, is different from ethnicity in archaic societies.

20 Most typical is the word of St. Paul: »There is neither Jew nor Greek, there is neither bond nor free, there is neither male nor female, for ye are all one in Christ Jesus« (Gal. 3,28).

that the killing of one single human being applies to humankind in general.[21]

For the philosophical perspective of universal history, the paradigm of the axial age implies the existence of a second epoch after the first epoch, the breakthrough of which we have just mentioned. This is characterized by the universalization and, at the same time, by the subjectivation of humankind vis-à-vis an ›objectivation‹ of the world. One point in this philosophical perspective has to be emphasized: in deviating from the traditional philosophy of history – as represented by Kant or Hegel – the epoch-defining feature of the axial age theory addresses the diversity of cultures existing alongside each other and does not attribute the philosophical importance of change to only one of them (in a temporal sequence with others). This Quality of Multifariousness is the reason why the axial age theory is so important for historical thinking in our era of globalization. It synthesizes a universal approach to history with an interest in difference, multitude, and diversity.

In this respect the axial age evolutionary turn in universal history can be regarded as a step towards the solution of the problems of intercultural communication today. But its universalization and subjectivation of humans and objectivation of the world in manifold different life forms is only a step in the right direction. Cultural difference remains in the universalized forms of humankind. It can even be an issue within cultures, not only an observation from an outsider's perspective. They refer to each other (if at all) in a negative way. One's own idea of universalism is thought to be the real, the true one; others are either a deviation or simply wrong. In a very radical form this is the case in the monotheistic concepts of religious belief. One almighty and all-encompassing God excludes every other divine being; only one's own belief is true; the others' belief is not only perceived as different (as in polytheism) but as wrong. And it is rather easy to devalue the humanity of others because of their differing beliefs.

21 See Qur'ān 5,32: »We decreed for the Children of Israel that whosoever killeth a human being for other than manslaughter or corruption in the earth, it shall be as if he had killed all mankind, and whoso saveth the life of one, it shall be as if he had saved the life of all mankind.«

The universalism of axial age civilizations in understanding man and his relationship to the divine world (the guarantee of the order of his life) is an exclusive one. This exclusion causes tensions and clashes, but since the different civilizations used to live apart from each other, they did not endanger the plausibility of single universalisms and their shaping of subjectivity, nor the ensuing awareness of nature and the human world. For thousands of years this coexistence of living beside each other has persisted. Even today on the level of everyday life it is still the dominant form of intercultural relationship, even in intellectual discourse. But it has no future, since globalization means that different life forms and their cultural regulations come closer and closer together, and they may even merge.

On the level of sense generation it is a question of common survival whether this exclusiveness can be overcome and even changed into its opposite. This is precisely a question of modernity, and I think that modern humanism as it was established in the West at the end of the 18th and the beginning of the 19th century is one first attempt to find an answer. I don't say that it is already an adequate answer,[22] but it indicates that one is possible and therefore indicates the direction of further historical development from the perspective of a philosophy of universal history.

(c) Modernity as a Second Axial Age

The step towards modernity took place all over the world. It was taken under the strong influence of Western culture, but it was more deeply and differently practiced than a mere process of westernization. To describe it one should follow the proposal of Shmuel Eisenstadt – one of the most prominent representatives of axial age theory – and speak of »multiple modernities« instead of

22 I have criticized this modern western humanism in the perspective of the demands for intercultural communication in the era of globalization and elsewhere. See Rüsen, Jörn: »Traditionsprobleme eines zukunftsfähigen Humanismus«, in: Vöhler, Martin/Cancik, Hubert (Eds.): *Humanismus und Antikerezeption im 18. Jahrhundert*, vol. 1: *Genese und Profil des europäischen Humanismus*, Heidelberg 2009, pp. 201–216.

one single unifying modernity.[23] In the framework of a philosophy of history this idea of a multitude of modernities, as has already been applied to the concept of an axial age, should be translated into the characterization of modernity as the third great epoch in universal history. This can easily be done on the philosophical level since the change to this epoch is a change in the logic of the already achieved (multiple) universalism in understanding humanity. I think that we can identify a lot of factual and theoretical evidence for the specific character of modernity as a *shift from exclusive to inclusive universalisms* in understanding mankind.

An established paradigm of this inclusive humanism is not yet in view. But particular elements of this paradigm can already be identified. A universalistic dimension of understanding humankind has already been established in the previous epoch, and there are no reasons for giving it up in favour of any kind of relativism. (Relativism may be useful to criticize dogmatic universalisms, but vis-à-vis the globalization process it is an intellectual hand up for the clash of civilizations, which relegates the effort of solving intercultural tensions to the power game of politics.)

But what about the inclusive character of this universalism? How can its historically pregiven logic of exclusion be changed into something completely contrary? We can observe developments in cultural orientation which may demonstrate the feasibility of this change. I cannot give a systematic account of these developments; this would demand an elaborate theory of modernity in the realm of cultural sense-generation orientation. However, I can spell out some signs and examples of a historical process of establishing inclusive universalisms in conceptualizing and understanding humanity. One of the strongest indications is, of course, modern Western humanism. Though this humanism has its shortcomings, it has a strong merit: it has brought about ideas of inclusiveness which could be interculturally accepted.[24] At the beginning of my paper I have already mentioned some of these ideas. The most

23 Eisenstadt, Shmuel N.: »Multiple Modernities«, in: Daedalus 29.1 (2000), pp. 1–30.

24 See the contributions of Dipesh Chakrabarty, Muhammad Arkoun and Longxi Zhang in Rüsen, Jörn/Laass, Henner (Eds.): *Humanism in Intercultural Perspective*, Bielefeld 2009.

convincing of these is that of human dignity – that every human being is more than a mere means to the purpose of others, and rather is a purpose within him- or herself. Difference in cultural orientation belongs within this dignity, but we should not at the same time overlook that dignity is a criterion for criticizing cultural orientations which violate basic elements of humanity.

As I have outlined in this paper, philosophy of history is in itself such an element of inclusive universalism. When reflecting upon modernity, it contributes to cultural efforts to give modernization in the guise of globalization a direction into the future. Here the hope for establishing humane factors in the cultural orientation of human life has a strong voice. Academic discourse may contribute to this if it picks up the challenge of globalization concerning cultural identity and works on the answer of humanism. Here otherness and selfishness should be designed as mutually enriching in their interrelationship in the framework of a shared idea of what it means to be a human being.

BIBLIOGRAPHY

Abelshauser, Werner: *The dynamics of German industry: Germany's path toward the new Economy and the American Challenge*, New York 2005.

Antweiler, Christoph: »Pankulturelle Universalien – Basis für einen inklusiven Humanismus?«, in: Rüsen, Jörn (Ed.): *Perspektiven der Humanität: Menschsein im Diskurs der Disziplinen*, Bielefeld 2010, pp. 93–144 (= Being Human: Caught in the Web of Cultures – Humanism in the Age of Globalization, vol. 8).

Antweiler, Christoph: *Mensch und Weltkultur: Für einen realistischen Kosmopolitismus im Zeitalter der Globalisierung*, Bielefeld 2011 (= Being Human: Caught in the Web of Cultures – Humanism in the Age of Globalization, vol. 10).

Arnason, Johann P./Eisenstadt, Shmuel N./Wittrock, Björn (Eds.): *Axial Civilizations and World History*, Leiden 2005.

Eisenstadt, Shmuel N. (Ed.): The *Origins and diversity of axial age civilizations*, Albany 1986.

Eisenstadt, Shmuel N.: »Multiple Modernities«, in: Daedalus 29.1 (2000), pp. 1–30.

Friese, Heidrun (Ed.): *Identities – Time, Difference, and Boundaries*, New York 2002 (= Making Sense of History, vol. 2).

Gethmann, Carl Friedrich: »The Special Status of the Human Being as a Topic of Practical Philosophy«, in: Duncker, H.-R./Prieß, K. (Eds.): *On the Uniqueness of Mankind*, Berlin/Heidelberg 2004, pp. 95–105.

Goethe, Johann Wolfgang: »Wilhelm Meisters Wanderjahre«, in: Trunz, Erich (Ed.): *Goethes Werke*, vol. III, Munich 1994.

Goethe, Johann Wolfgang: *Wilhelm Meister's Travels*, translation of the first Edition by Thomas Carlyle, Columbia, SC 1991.

Herder, Johann Gottfried: *Ideen zur Philosophie der Geschichte der Menschheit*, ed. Martin Bollacher, Frankfurt/Main 1989.

Huang, Chun-Chieh: *Humanism in East Asian Confucian Contexts*, Bielefeld 2010 (= Being Human: Caught in the Web of Cultures – Humanism in the Age of Globalization, vol. 9).

Humboldt, Wilhelm von: »Über den Geist der Menschheit«, in: Flitner, Andreas/Giel, Klaus (Ed.): *Werke in fünf Bänden*, vol. 1: *Schriften zur Anthropologie und Geschichte*, Darmstadt 1960, pp. 506–518.

Kant, Immanuel: »Metaphysik der Sitten«, in: Weischedel, Wilhelm: *Kant: Werke*, vol. 7: Schriften zur Ethik und Religionsphilosophie, second part, Darmstadt 1975, pp. 304–643: A 93 (English: http://praxeology.net/kant7.htm).

Koselleck, Reinhart: »Historik und Hermeneutik«, in: Koselleck, Reinhart/Gadamer, Hans-Georg: *Hermeneutik und Historik*, Heidelberg 1987, pp. 9–28 (= Sitzungsberichte der Heidelberger Akademie der Wissenschaften, Phil.-hist. Klasse, Jg. 1987, Bericht 1).

Koselleck, Reinhart: *Zeitschichten: Studien zur Historik*, Frankfurt/Main 2000, pp. 97–118.

Müller, Klaus E.: »Einführung«, in: Müller, Klaus E. (Ed.): *Menschenbilder früher Gesellschaften: Ethnologische Studien zum Verhältnis von Mensch und Natur*, Frankfurt/Main 1983, pp. 13–69.

Müller, Klaus E.: *Das kleine Dorf und die große Welt – Grundzüge des Humanitätsideals*, in: Rüsen, Jörn (Ed.): *Perspektiven der Humanität: Menschsein im Diskurs der Disziplinen*, Bielefeld 2010, pp. 145–190.

Osterhammel, Jürgen/Petersson, Niels T.: *Globalization: A Short History*. Princeton 2009.

Rüsen, Jörn/Laass, Henner (Eds): *Humanism in Intercultural Perspective: Experiences and Expectations*. Bielefeld 2009 (= Being Human: Caught in the Web of Cultures – Humanism in the Age of Globalizations, vol. 1).

Rüsen, Jörn: »Humanism in Response to the Holocaust – Destruction or Innovation?«, in: Postcolonial Studies 11.2 (2008), pp. 191–200.

Rüsen, Jörn: »Traditionsprobleme eines zukunftsfähigen Humanismus«, in: Vöhler, Martin/Cancik, Hubert (Eds.): *Humanismus und Antikerezeption im 18. Jahrhundert*, vol. 1: *Genese und Profil des europäischen Humanismus*, Heidelberg 2009, pp. 201–216.

Special Issue: »The Interaction between Self and the Others in the Age of Globalization«, Taiwan Journal of East Asian Studies 7.2 (2010).

Straub, Jürgen (Ed.): *Narration, Identity, and Historical Consciousness*, New York 2005 (= Making Sense of History, vol. 3).

I.3 Reinterpretation of Civilization

Two-way Interaction, Multiple Perspectives, and Awareness of Issues

ZHANG JIE

Interpreting civilization has always been an endeavor allowing multiple approaches and distinctive conclusions. In the academic community, the difficulty in differentiating civilization from culture is universally accepted. Researchers tend to generalize and define the word »civilization« from separate perspectives, using the method of scientific induction. Actually, the concept of civilization is very complex and profound, and thus is never to be interpreted from a single perspective. This paper provides a combination of different perspectives, such as the interaction between forward and reversed directions of the development of civilization, history, literature and language, in order to offer multiple interpretations of civilization. In general, civilization can be seen as the cultural achievement accumulated over the course of social evolution of mankind. However, from the historical perspective, this kind of cultural achievement is composed of a series of concrete historical events and social changes. From the literary perspective, civilization transcends those concrete historical events, becomes the result of the vicissitudes between the newer and older societies, and is of universal value. At the level of language, civilization is merely linguistic and semiotic representation by mankind, in which language and symbols serve as the carrier of civilization for the sake of its existence. Along with the development of human society, the interpretation of civilization will certainly present more changes. We do not seek an ultimate definition of civilization, yet we can always make further ap-

proaches towards it, because the interpretation of civilization requires multiple and dynamic perspectives.

From the earliest use of the term »civilization«, there have been complex and multiple interpretations about its meaning. Common grounds in this respect are hard to establish. Perhaps it is unlikely that a universally acknowledged definition will be found. Ru Xin writes in World Civilizations: »It should be pointed out that the interpretations of ›civilization‹ are just as diversified as those of ›culture‹. Different definitions coexist, without ever arriving at any consensus«. Therefore, the research project entitled »Studies on World Civilizations« administered by the Center for Comparative Studies of World Civilizations (Chinese Academy of the Social Sciences) has its focus laid on »the specific research of world civilizations« instead of »which definition is more suitable«.[1] However, it is necessary to interpret the term »civilization«, which not only determines whether we can define and represent civilization in verbal terms, but also suggests that different interpretations will lead to different research perspectives and methodologies, which in turn will directly affect our exploration of civilization itself.

During the specific research of civilization, one of the more generally practiced methods has been to approach the history of civilization, such as its genesis and origin. This method attempts to sort out a diachronic thread of development composed of cause-effect relationships in the complex phenomenon of civilization. Based on this effort, scientific induction, generalization and definition can be achieved. It can be said that any human civilization in history has a main and stable theme running through its development. One of the primary tasks of studies on civilization is to identify this main theme. For instance, Chinese civilization has undergone thousands of years of feudal regimes, during which the dominant Confucian civilization had »Confucian philosophy« as its main theme, namely the »Confucian philosophy« proposed by Dong Zhongshu, who insisted on the monopoly of Confucianism on social ideology, combining the theoretical achievements made by various theorists with Confucian teachings as the core.[2] Contrary to the situation in China, for American civilization, »perhaps the

1 Xin, Ru: »General Preface to *World Civilizations*«, in: Mansu, Qian: *American Civilization*, Beijing 2001, p 2.

2 Zhenduo, Ma et al.: *Confucian Civilization*, Beijing 1999, p. 4.

most striking feature lies in its youthfulness, with a history of less than four hundred years«. It is different from Confucian civilization in that »it has never been a indigenous civilization, but a creation by sophisticated European immigrants on the new Continent according to their ideas«. »Though the American people do not have a unified ideology, they share universally accepted ideas, namely the value system with liberty at the center«.[3]

Obviously, this research method, which starts from the historical perspective, has made a huge contribution to the studies on human civilizations, and has become one of the major methodologies in this field, paving the way for further explorations. However, the cognition of civilization has been complex and diversified, so it is hard to interpret the term from any single perspective. As a result, compared with the traditional mono-faceted interpretation, various and multiple interpretative perspectives can provide us with new channels for thinking, and can enrich methods in historical studies.

This paper offers diversified perspectives, such as the interaction between forward and reversed directions of the development of civilization, history, literature and language, and the awareness of problems in the interpretations of civilization. It attempts to achieve multiple interpretations of civilization. It is easy to verify that with the development of human society, interpretations of civilization are always changing. It is highly possible that we can never attain an ultimate definition of civilization, yet we can always make further approaches towards it, because the interpretation of civilization requires multiple and dynamic perspectives.

1. TWO-WAY INTERACTION IN THE DEVELOPMENT OF CIVILIZATION

In general, civilization can be seen as the cultural achievement accumulated over the course of social evolution of mankind. »The generally accepted practice in the international research community« is to »understand ›civilization‹ as ›culture‹ in its broad sense. In particular, it means the social and historical entity occupying a certain space (hence regional entity), including spiritual civilization and material

3 Mansu: »American Civilization«, pp. 1–2.

civilization. It is the agglomeration of the purposeful activities and achievements of mankind«[4]. In the General Reference Dictionary, there are two interpretations of civilization: the first states that civilization is equal to culture, such as material civilization and spiritual civilization. The second states that civilization refers to »the progressive state of human society, as opposite to the ›barbarian‹ state« (*General Reference Dictionary*: 1534). These definitions have been derived from the relationship between social development and the formation of civilization, which examines civilization from the perspectives of genesis and origin.

Indeed, when discussing the relationship between the development of a certain society and a civilization, people tend to treat social development as antecedent to civilization. Is it not true that the Confucian civilization in China's history has been the result of thousands of years of social evolution in China? The view that social development gives birth to civilization is undoubtedly correct when the genesis of civilization is in question. However, once a civilization has come into being in history, for later generations, this civilization is bound to exist prior to our current society, prior to our current context of social discourse. When we set out to evaluate a certain phenomenon of civilization, it is impossible to break away from the restrictions of the current social reality and the system of power discourse.

Before any history of civilization can be written, the writer has been conditioned by various factors, such as cognitive abilities, framework of thinking, level of science, and ideology. Our research tends to be tinted with a certain bias. It is in just this sense that absolutely objective civilization history can never exist. Most interpretations of civilization have been added by later generations. To a certain extent, it can be said that the history of civilization development has been »verbal construction« by later generations, or simply fragmentary interpretations of history. Therefore, the development of a certain civilization not only involves positive and forward formation or extinction, but also involves reversed development or counter-development.

In terms of time, the forward development of civilization is time- and space-restricted, because when this civilization dies out, there will be no further changes whatsoever. Yet the reversed development of civilization is infinite, which will be improved and completed along

4 Mansu: »American Civilization«, pp. 1–2.

with the lapse of time. As long as human beings continue to exist, interpretations about civilization will last. It is easy to see that after the extinction of a civilization, there will be no adding to its content, yet its interpretation will be increased. This development actually means that later generations have supplemented their understanding about civilization with the new knowledge they have acquired in this aspect. A civilization with true value shall enjoy eternal vigor, and later generations can always get inspiration from this kind of civilization.

In terms of the domain or space of thinking, the forward development of a certain civilization only contains the space of thinking and experience of the creators of such a civilization; however, the reversed development incorporates the intelligence and rich knowledge of all subsequent generations. In this way, when we are discussing a certain civilization, we should consider reversed development, which had been overlooked in the past. Studies on the reversed development of civilization aim to illustrate that the civilization in question usually consists of the understanding of later generations, with prominently subjective features.

When addressing the issues of China's Confucian civilization, we have experienced different understandings and evaluations over history, and we are coming up with reinterpretations of this civilization. Evaluations of different researchers, even during the same historical period, are unlikely to be the same. Their interpretations are also different. In addition to the influence from the ideological environment, interpretations are also affected by the cultural awareness, growth environment and research conditions of the researchers.

Therefore, the development of a certain civilization, as we understand it, generally includes two aspects. On the one hand, it is forward development that we are familiar with, namely the genesis and development of civilization. On the other hand, it is the reversed development that we often neglected in the past: once the civilization is created, later generations can still find new content and take new achievements from it. Along with the vicissitudes of time and environment, a civilization, which otherwise would not have changed, can continue to develop thanks to the evaluation of later generations. Obviously this development is not forward, but a reversed or counter-development. It is this two-way development, both forward and reversed, that constitutes the history of civilizational development.

2. Multiple Perspectives for Interpreting Civilization

From a diachronic perspective, the development of civilization has been realized through the interaction between forward and reversed development. From a synchronic perspective, the interpretation and research of civilization can be conducted from different angles. Although the research results from different perspectives indicate similarities to certain extent, differences are more obvious. As a result, the lack of awareness of multiple perspectives for interpreting civilization may lead to incomplete understanding and cognition.

Among most institutes of higher education, the specialized education or research of civilization is the responsibility of the history department. This is the case with the setup of the Department of American Civilization at Harvard University. In the academic community in China, studies on civilization are carried out in the historical context. From the historical perspective, this kind of cultural achievement is composed of a series of concrete historical events and social changes. The civilization of a certain nation or community has been centered on a particular ideology or spirit undergoing the process of formation or extinction accompanied by the changes of concrete historical stages. In China, Confucian civilization originated from ancient Chinese civilization and the Confucian ideological system based on three dynasties. With the efforts of representative figures of Confucianism in the Qin dynasty, headed by Confucius, Mencius, Xunzi and their disciples, Confucianism had become the most influential teaching at that time. After the brutal regime of Emperor Qin Shihuang with his notorious policy of »Burning down Confucian scripts and burying Confucian followers«, Emperor Wu, his successor in the Han Dynasty, accepted the proposal from Dong Zhongshu to »terminate all other schools and establish the monopoly of Confucianism«. Hence Confucianism, the core of Confucian civilization, could become the orthodox ideology of the ruling class. Thereafter, this civilization evolved through the Han, Tang, Song, Yuan, Ming and Qing dynasties before meeting its extinction in the »May 4th Movement« in the early 20th century. Historical approaches to civilization view each civilization as the result of history, as a civilization which originates, prospers and collapses in history. We should admit that the historical perspective has been a major one in studies on human civilization.

However, human understanding of civilization should be allowed to be done from multiple perspectives. Diversified researches from different perspectives are more thorough than those from single perspectives. Compared with historical perspectives, literary perspectives can transcend specific and superficial meaning to reach the level of universality. Seen from the literary perspective, civilization can transcend the changes of social stages and specific historical events, because civilization is the result of the alternative development of older and newer social institutions. Professor Lewis M. Dabney of Wyoming University writes in *Edmund Wilson: A Life in Literature* (2005)[5], »Edmund Wilson, the American literary and social critic of the 20th century, had depicted the track of American civilization with his writing.« He pointed out in the New York Times: »If American history does exist, it was Mr. Wilson who helped us find it, and he himself is an important part of this history«[6]. Obviously, Wilson's depiction is different from that of historians. Dabney's title for Wilson's biography is interesting in itself – a seemingly ordinary title with profound significance: »A Life in Literature«. Edmund Wilson worked with two features of literary criticism, »imagination« and »publicity«, to concern himself with the historical awareness and social problems in literature, thus enabling literary criticism to go beyond the sphere of literature and rise to the level of civilization. He always considered artists as individual »protagonists« in the history of literature and culture, and tried hard to represent their lives so as to reconstruct the history of civilization in which they had lived. Therefore, Edmund Wilson helped literary creation and criticism step out of the ivory tower through the channels of social history and reality; in addition, he employed literature to reveal the process of evolution of social civilization.

At the level of language, civilization is merely linguistic and semiotic representation by mankind, whereby language and symbols serve as the carrier of civilization for the sake of its existence. Under the influence of synchronic linguistics established by Ferdinand de Saussure, propelled by Roland Barthes and Derrida with their criticism of logocentrism, and based on the philosophical thinking of »language and being« by Heidegger and Gadamer and the analysis of linguistic logics and semantics by Wittgenstein, the theoretical community has

5 Dabney, Lewis M.: *Edmund Wilson: A Life in Literature*, New York 2005.

6 Dabney, Lewis M.: *The Edmund Wilson Reader*, New York 1997.

realized that language is of entity status and an »independent being« which serves as the foundation of human civilization. Be it truth or history, it is text constituted with language. It is language that legitimizes the »being« of our world. It is true that »man speaks language«; it is also true that language-based thinking controls human beings, that is to say, »language speaks of man«. The existence of social civilization is actually the existence of language, and the essence of civilization is represented with the essence of language. Language thus has become the »home of being«; »we reside in the homeland of language«.[7]

Obviously, from the perspective of language, the development of civilization has been changed from the relationship between man and world to the relationship between man and language. The achievements of civilization are no longer seen as conforming to the material world or being consistent with the subject or object. On the contrary, they are the opening of existence, and language becomes the major form of civilization. Language articulates civilization, including the current civilization as it is, the historical civilization belonging to the past, and the predictions of future civilization. Only by »constantly penetrating the homeland of language« can human beings reach the destination of civilization.[8] Therefore, between man and world there exists a reality of language, which enables our civilization to come into being.

In fact, the interpretations of civilization should coexist in pluralism. It is impossible to find an exclusively correct interpretation. Each way of interpretation can provide a unique method for us to understand civilization, and can complement others to achieve interdependence instead of mutual replacement. Since the development of civilization is complex and unfathomable, the researches made from single perspective cannot evade the insufficiency of being partial and biased.

---

7 Heidegger, Martin: *Poetry, Language, Thought*, New York 1971, pp. 191–92.

8 Heidegger: »Poetry, Language, Thought«, p. 123.

3. AWARENESS OF ISSUES IN INTERPRETATION OF CIVILIZATION

In general, the task of studies on civilization is to probe into the various historical events during the formation and development of a certain civilization. From among the complex phenomena of civilization, researchers can sort out and arrange its elements to arrive at some conclusive evaluations. This can facilitate the description of the evolution of this civilization and improve the understanding of the achievements of this civilization. Valuable lessons can be drawn from this kind of research to guide further studies on human society.

In the course of research on the history of civilization, the academic community has been used to the practice of starting from the origin of civilization, proceeding to the classification of phenomena of an individual country, period and civilization. This is an attempt to summarize the characteristics of a certain civilization during a particular period, together with the theme of this civilization and the rules for its development. Also, the origin of the civilization can be located, which is also the core spirit of the civilization.

However, it is interesting to note that once the achievements of a certain civilization are identified after analyzing various phenomena, this analysis would be reexamined or even criticized by contemporary researchers or later generations. It can also be refuted by the same researchers. The birth and development of Confucian civilization had undergone several major rises and falls in history. Emperor Qin Shihuang and Emperor Wu, both being monarchs of a great empire, took a totally different attitude towards »Confucianism«. This poses a bewildering question which has interested researchers for a long time: what is the mission of studies on civilization? In the face of diversified phenomena of civilization, shall we try to achieve some relatively unbiased evaluation and perform objective classification of the evolution of civilization, or shall we raise more issues? Shall we trigger new ideas? Are we able to solve the problems we encounter? Shall we look for new channels by replacing old questions with new ones, and promote our studies on civilization by reflecting more on the issues? In consideration of these questions, it is worthwhile discussing the awareness of issues for the research of civilization.

The academic tradition tends to divide philosophical development prior to the second half of the 20th century into three stages: ontology, epistemology, and the linguistic turn. The core issue for philosophical exploration in ancient Greece and Rome would be »What is the essence of the world«, and development in this field was based on ontological discussion about »being« or »existence«. All schools of theories at that time aimed to answer this question. Medieval philosophy and aesthetics actually had never deviated from the theme of theological ontology. In the 17th century, however, the European philosophical sphere witnessed a major event, »the epistemological turn«, with the focus on »how is it possible for human beings to know the world?« Rationalists headed by Descartes the French philosopher asked, »What is it that we know?« Empirical theorists represented by Francis Bacon wanted to know »how do we know what we know?« The »epistemological« philosophy established by Descartes had become the leading theory from the 17th century to the 19th century. At the turn of the 20th century, partly because of the influence of Saussure's linguistics, and more because of the positivism prevailing in the 19th century, the western philosophical sphere turned from the epistemological axle to the linguistic axle. The question taken up by theorists is »how can we express the essence of the world as we know it?« During the second half of the 20th century, scholars discovered that language should be the language of culture, so they turned to the axle of »cultural philosophy«. The focal point here is »In what cultural context do we express the essence of the world as we know it?« (Philosophy Institute of Academy of Social Sciences 1990).

Every time human beings discuss more sophisticated issues, they feel more dwarfed by the issues they discuss, and more convinced that the subjects cannot be thoroughly understood. However, it is this kind of »retreat« and change of question that has promoted the development of human civilization and social progress. Because human perception of truth is always changing, truth can never be absolute, and the existence of truth should be a chain of infinite questions, an eternal dynamic process. This is to say that truth does not exist in the form of a conclusion, but in the form of questions. The success of each exploration means the emergence of new questions.

Any conclusive understanding and evaluation can be critiqued or reconsidered. The research on civilization can best illustrate this point. However, questions can generate more room for thinking than conclusions. The answers to these questions are more diversified. In comparison, conclusive interpretations and understandings are more monotonous. Questions are for the readers to answer, yet conclusions have no such requirement. »Induction of the conclusion« is a closed frame of research, which is inevitable to incur language screening.

It is apparent that truth exists mainly in the form of questions. The development of civilization allows the process of continuous reversed interpretation. Studies on civilization should not be restricted in their scientific exploration, classification, induction and conclusion. Should they also involve the consideration of the issues brought about by the development of civilization? In this sense, is it necessary to stress the awareness of issues in the research of civilization? Should we raise more questions and draw fewer conclusions?

BLIOGRAPHY

Dabney, Lewis M.: *Edmund Wilson: A Life in Literature*, New York 2005.

Dabney, Lewis M.: *The Edmund Wilson Reader*, New York 1997.

Feng, Cao (Ed.): *General Reference Dictionary*, Shanghai 1980.

Heidegger, Martin: *Poetry, Language, Thought*, New York 1971.

Mansu, Qian: *American Civilization*, Beijing 2001.

Philosophy Institute of Academy of Social Sciences (former Soviet Union), Ovsyannikov, M.F. (Ed.): *History of Aesthetic Theories* (5th of six volumes), Moscow 1990.

Xin, Ru: »General Preface to World Civilizations«, in: Mansu, Qian: *American Civilization*, Beijing 2001, p 2.

Zhenduo, Ma et al.: *Confucian Civilization*, Beijing 1999.

II. The Breakthrough of Axial Times and Modernitites

II.1 On Axial Ages and other Thresholds between Epochs

BERNHARD GIESEN

The last national convention of historians in Germany showed that historical scholarship is, meanwhile, not only interested in different layers of analysis (event history, microhistory, regional history, structural history, cultural history, world history) but that it is also beginning to question the container model of nation states as a paradigm of historiography. Not only does the familiar spatial containment seem to be dissolving but also – and even more importantly – the temporal classification of its subject matter.[1] Together with national historiography, the customary periodization and differentiation into epochs comes under pressure. Today historians often choose a perspective that runs counter to the classic division into epochs: these are increasingly considered as constructions of historiography that do not match all fields equally well.[2] A classification according to functional fields or media, which differentiates explicitly in terms of pace of alteration and temporality, would be much more adequate: markets have a pace of repro-

1 See Giesen, Bernhard: »The temporalization of social order: Some theoretical remarks on the change«, in: Smelser, Neil J./Haferkamp, Hans (Eds.): *Social Change and Modernity*, Berkeley/Los Angeles 1992, pp. 294–319.

2 See Herzog, Reinhart/Koselleck, Reinhart (Eds.): *Epochenschwelle und Epochenbewusstsein*, Munich 1987 (= Poetik und Hermeneutik: Arbeitsergebnisse einer Forschungsgruppe XII); Seele, Peter: »Kategorien und Begriffe epochalen Wandels«, in: Seele, Peter: *Philosophie der Epochenschwelle: Augustin zwischen Antike und Mittelalter*, Berlin/New York 2008, pp. 35–61.

duction separate to that of constitutions, generations follow each other more rapidly than nation-states, etc.

However, the situation is even more rough in my own disciplinary field: following the distinctions of classical social theory, many sociologists still regard everything that happened before the French Revolution and the Industrial Revolution, those gateways to modern societies, as relatively stable, down-to-earth and clearly demarcated communities – in short: as »traditional« forms of society which succeeded timeless and stateless »primitive« societies, the investigation of which is mainly considered to be the business of ethnologists.

In the following remarks I will first address the question of whether and under which preconditions we can reasonably speak of such thresholds between epochs. Furthermore, I will outline the special cultural threshold that Jaspers[3] and Eisenstadt[4] have called the »axial age« and I will suggest how it may be rephrased in structural terms.

In the second step I will raise the question: why do we tend to make classifications which, when scrutinized more closely, are seen to be superficial and undifferentiated?[5] A preliminary explanation might refer to the logic of human narration: stories need to have a beginning and an ending, turning points and moments of decision have to be emphasized and discriminated from the regular »… so on and so forth«. Beginnings, turning points and endings are generally marked by mythical accounts that claim a greater believability than regular, normal stories. Myths can render improbable transformation plausible. They tell stories about creation and foundation, triumphs and traumata[6], in other words, about the extraordinary turned into narrative. At the conclusion of such a narrative, nothing is as it used to be; a new inception has been made.

---

3 Jaspers, Karl: *Vom Ursprung und Ziel der Geschichte*, Frankfurt/Main 1955.

4 Eisenstadt, Shmuel N. (1982): »The Axial Age: The Emergence of Transcendental Visions and the Rise of Clerics«, in: European Journal of Sociology 23.2 (1982), pp. 294–314.

5 Ehrlich, Leonard H./Wisser, Richard (Eds.): *Karl Jaspers Today: Philosophy at the Threshold of the Future*,Washington, D.C. 1988.

6 Giesen, Bernhard: *Triumph and Trauma*, Boulder 2004.

Some might argue that it is the mission of historiography to dismantle these mythical tales of inception as mere fiction.[7] Accurate research will dissolve the ruptures between epochs as gradual transitions and uneven changes that do not occur simultaneously. Ultimately, however, even the most thoroughly done analysis cannot escape the sequential order of narration.

Yet it is not only the format of narration that compels us to distinguish between epochs and to claim their inner unity. This assumption of the unity of an epoch is, in a distorted way, even fostered by the particular contortion of perspective that we associate with the spirit of modernity. Modernism focuses predominantly on novelty and tends to devalue the old and well known[8] – the old patterns seem to persist only as an anachronistic and exotic oddity, as a frivolous form of subsistence or as a »residue«, as Pareto once called it.[9] When we take the modern perspective we only see the new dress and forget the old body it covered.[10]

Thus, my thesis aims at this specific modernistic oblivion of continuity and its obsession with novelty and thereby also at the tendency of my own discipline to proclaim swiftly a new social order every other year to a label-addicted audience: from »late capitalism« to »risk society«[11], furthermore to »knowledge society«[12], to »network society«[13], to »global society«[14] – as if everything that so far has been gen-

---

7 White, Hayden V.: *Metahistory: Die historische Einbildungskraft im 19. Jahrhundert in Europa*, Frankfurt/Main 1991.

8 Giddens, Anthony: *Modernity and Self-Identity: Self and Society in the Late Modern Age*, Cambridge 1991.

9 Cf. for Paretos Term: Eisermann, Gottfried: *Vilfredo Pareto: Ein Klassiker der Soziologie*, Tübingen 1987, pp. 219–274.

10 Soeffner Hans-Georg/Max Miller (Eds.): *Modernität und Barbarei: Soziologische Zeitdiagnose am Ende des 20. Jahrhunderts*, Frankfurt/Main 1996.

11 Beck, Ulrich: *Risikogesellschaft: Auf dem Weg in eine andere Moderne*, Frankfurt/Main 2007.

12 Bell, Daniel: *The Coming of Post-Industrial Society: A Venture in Social Forecasting*, New York 1973.

13 Castells, Manuel: *Das Informationszeitalter 1: Der Aufstieg der Netzwerkgesellschaft*, Opladen 2003.

14 Luhmann, Niklas: *Die Gesellschaft der Gesellschaft*, Frankfurt/Main 2009.

erated by social and cultural evolution would not continue to exist in our society in one way or another. There may have been some translations, new dresses and arguably a different salience, but, they are still present, nonetheless. Little is actually new and, if it is, few contemporaries perceive it as such. Lévi-Strauss,[15] in his renowned preface to *Tristes Tropiques* (*A World on the Wane*), mentioned this blindness of contemporaries to novelty, when he wrote about the discoveries in Brazil of the 18th century; what phenomenal ethnological discoveries could have been made by Bougainville,[16] or even earlier by Léry,[17] had they been more sensitive to ethnic differences and less preoccupied with questions of geography and minerals.

Some evidence runs counter to the abovementioned modern perspective on novelty: nearly all institutional and cultural patterns that we relate to a »past« epoch still exist in our society today: when we adorn our T-shirts with names of football clubs, aren't we still totemists?[18] Aren't we still striving for courtly acclaim when we make the effort to appear on television? In organisations and associations we still discriminate between a patrons and clients; young men in the suburbs still want to be heroes who despise established rules. Let us not forget: even today the concept of the nation-state is not an archaic relic from times long bygone; rather, we still think in terms of nations[19] – at least on the soccer field and concerning issues of distribution within the European Union.

The actual copresence and simultaneity of patterns that we commonly relate to different epochs is not the remarkable exception, as one could still have assumed at the beginning of the past century, but rather the rule. Thus, the unity of an epoch is turned from a self-evident premise to a contingent field of research.

---

15 Lévi-Strauss, Claude: *Traurige Tropen*, Frankfurt/Main 1978.

16 Bougainville, Louis-Antoine de: *Reise um die Welt: Über Südamerika und durch den Pazifik zurück nach Frankreich*, Tübingen 2010.

17 Léry, Jean de: *History of a Voyage to the Land of Brazil*, transl. by Janet Whatley, Berkley 1990.

18 Cf. Freud, Sigmund: »Totem und Tabu. (Einige Übereinstimmungen im Seelenleben der Wilden und der Neurotiker)«, in: Freud, Sigmund: *Kulturtheoretische Schriften*, Frankfurt/Main 1997, pp. 287–444.

19 Giesen, Bernhard: *Die Intellektuellen und die Nation. Eine deutsche Achsenzeit*, Frankfurt/Main 1993.

Under which conditions, then, can we still conceive of the unity of an epoch? The traditional schoolbook response to this question refers to key events: the posting of Luther's theses in Wittenberg, the Peace of Westphalia, the Storming of the Bastille in Paris, the shots of Sarajevo et cetera. What holds true for novelty is also true, however, for events that mark a turning point: the epoch-making quality of such events is rarely acknowledged by contemporaries, and is frequently imputed only by later generations. The discovery of America by Columbus, the Boston Tea Party, even the Storming of the Bastille are examples of such epoch-making events the importance of which contemporary participants were not aware of immediately. We cannot escape the dynamics of shifting perspectives. They, in turn, support the assumption that the classification of epochs is, respectively, determined by the historical perspective.[20]

Also, the attempt to classify a certain epoch by means of then-prevalent engineering technology must fail once concede the co-existence of different technologies. The spreading of the railroad network did not make horses and camels obsolete; in the epoch of the Internet you still have mailmen and little corner shops; printing did not oust the lecture and the speech; genetically modified vegetables did not drive out the growing of tomatoes in one's backyard et cetera. Conversely, contemporaries experience some technological inventions as epoch-making that retrospectively appear rather inconspicuous. The Soviet Sputnik and the landing on the moon have been examples of such technological revolutions that did not affect society thoroughly.

We can only account for the unity of an epoch if we consider the effect it had in the minds of contemporaries. Such a suggestion can certainly not claim pristine originality. Rather, it is a kind of banal common-sense historiography. Furthermore, it solves the issue of periodization at the price of creating a possibly even bigger problem. The problem of demarcating epochs is simply shifted to the question of demarcating the boundaries of a culture.[21] Traditional conceptions of

---

20 Osterhammel, Jürgen/Petersson, Niels P.: *Geschichte der Globalisierung: Dimensionen, Prozesse, Epochen*, Munich 2003.

21 Cf. Zelle, Casten: »Nous qui sommes si modernes, serons anciens dans quelques siécles«. Zu den Zeitkonzeptionen in den Epochenwenden der Moderne«, in: Graeventiz, Gerhard v. (Ed.): *Konzepte der Moderne: DFG-Symposion 1997*, Stuttgart 1999, pp. 497–520.

culture tried to separate cultures in a spatial analogy – cultures were conceived of as containers like nation states. Contemporary cultural studies, however, no longer conceive of cultures as clearly demarcated spaces. Instead, they imagine cultures as consisting of distinctions and overlaps, transmissions and transitions. Yet I am not giving in to an entirely fuzzy conceptualization of culture. There are differences between cultures that cannot be dissolved into fuzziness and fluidity. I am speaking of the tacitly agreed viewpoints of a given epoch that are conceived by any sophisticated discourse in this epoch, that are habitually called upon, and that are considered to be self-evident. Reference to these unifying orientations has a binding force for participants of the debate, chains of doubts are stopped by it and further doubts remain latent. Questions concerning a more precise account of these core assumptions are not only not asked; they also cannot be answered. It is the impossibility of precise definition that makes for its success.

Just as the indexical reference to a given situation – »we« ... »here« ... »that there« ... – escapes precise definition and, by this very equivocality, generates meaning in everyday life, the cultural meaning which is created by highly abstract concepts such as »God«, »nature« or »reason« is generated by referring to an encompassing whole instead of referring to particular facts. We may call these notions concepts of synthesis or concepts of transcendence. These concepts of transcendence mark the unity of an epoch. They follow each other in a historical sequence. Thus, the concept of »nature« superseded that of a transcendent God in the 17th century. This, in turn, was replaced by the concept of »spirit« (similarly in Voltaire as well as in Hegel) at the end of the 18th century, followed by the concept of »life«[22] in the second half of the 19th century.

»Society« and »culture« are contemporary examples of these concepts. Concepts of synthesis are open to interpretation: they are »essentially contested concepts«. Classical social theory referred to those concepts of synthesis using different terms. Durkheim[23] speaks of the »sacred«, Weber[24] of »salvation«, Spengler[25] of »styles«, Simmel[26] of

22 Bergson, Henri: *L'Evolution créatrice*, Paris 1907.

23 Durkheim, Emile: *Die elementaren Formen des religiösen Lebens*, Frankfurt/Main 1981.

24 Weber, Max: *Gesammelte Aufsätze zur Religionssoziologie*, Stuttgart 1988.

25 Spengler, Oswald: *Urfragen: Fragmente aus dem Nachlass*, Munich 1965.

»life«, Parsons[27] of »values«, Habermas[28] of »preconditions of reasonable discourse«, et cetera.

In the second part of this essay I will argue that so-called »primitive« societies lack those concepts of synthesis. Those primitive societies center difference between the internal and the external realm or between »we and others«, and this leading difference is ethnocentric in an elementary way.

The above mentioned indexical constitution of meaning by hinting at the given situation at hand has an elective affinity to this ethnocentric orientation. As Garfinkel's[29] famous *breaching experiments* pointed out, the things that we label »we, here, now« do not need further clarification and often cannot be explained at all. In this respect they are similar to concepts of synthesis. These differ profoundly, however, from the elementary ethnocentricity of primitive societies in that they assume an exocentric unity of the world. Concepts of synthesis do not emerge before the big turning point that – since Jaspers and Eisenstadt – we call the »Axial Age«. Jaspers called this turning point »the most tremendous breach in world history«.[30] It occurred between 800 and 200 B.C. Great founders of religion appeared in this period – Laotse and Confucius in China, Buddha in India, Zarathustra in Iran, the Prophets in Palestine, the philosophers and tragic poets in Greece. Jaspers, verbatim:

»In this period the basic categories of our thinking were generated. [...] the innovation of this age is [...] that man becomes aware of life in general, of his self as a person and his limitations. He comes to know about the wholeness of the world and of his own powerlessness. He poses radical questions. [...] This

---

26 Simmel, Georg: *Lebensanschauung: Vier metaphysische Kapitel*, Munich 1918.

27 Parsons, Talcott: *Social Systems and the Evolution of Action Theory*, New York 1977.

28 Habermas, Juergen: *Theorie des kommunikativen Handelns*, vol. 1: *Handlungsrationalität und gesellschaftliche Rationalisierung*, Frankfurt/Main 1981.

29 Garfinkel, Harold: *Studies in Ethnomethodology*, Cambridge 1989.

30 Jaspers, Karl: *Vom Ursprung und Ziel der Geschichte*, Frankfurt/Main 1955, p. 19.

happened in reflection. Consciousness generated thinking and thinking turned to the process of thinking itself«.[31]

This thesis can also be found in Alfred Weber's[32] »Cultural History as Cultural Sociology«. It was developed and applied in terms of sociology by Shmuel Eisenstadt who elaborated it into an impressive comparative research program. His foremost interest refers to groups of intellectuals who, by interpreting sacred scriptures, founding schools and by the so-called thinking of the second order,[33] created a specific self-centred realm of communication, while the charismatic founding figures recede to the background. This scripture-based and discourse-based mode of communication also generated the conception of an eternal order of afterlife.

This timeless and transcendental order no longer warranted the unity of the world in an analogous manner – that is, by imagining the unknown as analogous to the pattern of the known – but rather was contrasted with visible and tangible things, to the peculiarity of profane interests and to the world of money and power. Since then, the »here and now« and the other world have been represented in sharp contrast. Man could no longer make herself comfortable with the world at hand. This world was suspected of being unholy, meaningless and inconsistent. By contrast, the order of the transcendent world was not restricted in terms of time and space; rather, it exists at all times and everywhere and claimed universal validity. The sacred, the divine and principled order had no longer a special place nor moment in this world. It became disembodied, timeless and placeless. Everything that opposed this universality or that claimed an exception challenged the unity of the world. The problem of salvation emerged.

Because of their claim to universal validity, the great scripture-based religions developed a missionary zeal and an expansive dynamics: they tried to change those realms of the world which still opposed the eternal order. From this cultural matrix the great monotheistic religions, especially Judaism, Christianity and Islam, developed a fundamental intolerance towards everybody who still adhered to the »false

31 Jaspers: *Vom Ursprung*, p. 20.

32 Weber, Alfred: *Kulturgeschichte als Kultursoziologie*, Munich 1963.

33 Ger: Denken 2. Ordnung: this basically means the thought process about thinking itself.

faith«. Jan Assmann[34] has outlined this fundamental change from locally embedded sacrificial rites to the – as he labelled it – »mosaic distinction« between »true« and »false« faith. This sets limits to the dialogue between religions which is nowadays so often talked about. Since this dialogue ought not to be just a shallow courtesy of intellectual diplomacy, and bound to question the universal and missionary claims of other religions, monotheism might thereby forfeit its unifying aspect. In times of global media news coverage, this claim of universality is heading into risky terrain: If God is eternal and everywhere and facing all of mankind, then there is always also an insuperable conflict of true and false belief.[35] Things that used to be ignored due to lack of information and possible answers can wreak worldwide havoc nowadays. In this way, global media coverage primarily uncovers the true potential of the fight for the one true faith.

The »false faith« that is so strongly opposed by the major scripture religions used to be the old practice of the sacrificial rites. The theurgy, the coercion of the Gods or the bargaining with the Gods who still carried human traits – this, the tolerant world of polytheism, in which the worship of one god did not exclude the worship of another, the old pagan world with the limited power of tutelage and its tribal gods, in which the sacrifice of the innocent, also the innocent human, appeased the gods and had a cathartic effect on the ones performing the sacrifice – this world was over now. These primordial and pristine sacrificial rites were either ridiculed – as in the ancient Greece of the sophists – or fought bitterly as pagan worship. Iconoclastic movements from Echnaton and ancient Judaism to the Byzantine iconoclasts of the 8th century up to radical reformation protestantism by Calvin and Zwingli attacked and destroyed the imagery and statues of the old gods – the only legitimate connection between the profane and the otherworldly realm was the revealed »word of God« delivered in the sacred scriptures.[36] The primacy of scripture was created and established by axial-age-type breakthroughs. The old rites of sacrifice, in contrast, mostly survived as a clandestine practice, on the margins of society or as arbi-

34 Assmann, Jan: *Die Mosaische Unterscheidung: Oder der Preis des Monotheismus*, Munich/Vienna 2003.

35 Assmann, Jan: *Monotheismus und die Sprache der Gewalt*, Vienna 2006.

36 See Barnes, Robin Bruce: *Prophecy and Crisis: Apocalypticism in the Wake of the Lutheran Reformation*, Stanford 1988.

trary everyday life. Occasionally we still practice it but we do not assume a serious claim with it.

Of course, all this had political consequences, too: while in the old polytheistic world of sacrificial rites the prince was also the priest, the axial-age-type splitting of the world engendered a strict separation between religious leadership and political authority.[37] Now the king could be held accountable in the name of an eternal order; his authority was no longer based just on success, influence and custom, but was subordinated to a higher set of beliefs. This subordination of political power under a divine command or under a transcendental order meant a breakthrough of a differentiation whose consequences for the development of the spirit of modernity can hardly be overestimated.

Some historical detail, of course, can be mobilized in order to oppose this general thesis of an axial-age-type revolution. This thesis it resembles the assumption of a neolithic »revolution« which is commonly assumed in materialistic theories of evolution: both, neolithic as well as axial-age-type »revolutions«, did not take place instantly but needed long periods; both refer to a set of profound changes that emerged independently in different regions; and finally, both are challenged by a set of remarkable exceptions. Echnaton, the first great monotheistic revolutionary, was, as pharaoh, political sovereign as well as demigod. In the 7th century, the Caliph of Baghdad as well as the Byzantine emperor unified the political as well as the religious leadership in one position. Chinese Confucianism did not develop from out of a profound dislike of the this-worldly realm, a tension typical of the Axial Age. Even the late medieval conflict between emperor and pope originated from the claim of the pope to unify religious and mundane power in one person.[38] Furthermore, in popular religious practice the assumption of one eternal and omnipresent God could not replace the worship of certain locations or the marking of special times as sacred.

---

37 For a contemporary perspective on this issue see Carter, Stephen L.: »Reflections on the Separation of Church and State«, in: Arizona Law Review 44.2 (2002), pp. 293–312.

38 Cf. Giesen, Bernhard: »Tales of transcendence: Imagining the sacred in politics«, in: Giesen, Bernhard/Suber, Daniel (Eds.): *Religion and Politics: Cultural Perspectives*, Leiden/Boston/Tokyo 2005, pp. 93–137.

Also, the assumption of one single axial-age-type breakthrough is challenged by historical details: two of the most fervid axial-age-type breakthroughs, Islam and reformatory Protestantism, emerged only one thousand and two thousand years later, respectively, than Jaspers and Eisenstadt initially assumed. That is why Alfred Weber introduced the concept of so-called »secondary breakthroughs«.

Nevertheless, this should not foster a premature discarding of the historical ideal type of Axial Age. Similarly to other ideal types it cannot, by principle, be challenged by the existence of hybrid forms. Quite to the contrary, it hones the search for facts deviating from the ideal and functions as a sort of gauge. And just like other ideal types it establishes an analytical perspective that enables inter-cultural comparison, a field whose proliferation is meanwhile approved.

Finally, we can elude the indicated difficulties by shifting the axial age thesis from a theoretical approach based on epochs to one based on structure. Accordingly, an Axial Age does not denote a specific epoch in historical development, where a profound readjustment of a world view took place at different locations simultaneously, but rather hints at a specific socio-structural set of conditions. Under those conditions, certain intellectuals – within special discourse rituals, and at a notable distance from the economic as well as political centre – imagined and created an abstract entity that they opposed to existing circumstances. The resulting tension is not restricted to the relation of spirit and power, or immanence and transcendence, but it can also unfold between intellectual groupings. Here, it is typically characterized as the opposition of orthodoxy and heterodoxy or the shift between asceticism and worldly pleasure.

The history of medieval monastic movements provides rich material for illustrating this shift between ascetic distancing and secularization. The cluniacensic reformatory movement under abbot Odo in the 10th century claimed to replace the secularized way of life of the clergy by a return to the pristine asceticism of Benedictine rules. After few generations, with the ending of the 11th century at the latest, however, it fell for the seduction of worldly influence and became a scandalized display of ecclesiastic splendor, backed up by a strengthened papacy. The monastic movement founded by Bernard de Clairvaux in the 12th century took up the ascetic approach and established a fervid distance between itself and the worldly splendor and power of the Cluniacense

Order.[39] At the beginning it rapidly attracted intellectuals, then it gained political influence; finally, however, it gave up its former aspirations and predominantly increased the wealth of the order without admitting a luxurious lifestyle to the members of the order. The *Fratres Minores* appeared at the beginning of the 13th century, succeeding Francis of Assisi in order to radically renew the monks' ascetic rules, and so forth.

Similar stories of decadence of ascetic heterodoxy can be found in different fields. These fields do not necessarily have to be religious ones. The romantic poets of the early 19th century in Germany, for instance, developed a similar distance to society, to the world of power and monetary interests and imagined the identity of the German nation as an encompassing aesthetic alternative. The trivialization of romantic lifestyle in the first quarter of the 19th century, in its turn, lead to a new intellectual distancing by Heine and Börne, the Young Hegelians and the group Young Germany in the Vormärz.[40]

In a nutshell: The common structural precondition of all those axial-age-type processes is, firstly, the discrimination between the center and the periphery and, secondly, a partial de-sacralization of the societal center. In axial-age-type perspective it is no longer analogy and ethnocentrism that warrants the unity of the world but, instead, exocentrism and principles. The unity of the whole cosmos transcends the diversity of its elements. This transcendent unity presupposes notions of synthesis that engender the unity of an epochal discourse. However, only in marginal cases we can assume that complex societies harbor just one of those notions of synthesis. Different communities, subcultures, fields and arenas in these societies are directed by others, respectively. The fine formulation by Weber about the »return of the ancient and believed-to-be-dead polytheism«, matches, in an oddly contorted way, the situation in modern societies. However, just because not only the reality of our society, but also the discourse about it, are decentralized and polyphonic, we have a strong need for unifying and encom-

---

39 For his appearance in the history and literature see the illuminative work of Botterill, Steven: *Dante and the Mystical Tradition: Bernard of Clairvaux in the »Commedia«*, Cambridge 1994.

40 See Hinderer, Walter: »Nazzarener oder Hellene. Die politisch-ästhetische Fehde zwischen Börne und Heine«, in: Monatshefte 66 (1974), pp. 355–364.

passing labels. And it is sociology that caters to these needs. Those labels, no matter how simplified, counterfactually proclaim an assumed unity of the society with one term: i.e. »risk society«, »knowledge society« et cetera. What used to be the accomplishment of sophisticated discourse itself, namely, to conceive of the synthesis of the whole, has now been turned into a niche for sociological soothsaying.

Finally, I should add that axial-age-type breakthroughs are by no means the only epoch-making thresholds in the cultural evolution of human societies. The shift from simple hunter-gatherer societies to the societies of horticulturalists and herdsmen already decentralized the plain ethnocentric world-view by introducing the centrifugal dynamic of male hero cults. The call of peril, the temptation of the extraordinary engendered the zest of violent warfare by which the male subject could constitute himself in this framework of the hero myth. With it came – in addition to simple internal-external discrimination – the exocentric tendency to look for the extraordinary beyond the common form.

Another form of decentering resulted from the renowned »neolithic revolution« that led to the formation of stratified large societies.[41] By this transformation the center of society disappeared as a visible locality at hand. The center was transferred to the conqueror, the prince and the mounted aristocracy who were able to move quickly between locations and who were separated from the down-to-earth peasants by corporate barriers. Society dissolved as the community of those that knew each other by face and by name; it now included a great number of strangers and unknown people and was held together by the conqueror's threat of force.

The decentering of the world by the Axial Age revolution has already been outlined.

Finally, we should mention the transition from empires with flexible border zones to nation states with precisely defined border lines and a rationally administered internal economic realm. In the early modern age territorial states shifted the dynamics of growth from mere enlargement of the conquered territory or subjugation of barbaric peoples beyond the borders to a more intensive use of the available re-

41 See Arnason, Jóhann P. (Ed.): *Axial Civilizations and World History*, Leiden/Boston/Tokyo 2005.

sources of terrain and people within the borders. This was the foreshadowing of a new synthetic frame of reference that enunciated the transition to the modern age: a shift of synthesis and the postponement of perfection into the future. Secular progress takes over the command of the future.

The shift from princely territorial states to modern democratic nation states could tie in with that. Nation states differ from the princely state by completely decentralizing and depersonalizing the political sovereign: all citizens included in the nation are equal but the justification of the nation's boundaries becomes a pivotal issue.

BIBLIOGRAPHY

Arnason, Jóhann P. (Ed.): *Axial Civilizations and World History*, Leiden/Boston/Tokyo 2005.

Assmann, Jan: *Die Mosaische Unterscheidung: Oder der Preis des Monotheismus*, Munich/Vienna 2003.

Assmann, Jan: *Monotheismus und die Sprache der Gewalt*, Vienna 2006.

Barnes, Robin Bruce: *Prophecy and Crisis: Apocalypticism in the Wake of the Lutheran Reformation*, Stanford 1988.

Beck, Ulrich: *Risikogesellschaft: Auf dem Weg in eine andere Moderne*, Frankfurt/Main 2007.

Bell, Daniel: *The Coming of Post-Industrial Society. A Venture in Social Forecasting*, New York 1973.

Bergson, Henri: *L'Evolution créatrice*, Paris 1907.

Botterill, Steven: *Dante and the Mystical Tradition: Bernard of Clairvaux in the »Commedia«*, Cambridge 1994.

Bougainville, Louis-Antoine de: *Reise um die Welt: Über Südamerika und durch den Pazifik zurück nach Frankreich*, Tübingen 2010.

Carter, Stephen L.: »Reflections on the Separation on Church and State«, in: Arizona Law Review 44.2 (2002), pp. 293–312.

Castells, Manuel: *Das Informationszeitalter 1: Der Aufstieg der Netzwerkgesellschaft*, Opladen 2003.

Durkheim, Emile: *Die elementaren Formen des religiösen Lebens*, Frankfurt/Main 1981.

Ehrlich, Leonard H./Wisser, Richard (Eds.): *Karl Jaspers Today: Philosophy at the Threshold of the Future*, Washington, D.C. 1988.

Eisenstadt, Shmuel N. (1982): »The Axial Age: The Emergence of Transcendental Visions and the Rise of Clerics«, in: European Journal of Sociology 23.2 (1982), pp. 294–314.

Eisermann, Gottfried: *Vilfredo Pareto: Ein Klassiker der Soziologie*, Tübingen 1987.

Freud, Sigmund: »Totem und Tabu. (Einige Übereinstimmungen im Seelenleben der Wilden und der Neurotiker)«, in: Freud, Sigmund: *Kulturtheoretische Schriften*, Frankfurt/Main 1997, pp. 287–444.

Garfinkel, Harold: *Studies in Ethnomethodology*, Cambridge 1989.

Giddens, Anthony: *Modernity and Self-Identity: Self and Society in the Late Modern Age*, Cambridge 1991.

Giesen, Bernhard: »Tales of transcendence: Imagining the sacred in politics«, in: Giesen, Bernhard/Suber, Daniel (Eds.): *Religion and Politics: Cultural Perspectives*, Leiden/Boston/Tokyo 2005, pp. 93–137.

Giesen, Bernhard: »The temporalization of social order: Some theoretical remarks on the change«, in: Smelser, Neil J./Haferkamp, Hans (Eds.): *Social Change and Modernity*, Berkeley/Los Angeles 1992, pp. 294–319.

Giesen, Bernhard: *Die Intellektuellen und die Nation: Eine deutsche Achsenzeit*, Frankfurt/Main 1993.

Giesen, Bernhard: *Triumph and Trauma*, Boulder 2004.

Habermas, Juergen: *Theorie des kommunikativen Handelns.* Vol. 1: *Handlungsrationalität und gesellschaftliche Rationalisierung*, Frankfurt/Main 1981.

Herzog, Reinhart/Koselleck, Reinhart (Eds.): *Epochenschwelle und Epochenbewusstsein*, Munich 1987 (= Poetik und Hermeneutik. Arbeitsergebnisse einer Forschungsgruppe XII).

Hinderer, Walter: »Nazzarener oder Hellene. Die politisch-ästhetische Fehde zwischen Börne und Heine«, in: Monatshefte 66 (1974), pp. 355–364.

Jaspers, Karl: *Vom Ursprung und Ziel der Geschichte*, Frankfurt/Main 1955.

Léry, Jean de: *History of a Voyage to the Land of Brazil*, transl. by Janet Whatley, Berkley 1990.

Lévi-Strauss, Claude: *Traurige Tropen*, Frankfurt/Main 1978.

Luhmann, Niklas: *Die Gesellschaft der Gesellschaft*, Frankfurt/Main 2009.

Osterhammel, Jürgen/Petersson, Niels P.: *Geschichte der Globalisierung: Dimensionen, Prozesse, Epochen*, Munich 2003.

Parsons, Talcott: *Social Systems and the Evolution of Action Theory*, New York 1977.

Seele, Peter: »Kategorien und Begriffe epochalen Wandels«, in: Seele, Peter: *Philosophie der Epochenschwelle. Augustin zwischen Antike und Mittelalter: Augustin zwischen Antike und Mittelalter*, Berlin/New York 2008, pp. 35–61.

Simmel, Georg: *Lebensanschauung: Vier metaphysische Kapitel*, Munich 1918.

Soeffner Hans-Georg/Max Miller (Eds.): *Modernität und Barbarei. Soziologische Zeitdiagnose am Ende des 20. Jahrhunderts*, Frankfurt/Main 1996.

Spengler, Oswald: *Urfragen: Fragmente aus dem Nachlass*, Munich 1965.

Weber, Alfred: *Kulturgeschichte als Kultursoziologie*, Munich 1963.

Weber, Max: *Gesammelte Aufsätze zur Religionssoziologie*, Stuttgart 1988.

White, Hayden V.: *Metahistory: Die historische Einbildungskraft im 19. Jahrhundert in Europa*, Frankfurt/Main 1991.

Zelle, Casten: »›Nous qui sommes si modernes, serons anciens dans quelques siécles‹. Zu den Zeitkonzeptionen in den Epochenwenden der Moderne«, in: Graeventiz, Gerhard v. (Ed.): *Konzepte der Moderne: DFG-Symposion 1997*, Stuttgart 1999, pp. 497–520.

II.2 The Axial Age and Islam

Reflections on ›World‹ and ›History‹ Today

GEORG STAUTH

1. INTRODUCTION

For the German Philosopher Karl Jaspers the shattering events of 1945, the end of the Second World War, marked the beginning of a new era, the turning point leading to something »new«, a break in history which was decisive for the future of Europe. Signifying the conditions as much as the potentials of a »new humanism«, for him »1945« stood for the end of 12 years of Hitler's Third Reich and German fascist rule and its hegemonic dominance of European affairs.[1] As the then-influential journalist and political philosopher Dolf Sternberger remarked, this event was also the break that turned Jaspers into a political philosopher.[2] I wish to stress with this paper that what is known as Jaspers' Axial Age Theory can only be understood in terms of the historical break of 1945 which shaped recent modern European and Western history.

In addition, I wish to give reference to some reflections of Michel Foucault which were developed in the context of another, a second turning point in recent modern history about 30 years later, namely, the Islamic revolution of 1978/9 in Iran. Indeed, in Iran Foucault took

1 Cf. Jaspers, Karl: »Über Bedingungen und Möglichkeiten eines neuen Humanismus«, in: Jaspers, Karl: *Rechenschaft und Ausblick: Reden und Aufsätze*, Munich 1951, pp. 265–292.

2 Cf. Sternberger, Dolf: »Jaspers und der Staat«, in: Frankfurter Allgemeine Zeitung, 22.02.1963, p. 2.

the »Islamic Revolution« as a turning point of »humanism«, the end of the »outdated project« to modernize Islam in European terms. In fact, he applied his idea of »empowerment of the body« and »political spirituality« and »new techniques« of mass communication in describing the process of this revolution in his »reportages des idées«.[3]

These two momentums in contemporary European thought, Jaspers and Foucault, both interweave the breaks in current modern history with events and processes in earlier history. Karl Jaspers' »Axial Age« and Michel Foucault's spiritual »empowerment of the body« are crucial concepts for understanding what happened with »Islam and the West« in recent years. Both concepts signify decisive changes in human history which relate to trans-cultural and trans-civilizational processes. However, if they were to signify »progress«, they were at the same time blatantly used in reverse for limited cultural reconstructions of power, both West and East. I wish, therefore, to review in this paper some aspects related to Jaspers and Foucault, with respect to more recent approaches to Islamic and Western reconstruction.

2. Jaspers' Post-fascist Political Philosophy

Jaspers' political and historical philosophy in the years from 1945 to 1950 is a complete expression of the condition of »*Neuanfang*«, the condition of a »new beginning«, and of his will to contribute to a complete humanitarian transformation of Europe and the West. For him this meant to actualise a »new« essence of the idea of humanity and the human based in their »origin«. Here two main questions are invoked by Jaspers. First, he reflects on how to appropriate anew the ideals of human formation and education from the classical, the Greek tradition. Second, he asks how to reconstruct the present concept of man from its origins.

Jaspers links both questions to the breakthroughs in history and the ascendance of new visions of transcendence from 800 B.C. to 200 A. C. Thus, Jaspers' operating on »Germany«, »Europe« and the »West«,

---

3 Cf. Stauth, Georg: »Revolution in Spiritless Times: An Essay on Michel Foucault's Enquiries into the Iranian Revolution«, in: International Sociology 6.3 (1991), pp. 259–280.

his pledge for the renewal of modern history after the Second World War[4], stands in close connection to his overall political and historical philosophy, which included what happened in China, India, Palestine and Greece to the ››millennium of transcendence«, his theory of the »Axial Age«.[5] In fact, Jaspers' »*Achsenzeit*« – to use the German word – announces the need for historical theory and an all-inclusive reflection of world history and »humanity as a whole«. In sharp contrast to the indirect utilisation of his ideas in contemporary »clash of civilization« theories, Jaspers expresses the need for recognition of the other and of the human ethos in every single human being. He brings about a decisive step in the inherent understanding of »world« and »ethos« beyond bondage to one single religion or nation.

However, in his explicit discussions of the »Axial Age«, Jaspers' speechlessness about Islam and Judaism is painstakingly evident. Today this is difficult to understand. As he formulates world history on a new stage, the exclusion of Islam and Judaism from his reflections on ›world‹ and ›history‹ can only be interpreted as an internal contradiction to his own project. In connection with his sort of absolutist focus on »*Abendland*«, the West and the »origins«, this eclipse of Islam and Judaism can only be explained as a sort of implicit recognition of both, seen as being – sort of silently – part of the pre- or post-axial evolution of the West.[6]

Like Judaism, which he silently included into the pre-axial »biblical tradition«, Islam was otherwise silently included into a late branch of post-axial civilizational evolution. For someone who was so decisively self-oriented towards European and Western history in 1945–1950, perhaps this may appear to be a necessary negligence. However,

---

4 Cf. Jaspers, Karl: *Rechenschaft und Ausblick: Reden und Aufsätze*, Munich 1951; Jaspers, Karl: *Erneuerung der Universität: Reden und Schriften* (1945/46), ed. Renato de Rosa, Heidelberg 1986.

5 Jaspers, Karl: *Vom Ursprung und Ziel der Geschichte*, Munich 1949, cf. pp. 15–105; Jaspers, Karl: »Die Achsenzeit der Weltgeschichte«, in: Der Monat 1.6 (1949), pp. 3–9; Jaspers, Karl: *Europa der Gegenwart*, Vienna 1947.

6 Cf. Jaspers, Karl: »Schema der Weltgeschichte«, in: Jaspers, Karl: *Vom Ursprung und Ziel der Geschichte*, Munich 1949, pp. 43–48; Jaspers, Karl: »Von der biblischen Religion«, in: Die Wandlung I.1 (1945/46), pp. 406–413 (s.a. Jaspers: »Rechenschaft und Ausblick«, pp. 65–75).

it was also linked to his methodological reductionism. Notwithstanding his silence on Judaism (which is not the subject here and needs separate treatment),[7] Jaspers' silence on Islam can only be understood within the context of his task-program for post-Hitler Germany and Europe, and his specific type of self-reflexivity with respect to Nazism, secularism and Christianity after the Catharsis. The failure of »Science« and of German »*Geist*« in preventing it sets the limits for Jaspers' reflection. His focus on Christianity, Hinduism and Confucianism in terms of cultural history and his view of America, Europe and Russia in terms of world politics lead to a narrow self-reflexive deadlock. And even in reflecting on »Science« and »*Geist*«, Jaspers' political philosophy, as Sternberger remarks, limits itself largely to the vast »*Feld der Ämter*«, the »field of offices«.[8]

However, if Jaspers – against his own intentions – remains the momentum in contemporary Western theory that seems to be the configurative point of necessary self-affirmation and of distinction turned against the non-western, the non-modern, we think it is important to trace some misunderstandings in this conception of the Axial Age with respect to Islam.

Today, the surge of Islam in Europe and America is obvious. However, where Jaspers spoke of »What is Europe?«, he spoke of the »biblical religion« that extends to America and Russia, a spiritual unity that evolved in the struggle against the Persians, the Mongols, the Turks, against Islam.[9] »Spiritual Unity« means in this context to decline the existence of exchange, mutual learning and dialogue and engagement with the cultural other. Jaspers, here, reflecting in his famous Geneva speech of 1947 on »*Europa der Gegenwart*«[10] – contemporary Europe – centres his view on »world history« as a history of »parallel« events of thinking and the development of ideas, rather than on exchange and mutual impingements.[11] The question is how to apply

---

7 Cf. Jaspers, Karl: »Die Schuldfrage«, in: Jaspers: »Erneuerung der Universität«, pp. 113–213.

8 Sternberger, Dolf: »Jaspers und der Staat«, p. 2.

9 Cf. Jaspers, Karl: »Was ist Europa?«, in: Jaspers: »Erneuerung der Universität«, pp. 246–47.

10 Jaspers: »Was ist Europa?«, pp. 245–274.

11 This holistic approach is also maintained by Jaspers in »Vom Ursprung und Ziel der Geschichte«.

Jaspers to the contemporary problem of integration and dialogue of Islam in Europe and the West. The paradox is that further to the Islamic revival as a world religion and its historical presence in Europe, Islam seen in mutual eastern western terms of self-reflection seems to be enshrined in perceptions of the pure cultural ›Other‹, a European antipode. This indeed is a point to be considered with respect to the present conditions of cultural renewal of the West itself. Islam is one – a major – issue on the agenda of ›world‹ and ›history‹ today. It was not in the time of Karl Jaspers, and to excuse him, really, it was not an issue of the years following the end of the Second World War.

The operating idea of this paper, therefore, is to review Axial Age Theory in the context of the developments that have changed the world since 1945–50. I will, therefore, attempt to evade the tiresome debates about the justification of the concept of an »Axial Age«.[12] In fact, the most recent and dramatic changes have turned »Islam« into a core issue of global modernity. I will, therefore, first look into the meaning of Jaspers' silent inclusion of Islam into Western history and renewal. Second, I will refer to some traits and effects of Jaspers' theory with respect to our contemporary condition of trans-civilizational communication, »body«, »governance«, humanism and spirituality, and power formation.

3. THE ›ESSENCE‹ OF THE AXIAL AGE

Although there were many debates about the Axial Age and its relation to modern culture and civilization, they did not crystallise with respect to Jaspers' focus on »revelation«. It should be clear, however, from the start of this discussion that despite its universal humanistic intentions, Karl Jaspers' concept of Axial Age refers in essence to this very – heuristically and semantically – Christian idea, namely, to the high-ranking Protestant theological issue of »*revelation*«. Jaspers made it the central ground of his understanding of universal civilizational formation. Jaspers used the concept of revelation analytically as a type of egalitarian parameter of comparison; Christianity, Hinduism and Confucianism, in the main. Revelation, as he sees it, revealed truths (and

12 For the start of this Jaspers renaissance, see the special issue 104.2 of Daedalus (1974).

respective truth claims), which meant for Jaspers that in the first time in history, »communication« between World Civilizations was made possible by the event of parallel, similar, common spiritual experiences leading to the constitution of a common ground where humanity as such began to share an appeal to »one truth«. On a second level, for Jaspers the turning point, the »*axis*« of world civilization relates to revelation also, in that it takes the initial historical momentum that separated interpretative power – the field of the priests, or of »*Amt*« – from executive power – the realm of power politics itself. This separation seems to be another point of ›origin‹ to begin with, a point where modernity took its roots as best expressed in the contrasting images of the »Prophet« challenging the »Pharaoh«, historically first emerging with Moses' and his people's exodus from Egypt.[13] Power and Spirit became two separate (however, possibly in different forms interrelated) poles, setting the terms of discourse about world and order.

Since then the dialectics of »King« and »Prophet«, the secular world of power contrasted with the ordering power potentials of referring to the Beyond, took hold in the holy scripture of the Jews. Certainly, this laid the roots of a new dynamic between Orthodoxy and Heterodoxy, which, as Shmuel N. Eisenstadt sees it, established a bipolarity of discourse which later shaped the various patterns of institutionalisation of protest in modern political culture.[14] Unfolding a

---

13 Certainly, as a historical philosopher Jaspers stands in the shadow of Nietzsche, who saw in Socrates the turning point, when ›will to truth‹ in morality was developed as a nihilistic tool of ›will to power‹. Jaspers abolishes Nietzsche's critical perspective and takes a positive scientific view which certainly sets the path for all subsequent discussions on the Axial Age. However, Nietzsche should be mentioned in this context in order to understand Jaspers' affirmative turn. This treatment of Nietzsche's critique silently parallels Max Weber's earlier reversions of Nietzsche with respect to the genealogy of the ›priest‹, modern professional man and ›office‹ in modern institutional foundation. Compare my »Nietzsche, Weber, and the affirmative sociology of culture«, in: European Journal of Sociology XXIII (1992), pp. 219–247. See also »The Priest is a Beefsteak Eater – Rationalisation and Cultural Control«, in: Stauth, Georg/Turner, Bryan S.: *Nietzsche's Dance*, Oxford 1988, pp. 99–122.

14 Eisenstadt, Shmuel N.: *Die Antinomien der Moderne. Die jakobinischen Grundzüge der Moderne und des Fundamentalismus: Heterodoxien, Uto-*

»permanent revolution« of thought which related to the interplay of this-worldly and extra-worldly powers, the Axial Age, here, means the global event of this continuous process of institutionalisation, originating in the strict conceptual break between »One God« and the »World«. Certainly, in Christ and early Christianity this separation took a very special momentum, a momentum that made this break definitive. It was the martyrdom of Christ, and his rejection by his own people as a prophet and leader, that had irreversible and unique consequences. »Religion«, which so often parallels »Christianity« in Jaspers' discourse, would come to have an important effect as a spiritual idea beyond worldly powers, setting the path towards a new human universalism: The ›Church‹, in fact, emerged as a unique institutional formation, as the administrator of universal truth, in the margins of political power and the state. For Jaspers, this is precisely the point that counts: »revelation« turned it into – in different degrees – relatively autonomous institutions of cultural formation – and of course with it, limiting absolutist politics and the power of political rulers or ruling centres.[15] Jaspers took »revelation« as an axial breakthrough.

However, for Jaspers revelation was not only a sort of starting point for interactive comparison of different civilizations; it also meant for him a sort of parameter of social development and modernity, a meditative tool for peaceful communication and interaction between the different cultures and world civilizations. In a way, Jaspers was here anticipating a model of thought which was later developed around the myths that »democracies do not attack each other« and live in relative peace with one another.[16]

---

pismus und Jakobinismus in der Konstitution fundamentalistischer Bewegungen, Frankfurt/Main 1998; also »Culture and Power. A Comparative Civilizational Analysis«, in: Erwägen – Wissen – Ethik 17 (2006), pp. 3–16.

15 This point deserves attention on its own, specifically with respect to the formation of and struggle against heterodoxies. It is to my understanding again a limitation – in this case of Eisenstadt – to reduce this to ideological dissent. In most cases »orthodoxy« started with the suppression of ›popular‹ traditions and conventional cultic practices.

16 This is not the place to reflect in detail upon the question of why and how the construction of »Church« in Christianity takes a unique stand as with respect to »revelation«. In the thinking of Karl Schmitt and Eric Peterson,

If the main topic of cultural studies and philosophy in the period of World War Two and shortly after was how to concretise the Unity of Humanity, it was Karl Jaspers' outspoken aim to view this in terms of ›origin‹, i.e. the lasting facts and effects of the Axial Age. For him there are three dimensions of the Axial Age (in his terms limited to the period from 800 to 200 before Christ) that contributed to the foundation of our modern universal idea of common history:

First, the transformative effects of revelation were decisive for creating a very specific bond of particular religious belief, which at the same time was turned into the quest for cognition and experience (i.e. the quest for universal cognition and knowledge). For Jaspers, revelation simultaneously led to a basic universal mutation of humanity, an experience that was possible in China, India, and the West, and that led the foundation, here, of a universal concept of history that spiritually integrated all humanity.

Second, this historical modification of the perception of humanity linked to the axial breakthrough also lead, according to Jaspers, to a sort of unlimited demand for human communication. This call for unlimited communication became a sort of inner need linking one's own consciousness with that of all others, even with that of strangers.

---

both Catholic thinkers antedating the advent of the »Third Reich« in the 1920s and early 1930s, a certain political functionality of »revelation« can be observed. According to Taubes, for them, »the Church is only because Jews did not accept, because they do not live in faith«. (»Die Kirche ist nur, weil die Juden nicht angenommen haben, weil sie nicht im Glauben leben«.). Cf. Taubes, Jacob: *Ad Karl Schmitt: Gegenstrebige Fügung*, Berlin 1987, p. 60. One could reverse this: The Jewish Prophets and Muhammad stood in the midst of »their« people, only Christ did not. ›Church‹, in this way, meant from the beginning a structural determination of enmity towards ›Jews‹. However it also meant from the start a certain neutrality towards ethnic or national background. It is not without sadness that one can observe today how such questions return into the forefront of inter-religious discourse again. The silent affirmation of the »Church«-model in Jaspers certainly plays a part in his genealogy of the »Axial Age«.

Third, Jaspers stresses the point that unlimited communication at the same time also leads to a type of self-reflection which includes the doubting of all attempts to generalize ultimate truth.[17]

Jaspers' idea is that there was an »axis« in world history around the time of 500 B.C. which could form a common framework for all peoples, for their historical self-reflection and self-consciousness. It created »transcendence«, prophetical revelation and philosophical reflection on the limits of humanity and this-worldliness, the source of an emerging universal pattern of separation and difference between the institutions of worldly power and political rule on the one hand, and those institutions founded on the search for knowledge and ultimate truth on the other. For Jaspers this meant the foundational setting of universal regulative communication as the foundation for any new world order, or rather a new world order in itself.

To sum up, Jaspers puts two main issues into the centre of modern self-understanding with respect to Axial Age Theory. First, he positions the search for »origin« and »axis« into the centre of »world history«, certainly evoking the question of empirical evidence and of competitive and comparative study and putting it into the forefront of trans-civilizational discourse. Second, he puts the problem of the foundational and regulative powers of transcendence and ultimate truth (religion and philosophy) into the centre of »world-culture«, paradoxically making them the centre-subject of the secular scientific enterprise.

With respect to evidence, we may note that an increasing number of historians, cultural theorists and sociologists of comparative civilizational analysis would today subscribe in broad terms to the narrative

17 Cf. Jaspers, Karl: »Die Achsenzeit der Weltgeschichte«, p. 8. The ambiguity of this statement is obvious, especially if one reads today a variety of reactions to it. One comes immediately to my mind – a statement of an important Malaysian Islamic Scholar, Sayyid Naquib Al-Attas, in a personal discussion on Nietzsche, Islam and Modernity in 1995: »There is no doubt in Islam […]«; al-Attas, inspired by Iqbal and Nietzsche developed an Islamic »De-Westernisation« program which was influential in Malaysia in the 1990s: Al-Attas, Syed Muhammad al-Naguib: *Islam, Secularism and the Philosophy of the Future*, London 1985. See also my article on *Protestantisierung des Islams* (2006) (http://www.ifeas.uni-mainz.de/workingpapers/AP70.pdf).

of facts, emphasising axial theory as a broader pattern of historical and cultural historical understanding of world history. At the same time, axial age theory has contributed to the questioning of mainstream methodological conventions in the disciplines concerned.[18] However, the dimension of looking at facts and sources from the different angle of an axis, rather than continuity, preoccupied most of the research and debate among scholars. Debating the »breakthrough« problem within given historical and civilizational conditions with respect to the unfolding of new religious ideas, the question remained based on the problem of facts and empirical evidence of an axis, not on questioning the genealogical conditions of what ›axis‹ could mean in terms of essentialist enshrinement of concepts.

The paradoxes and ambiguities of Jaspers' philosophy of history can also be traced, in that the premises of axiality largely relate to the emergence of priest-power (or, if you will, the relatively independent power of literati, virtuosi, priests) and the »Church«. This was not and is not today a universal model. It certainly relates to a prehistory of modern functional differentiation and science (notwithstanding the functional continuity of religion); however, doubts remain today as to whether this can serve as a sustainable model of global society. Furthermore, Jaspers understood this as a development of an inner human sense that was emerging in this period, a cultural power of unlimited communication over the borderlines of belief systems based on revelation, and making it a foundational pattern of modern consciousness. Again, one is tempted today to ask whether this is Western utopia or human fact.

Jaspers' philosophy of the inner universal mind failed: It was challenged in many ways precisely by those who took his call to study axial breakthroughs seriously, and reversed into modern philosophies of

18 For preliminary evaluations see the contributions to the Karl Jaspers issue on »Wisdom, Revelation and Doubt: Perspectives on the First Millenium B.C.«, in: Daedalus 104.2 (1974) and specifically Eric Weil's »What is a Breakthrough in History?«, ibid. pp. 21–36. Recent discussions cf. Arnason, Johann P./Eisenstadt, Shmuel N./ Wittrock, Björn (Eds.): *Axial Civilizations and World History*, Leiden 2005; Arnason, Johann P./Salvatore, Armando/Stauth, Georg (Eds.): *Islam in Process: Historical and Civilizational Perspectives*, Bielefeld 2006 (=Yearbook of the Sociology of Islam 7).

intellectual and spiritual superiority of the West, or into patterns of comparative civilizational analysis, measuring religion and revelation as such into parameters of relative superiority of institutional and social settings by authenticating the western experience, and through this defining the lifestyles and beliefs of so many peoples as heterodoxies of the modern age.

Certainly, this prolongs the age-old pattern of reflecting Western instrumentalism and pragmatism into philosophical patterns of progress and renewal, while on the other hand the philosophical otherness of many peoples, and certainly of Islam, was then proclaimed in terms of its political suppression of philosophy as such.

4. ISLAM AND JASPERS' PARADIGM

For Karl Jaspers, the Axial Age meant the earliest clear-cut momentum, a true breakthrough in history, that paved – through ›Monotheism« and revelation – the way to Modernity. This is seen, certainly, as the breakthrough of scripture. However, if scripture means a one-way monolithic *interpretatatio*, a pure, »orthodox« setting, this is not what Jaspers meant. Rather, it was meant as the very opening of a new discursive level, with a variety of levels of interaction among social milieus, and indeed as Eisenstadt later stresses, the ascendance of new elites and »*Kulturträger*«.[19] And indeed, the ascendance of Islam over a period of more than 300 years precisely meant a very complicated development, one that hardly fits into »world history« European style, as van Ess shows in his recent essay.[20]

When Karl Jaspers speaks of »biblical religions«, one is immediately struck by the question: what then is Islam? Without doubt, Islam stands in the biblical tradition, and to varying degrees Muhammad

---

19 Eisenstadt, Shmuel N.: »Allgemeine Einleitung: die Bedingungen für die Entstehung und Institutionalisierung der Kulturen der Achsenzeit«, in: Eisenstadt, Shmuel N. (Ed.): *Kulturen der Achsenzeit I*, Frankfurt/Main, 1987, p. 10.

20 Ess, Josef van: »Islam and the Axial Age«, in: Arnason, Johann/Salvatore, Armando/Stauth, Georg (Eds.): *Islam in Process: Historical and Civilizational Perspectives*, Bielefeld 2006 (= Yearbook of the Sociology of Islam 7), pp. 220–240.

perceived himself as a ›new‹ Jesus, or as an authentic final point crystallising in the line of Jewish Prophets; his teachings were accepted by Jewish priests as an expression of the Jewish prophetic myths, and until today the literary tradition of the Qur'ān with respect to the tales of the prophets is not questioned. How could this lead to a revelation of its own, to a completely separate »religion«? Following Jaspers, could one apply axial theory with respect to the ›essence‹ of Islam?

And perhaps there is a third, even more important question related to this, namely, did not Islam attempt to accomplish »revelation« in the very sense of realizing conceptually the unfulfilled promises of the »biblical religions« with respect to monotheism, human equality, and revealed scripture?

Jaspers' intentions, as we have seen above from viewing »Vom Ursprung und Ziel der Geschichte« in the context of the German and European post-World War Two scenario of »break«, were twofold. First, he intended to reposition Germany and Europe within the new world-historical situation: What are the roots and essence of Europe and the West, and what are we to learn from axial breakthroughs and the path to European and Western dominance? Second, he intended to approach world-history not merely to make it an exercise of civilizational comparativism, but rather to understand it as an endeavour for reflecting the patterns and potentials of common communication. This is where, I think, we should take Jaspers seriously and my question remains: what can we learn from his axial breakthrough theory for our »time«, the given world context of an obviously re-installed confrontation of Islam and the West?

Here, we can limit further investigation to two questions: First, what is (the position of) Islam with respect to Axial Age theory? Second, what is Axial Age theory with respect to our »time«, the so-perceived confrontation of Islam and the West (even if this might only be considered a prelude for other such confrontations to come)?

Although Jaspers – not surprisingly – never dealt openly with Islam, he seems to have approached it vaguely within the framework of »biblical religions«. This is why one easily could incorporate Islam – the revelation, the specific forms of personal morality, the ›philosophy‹, the institutional settings and structural conditions – into the framework of Jaspers' ›breakthrough‹-theory. This certainly occupied Western Orientalists in the 1960s and 1970s, at first in a sort of attempt to modify conventional views on structural ›hydraulic‹ underdevelopment and ›Asiatic‹ influence. However, without referring to Jaspers' Axial Age, but rather to Max Weber's Protestantism thesis, Maxime Rodinson, Bryan Turner and Ernest Gellner, to name the most known and important contributors, acknowledged Islam in the tradition of ›breakthrough‹ as a modern religion.[21] In the 1980s, after the Iranian Islamic Revolution, a new dimension came into play; the religious genealogy of Islam was now discovered in a broader framework which gave rise to anxiety, a rediscovery of the ›politics of transcendence‹ and political theology at large.[22] Certainly, the 1987-issue of *Telos* signified the broad ›renaissance‹ of political theology.[23] It is interesting to see how these discourses relate directly or indirectly to the Heidelberg of Max Weber and Alfred Weber and of Karl Jaspers.[24]

Of course, if one speaks of the aura of inherited religious narratives and metaphors of thought, one would first ask how closely Mecca and Medina were related, in their cultural worlds, to the higher civilizations which surrounded the Arabian Peninsula. The question would then be how far Muhammad and Early Islamic religious discourse were influenced by the religious ideas which were prevalent in the

---

21 Cf. Rodinson, Maxime: *Islam and Capitalism*; Rodinson, Maxim *Islam und Kapitalismus*, Frankfurt/Main 1971; Turner, Bryan S.: *Weber and Islam: A Critical Study,* London 1974; Gellner, Ernest: *Muslim Society*, Cambridge 1981. It remains to be discussed to what extent this applies to Muhammad Iqbal, the philosopher of Pakistan: Iqbal, Mohammad: *The Reconstruction of Religious Thought in Islam*, Lahore 1954 (reprint of 1927 edition). The reprint was influenced by Max Weber and Jaspers in Heidelberg.

22 It is unnecessary to give an account here of the rich stream of literature debating the relevant literature from the nineteen thirties, namely, the works of Carl Schmitt, Leo Strauss and Erich Voegelin. For Germany, Jacob Taubes was one of the most interesting as well as ambiguous protagonists; see Taubes, Jacob: *Die politische Theologie des Paulus*, ed. Aleida and Jan Assmann, Munich 1993, and also his *Der Preis des Messianismus. Briefe von Jacob Taubes an Gershom Scholem und andere Materialien,* ed. Elettra Stimilli, Würzburg 2006.

23 See Telos. Special Issue: *Carl Schmitt, Enemy or Foe?* 72 (1987).

24 As for Voegelin, for example, see: Assmann, Jan: »Axial ›Breakthroughs‹ and Semantic ›Relocations‹ in Ancient Egypt and Israel«, in: Arnason/Eisenstadt/Shmuel: *Axial Civilizations and World History*, pp. 133–136.

Hellenistic world, Gnosticism, Christianism and Judaism and Greek and Roman Philosophy and science. Both ways, Greek and Roman (and at the most, some Persian influence) are considered to be predominant. So in both perspectives, old oriental continuities, whether religious or philosophic, were traced as the dominant sources of later Islamic discourse.

A further dimension has recently shaped much of our perspective on Islam; this concerns the originality of Muhammad's revelation and the type of striking effects this brought in breaking with all types of prevalent cultural constructions. This later view comes close to the self-perception of Arabs, acknowledging »that their race did not share in philosophy, although they surpassed other nations in rhetoric and poetry«.[25]

As with all religions, myth seems to have been the most important ideological motive, not logic or philosophy. The predominant myths in Central Arabia, those not deriving from bare Arab tribal history, depended largely on Ancient Judaism and Egypt.

In terms of the early German ›*Islamwissenschaft*‹ – to name Ignaz Goldziher and Carl Heinrich Becker – Islam emerged as a movement which was largely reflective of earlier axial developments in Judaism, Hellenism and Christianity: an over-reflexive monotheism manifests itself in the idea of an unreachable, absolute God; a highly regulative concept of (revealed) Law extending to all spheres of everyday live; self-responsible scholarship based on personal knowledge and reputation; social and civil attainment of spiritual power and transcendence. Ideally speaking, all these dimensions are based on *'ilm*, the knowledge of scripture and law (science), and *ma'rifa*, spiritual knowledge and qualities of the individual. In a kind of original egalitarian radicalism, the early Islamic movement responded to Judaism and Christianity by radicalising the position of the individual before of the One God. This self-affirmative, this-worldly stabilisation of the individual led, on the other hand, to lowering his sense of responsibility with respect to these institutions; and with respect to these there always remained a sort of absolute freedom to follow or not to follow, to be ›knowing‹ ('ālim), or to remain ›not knowing‹ (*jahl*). In this framework of religious democratism, affirming the individual self, the parameter of knowledge leads at the same time to a sort of hieratic differentiation,

25 El-Ehwany, M.: *Islamic Philosophy*, Cairo 1957, p. 1.

which itself makes personal institutional responsibility virtually impossible. Belief, honour, law remain potentialities of the individual, but remain ineffective against tyranny and power. The paradox is that this does not mean that modern institutions are obsolete in countries with Islamic populations; where they have been established and guarded, they function brilliantly within their given realms. What is obvious, however – and this shows the failure, and in the end, the disaster of an applied Jaspers project in Islam – is that basing Islam today within the framework of a communicative discourse on »revelation« is a *contradicio in adjecto*. Revealed issues – whatever their historical context – are treated as non-communicators; this is what happened in reality, and in the period of post-colonialism led to the disasters and conflicts which we are witnessing today.

We could add that contrary to the radical integration of science and secular knowledge into an over-arching religious discourse in post-medieval Europe (Jaspers speaks of a second term of Axiality), in the Islamic East a gradual process of separation of secular knowledge (the sciences, architecture, *'ilm al-qādim* – the knowledge of the pre-Islamic ›Old‹) and philosophy (*kalam*) took place. This disintegration of the sciences from religious discourse led – it has been argued – to a sort of cultivation and preservation of the knowledge of the old cultures on its own. Similarly, one could argue, it also led to a certain conventionalisation and retarding of the sciences and gradual decline. However, in Islam today, there is no such thing as religion retarding the application of science and technology, or access to resources; at least, it is hardly to be seen in Islamic countries.

Finally, the integration of non-Arabic and non-Islamic ethnic and religious groups and communities under an over-arching administrative and political system which was ideally considered a »revealed« order was in practice always an order of co-existing cultures and secular rule, military in nature. Again, this shows how futile and paradoxical it is to introduce democracy through Western impingements based on a discourse of »revelation« and religious politics. Perhaps it is good not to forget, at least, that a great Arab philosopher and civilization theorist, Ibn Khaldun, was clear enough about the military nature of »power«, in its purest secularity, when it expresses itself in ›civilizational‹ terms.

Jaspers describes the Axial Age as an era in which the conditions were set up to make possible a sense of knowledge and truth that developed increasingly separate from political rule. Following Nietzsche, who developed the complex relation of truth to power, Jaspers instigated the will to knowledge and truth as a separate realm, differing essentially from the will to political power and rule. Reversing Nietzsche's critique – which, like for many others and specifically Max Weber, was seen as pure nihilism – Jaspers identified this separation as a historically necessary and productive precondition of Modernity[26]. For Jaspers, modern science and objectivity depended largely on the independence of knowledge and truth and the respective institutions and cultural pretenders that were created in this age of prophetical revelation against the preceding holism. In other words, the discourse of the Axial Age would immediately include the discourse concerning religion in that very specific sense of how far the prophets and the revealed scriptures bear witness to certain potentials for varying degrees of independence, neutrality and sovereignty of knowledge from the ruler.

With respect to Islam, to speak of the Axial Age would immediately lead us into this very specific question about how far Muhammad's revelation and the Qur'ān as such, from the very beginning, contributed – in the respective cultural spaces where they were located, in vary-

26 Nietzsche indeed understood largely modern individualism as a result of the ›event‹ of Christ and believed that the world as a whole would move on to shaping an in itself lonely modern subject, devaluing as much his own nature, also all living ›nature‹ as such. This, in fact, was a point that Jaspers raised with respect to how to deny Nietzsche's nihilism. Jaspers insisted in »Weltgeschichte als Weltwissen« that the preservation of the external world turns into a human task which makes new arrangements possible. This point – as in general with his intense and sophisticated, if not theological, rejection of Nietzsche – is best developed in his *Nietzsche und das Christentum* (Hameln 1938). As for Jaspers' dependence on Weber, regarding these issues see Henrich, Dieter: »Karl Jaspers: Thinking with Max Weber in Mind«, in: Mommsen, Wolfgang J./Osterhammel, Jürgen (Eds.): *Max Weber and his Contemporaries: The German Historical Institute*, London 1987, pp. 528–544. See also Manasse, Ernst Moritz: »Jaspers' Relation to Max Weber«, in: *The Philosophy of Karl Jaspers*, New York o. J., pp. 369–391, spec. 386; compare aswell Jaspers, Karl: »Über meine Philosophie«, in: Jaspers, Karl: *Rechenschaft und Ausblick: Reden und Aufsätze*, Munich 1951, p. 340.

ing degrees over history – to this type of independence of »knowledge« which is associated with the modern perception of science. Does it matter?

I can name, perhaps, some ›axial‹ issues of debate which could narrow the perspective of the Axial Age in order to make it applicable to the subject of Islam.

First, there is Jaspers' limitation of temporal fixity, limiting his view to a period between 800 B. C.–200 A. C., which would immediately exclude Islam.

Second, there is the problem of separation of »prophet and king« which again would exclude Islam, given the fact that Muhammad acquired a sort of status of »king«, a positional relation which in Jaspers' terms would count as pre-axial.

Third, there is the problem of Script and priest, where again Islam would fall out because of its abolishment of the institution of the priest as the sole ›interpreter‹ of scriptural truth.

There are many sorts of smaller problems which relate to institutional and knowledge development in Islam which would not fit Jaspers' conceptualisation. The major problem among these, certainly, is the fact that in Islam the scripture of the book that counts as »revelation« – and more generally the large body of canonical texts largely referred to today as »*shari'a islamiyya*«, Islamic Law – is considered revealed and holy scripture as such. Sufism, first in contradiction with, then in affiliation to canonised scripture, certainly forms a very complex source of religious inspiration, beyond the revelation (or continuous re-instigation of it), which is, however, of overall importance in Islam, which again is a sort of »non-independent« fall-out with respect to the institutional and knowledge formation Jaspers had in mind. So Jaspers was indeed quite consequential in that he did not treat Islam within his conceptual framework; also in that where he clearly names Islam, he puts it in a consequential position as sort of a follow up of the Axial Age, which would perhaps give us a key to discuss Islam here, within this broader concept, and from there put it back into that question of what the ›authentication of Islam‹ would mean to modernity within Jaspers' conceptual framework. Certainly, it would be quite worthwhile to analyse ongoing projects in the modern reformulation of Islam.

5. COMMUNICATION, WORLD, ISLAM

I wish to present a second momentum in contemporary European thought which relates to Michel Foucault, turning the modern discourse about humanism and civilization into a new dimension: the forces of individualism in relation to the physical net of social relations culminating in the ›empowerment of the body‹. In the context of Foucault's discussion of »bio-power« the thematic of ›Islam‹ became important. To include Foucault within the civilizational perspective and to advance his complementary role in it, it is important to give the following three reasons: One, Islam and the Islamic Revolution in Iran mark an essential change in Foucault's thinking of »civilization«: the »prophetic« origin in the »Orient«. Two, it stands in a close and effective – however, in a way suppressed – relation to the discursive re-invention of religion in modern discourse. Three, it relates to reactive attempts to mount a reversion of the project of modernity, basing ›freedom‹ of religious expression at the centre of a ›liberalist‹ project of ›post-secularism‹. Perhaps it is worth noting that it is paradoxically only with Foucault's identification of »Islam« in the process of events of 1978/79 in Iran that the formation of religion as a dispositif of ›global‹ modernity became prominent in recent intellectual history. By putting forward some very sublime and once-marginal forms in the making of Islam in the aftermath of Iranian events, it was made possible to take religion as a primary medium for attempts to frame it as an issue of global governmentality.[27]

---

27 This remaking of Islam was largely related to the project of reversing the ideas of the European »Left« into a new modernist ideology of political Islam. Possibly the genealogy of the project leads back more to American Orientalism, ›Chicago‹ and Pakistan than to Heidelberg and Paris. With respect to Foucault and Iran, it is interesting to note that Paris was the place that influenced the leading protagonists of the new »Islamic Left«, certainly Ali Shariatti for Iran. A very interesting shift from ›traditionalism‹ to the new fashionable »blend of Islam and socialism« of Islamic leftism in pre-revolutionary Iran is observed by Mark Sedgwick in his admirable »Against the Modern World« (Oxford 2004, cf. pp. 158–159). It is on the back of this ›Islamic Left‹ that the so-called Cairo-Mecca inspired Salafis, the so-called reformist movement which later gained momentum in the Arab Middle East and Africa with a new ›radicalist‹ orientation.

In 1978 Michel Foucault, together with some of his friends in Paris (specifically André Glucksmann and Alain Finkielkraut), developed the project to study the real processes of the »event of ideas« among people and their movements as events of geo-political importance. The event of Islam in Iran appeared in the current stream of time as an idea in which life expressed itself in its most vivid form. It was perceived as an event of change not only in Iran but in history as such. Foucault's studies on »*governementalité*« also seem to have been influenced by this »idea«; it marked a change in his perspective, the focus on government and state turning into the body-problematic which marked the years of 1976 to 1980. Foucault in 1976 first used the concept of »bio-power« and then »bio-politic«, the governmental regulation of bodies, »power over the living«, in his lecture on »Du gouvernments des vivants« which was then subsequently turned into the perspective of »self-government among the selves« and »ethics of the subject« in 1979.[28] It is to be noted that already with the publication of »La volonté de savoir« in 1977 Foucault developed his concept of »*dispositif*«, meaning a heterogeneous whole of discourses, institutions, architectural settings, regulative decisions, laws, administrative interventions, scientific statements, etc., a present coherence of expressed and unexpressed components forming a »net« or being made connected into a »net« at any stage of historical action (see Foucault's 1977 lecture on »The game of Michel Foucault«).[29]

---

28 Sennelart notes the last lecture of the 1975–1976 turn on »In Defence of Society« and of course in 1979 »The Birth of Bio-Politic«. Cf. Sennelart, Michel: »Situierung der Vorlesungen«, in: Sennelart, Michel: »Situierung der Vorlesungen«, in: Foucault, Michel: *Geschichte der Gouvernmentalität I: Sicherheit, Terriorium, Bevölkerung*, Frankfurt/Main 2004, pp. 527; Sennelart, Michel: »Situierung der Vorlesungen«, in: Foucault, Michel: *Geschichte der Gouvernmentalität II: Die Geburt der Biopolitik*, Frankfurt/Main 2004, pp. 445f.

29 Foucault, Michel: »Das Spiel des Michel Foucault«, in: Foucault, Michel: *Dites et Ecrits: Schriften*, vol. III (1976–1979), Frankfurt/Main 2003, pp. 391–429; p. 392. There are good reasons to stress this, as recent applications of Foucault by historians seem to stress the rather pessimistic effect of ›net‹ as a ›dispositif‹; cf. Gießmann, Sebastian: »Canalize is to Colonize. The Saint-Simonians Invent Modernity« (http//www.atopia.tk). This

Certainly, it was the momentum of interrelatedness and connectedness of this »net« that interested Foucault in Iran. During the Iranian Revolution in autumn/winter 1979, however, it is the mass subject, empowered by a broadly communicated new idea of ›Islam‹, which seems to have interested him. At first he raised a variety of questions which relate indirectly to his lecture themes of spring 1979. However, in these lectures he deals with perceptions of European governance since the 18th century and largely abolishes the ›Orient‹ and certainly ›Islam‹ from his perspective.[30] As with his ›reportages‹ from Iran, he starts by symbolically comparing to the masses to the earthquake of Tabass, 10th October 1978. This reference embeds a certain exasperation at the inherent connection made between the ›natural‹ disaster and the social erosion of governmental and military power: the loss of organised power of the state precedes the loss of life and the dead bodies of the earthquake victims.[31] Most significantly, all his discussions with leading protagonists of the »revolution« evolve around a keyword with which the new religious embodiment of power within the mass movement came to be conceptualised as the »political spirituality of Islam«. With this term, intellectuals of the Iranian left framed a sort of live-to-live power of social regulation and the essential message of a utopian post-revolutionary ›regulatory system‹ in Iran. In the more general sense of Foucault's lectures on Spring 1979, »spirituality« became one focus of »guidance of the Self by the Self itself in its relation to others« or of the »ethics of the subject«. Certainly, here – as mentioned above – in the lectures these concepts were deprived of any concrete reference to Iran and turned into key concepts of Foucault's perspective on occidental processes. However, Foucault's descriptions and partly participatory observations of the 1978/9 events, the manifesta-

---

indeed leads to a revision of Foucault's analytical ›positivism‹ and civilizational optimism with respect to ›technologies‹.

30 Although it needs no further discussion in this context, I certainly maintain my point that this is largely related to the blunt attacks by Glucksmann and others on Foucault's initial sympathies with the idea of »Islamic Revolution« as expressed in his early ›reportage‹ from Tehran.

31 There inner connectedness of events is important: the ›net‹ evolves. In this context is perhaps interesting to note »Haiti« and to point to the remaining question mark of what it signifies with respect to present issues of global humanism and ›net‹-issues of ›connectedness‹.

tions of mourning, the ›naked hands‹ of mourning women in front of machine guns, the clandestine usage of common media such as cassette recorders (the new power of which in uncontrolled communication he witnessed himself in his own lecture hall), all this seemed of symbolic and practical importance with respect to the construction of the new ›spirit‹, the ›political spirituality of Islam‹. Thus, it seems quite clear that the discovery of the idea of ›political spirituality‹ of religion in the context of Iran runs parallel to his lecture-thematic of ›body and population‹ and the ›genealogy of bio-power‹ in 18th century Europe. Certainly it needed the historical momentum and the sense for comparison of ›movements‹, as with the French revolution of break and continuity – which was facilitated and certainly intellectually inspired by the socio-political atmosphere in Paris. There were mutual meetings between the Entourage of Khomeini (Bani Sadr), the appearance of Ali Shariati's religious Marxism and the »Second Left«.[32] The Iran Project, as much as the largely failed project of philosophical »*reportages des idées*«, took its presence in the framework of Foucault's general activities and his »attempt to participate in a renewal of the leftist culture« in Europe.[33]

Jaspers viewed axial civilizational progress in terms of revelation and the communication effects it offers in exchange for ultimate truths and reason (and with forms of ›rational‹ comparison). Depending on Max Weber, the regulative power of world attitudes through ›belief‹, in terms of their sublime effects on related forms of institutional regulation, remained his focus. Foucault, on the other hand, turned out to be largely taken by the reality of the mass effects of spiritual inhibition of the individual, the ›self‹, which marks a complementary perspective to his early work. Certainly, he was aware of the fact of the lack of

32 For mutual exchanges with Shariati see Aysha, Emad El-Din: »Foucault's Iran and Islamic Identity Politics Beyond Civilizational Clashes, External and Internal«, in: International Studies Perspectives 7 (2006), pp. 385–388.

33 Sennelart, Michel: »Situierung der Vorlesungen«, in: Foucault, Michel: *Geschichte der Gouvernmentalität I: Sicherheit, Terriorium, Bevölkerung*, Frankfurt/Main 2004, p. 531; Stauth, Georg: »Revolution in Spiritless Times. An Essay on Michel Foucault's Enquiries into the Iranian Revolution«, in: International Sociology 6.3 (1991), pp. 259–280.

»*Amt*« (to use Weber's term) among Shiite clergy.[34] Iran, however, added the importance of the sublime powers of pure live expression through mass events like religious rituals, body power and mass communication and new communication technologies interlocking the ›body‹ and the ›self‹ into one »net« through the shattering event of the revolutionary process.[35] Both, Jaspers and Foucault, represent momentums which are guiding for ideas of cultural and civilizational change and for global human understanding. However, it is obvious that the two philosophies – in spite of their intentions – were blatantly used for cultural reconstructions in reverse, for the construction of cultural concepts of »difference« and for religious and anti-religious power-constructions, dividing Islam and the West and modelling »Islam« in various forms as a »*dispositif*« of resisting and hindering universality and humanism, and turning it into a governmental game with the source ›par excellence‹ of ›global‹ heterodoxy.

The ›mistake‹ – according to the reaction of Paris and dominant opinion leaders – of Foucault was that he developed the intrinsically European issue of sovereignty, liberalism and the modern democratic subject into the revolutionary ascendance of the modern political idea of Islam. In Iran he identifies »spirituality«, deriving it from an in-depth concept of European essentialism, in terms of a responsive re-version in the religion of the other. The utopia of a potential mode of governance related to face-to-face social regulation and new order, giving way to a new, modern individualistic political sensitivity based

34 For a short discussion of Foucault's belief of the ›unprecedented‹ role of Shiism in ›fomenting political awareness‹ and the lack of organised institutions, see Aysha: »Foucault's Iran and Islamic Identity Politics«, pp. 377–394.

35 Stauth: »Revolution in Spiritless Times«, pp. 271–277. These are ›positive‹ analytical descriptions of ›what happened‹; they have nothing to do with »naïveté«, as claimed by his critics. With respect to social and politico-religious movements, the issues of uncontrolled action, free or opportunity spaces has been widely discussed after the events of Iran in 1978/9: e.g. Polletta, Francesca: »Free Spaces in Collective Action«, in: Theory and Society 28 (1999), pp. 1–38; Yavuz, Hakan: »Is there a Turkish Islam? The Emergence of Convergence and Consensus«, in: Journal of Muslim Minority Affairs 24.2 (2004), pp. 213–232.

in religion, seemed to emerge.[36] While the tenuous relation between »king« and »prophet« – the Shah and Khomeini, which he observed in an interview with Khomeini waiting for his return from exile in Paris – was maintained by his contemporaries to be a purely »oriental« issue, Foucault saw its deep affinity with the religious »origins« of Europe and the problem of sovereignty in emerging modern institutions and the »ubject« in modern Europe.[37] However, Foucault remains a critical theorist insofar as he clearly exposes the processes of monopolisation

---

36 It is indeed true that in the ›nutshell‹ perspective of Foucault on Iranian events, he in fact traced the new forces of religion »for moving forward in time towards something *other than* what existed in the Islamic past and the Western present«; Aysha: »Foucault's Iran and Islamic Identity Politics«, p. 378. Aysha gives us a »correct« account of the later political and ideological reversions of ›Foucault's Iran‹, however, where Foucault – in responding to the critique of a feminist reader of his encounter with Khomeini – insisted on the »problem of Islam as a political force«, to be »an essential one for our time and for the years to come« (Foucault, Michel [NO]: »Réponse à une lectrice Iranienne«, [reply to an Iranian Female Reader], in: Le Nouvel Observateur 731 [1978], 13.–19.11.1978, p. 26) (Foucault: *Dites et Ecrits: Schriften*, vol. III [1976–1979], p. 887). His instincts were already electrified with respect to what the following respective instalment of ›religion‹ as a ›dispositif‹ of East/West-governmentality could lead to in the future. Perhaps it is an irony of these developments that »Iran« today in fact stands for »things to come« not only in the Muslim world. That is to say, the invention of religion as a ›dispositif‹ of global governmentality and in terms of civilizational clashes was indeed one of the things that came – which, however, contributed little more than re-invoking the technicalities of selective recognition and hatred that have long pre-existed. This also could point to the momentum by which Foucault's instincts as a philosopher led him to return to his »old« issues after 1978.

37 There was, clearly, a reaction to the acclaimed ›mistake‹ of the preoccupation with Iran and Islam in Foucault's Collège de France lectures of the spring of 1979 and 1980; however, the »Gouvernement des vivants« remained the main issue of his political philosophy. For the latter see Landry, Jean-Michel: »Confession, Obedience and Subjects. Michel Foucault's Unpublished Lectures on the Government of the Living«, in: Telos 146 (2009), pp. 11–123.

of power and its effects, and the underlying need for »synchronisation« between the »sentiments of the masses« and power – here, in a new turn in a »revolt of culture«, as he saw it; yet the event of »spirituality« in a framework of civil insurgence and manifest communication between actors remained his focus.[38] No doubt, though, he himself soon became aware of the deadlock of this »solution« while the process of the new Islamic government came into play.

It is not without irony that serious and influential applications of Foucault in the current discourse of Islam and feminism, for example, have come into play in identifying new ›physical‹ media of the Islamic »*dispositif*« in general and in particular with respect to the »niqâb«, »burqua« or female Islamic attire in general[39], or with respect to public expressions of inner religious ›spirituality‹. I am certainly aware of the influential work of anthropologists like Talal Asad[40] and Saba Mahmood[41], who silently turn the Foucault/Iran treatment of body politics

---

38 For further discussion see Foucault, Michel: *Politics, Philosophy, Culture: Interviews and Other Writings (1977–1984)*, transl. by A. Sheridan et al., ed. and introd. L. D. Kritzmann, New York/London 1988, pp. 217ff.; also my »Foucault und Islam«, in: Stauth: »Protestantisierung des Islams«, pp. 7–12.

39 Certainly, this includes the field of repulsive »aesthetic sensibilities« and even varieties of competing aesthetic utopianisms, as well as the general idealisation of modernism in grounding its aesthetics in antiquity and premodern ›Gestalt‹ in general. For Germany see e.g. the very interesting work of Stefan Breuer, although much criticized by the new George-Clan on Breuer, Stefan: *Ästhetischer Fundamentalismus: George und der deutsche Antimodernismus*, Darmstadt 1996.

40 I do not wish to enter into a debate on the religious anthropology of Talal Asad. His concept of ›discursive tradition‹ appears to me as a sort of religious, and more specifically Islamic, simplification of Foucault's ›dispositif‹, alternising a variety of reflections of continuity, both religious and secular, into a pattern of inner, historically loaded bondage. Asad has won much attention in America, setting the stage for essentialist identifications of Islamic specificity. For his influence in Europe see Peter, Frank/Arigita, E.: »Authorising Islam in Europe«, in: Muslim World 96.4 (2006), pp. 537–737.

41 Cf. Asad, Talal: *The Idea of an Islamic Anthropology of Islam*, Washington D. C. 1986; Asad, Talal: *Genealogies of Religion: Discipline and Rea-*

and »religious spirituality« into a new stage of global governmental research, in which »spirituality« in the various forms of re-invented Islamic »tradition(alism)« take on a more sublime form, specifically in Mahmood's work where the issue of »political spirituality« turns into a new Islamist feminist *»dispositif«*: »politics of piety« as the »great challenge« for Western secularism and liberalism. In Cairo Mahmood studied a group of middle class women in a fashionable quarter, reporting their »discursive engagement with sacred texts«.[42] In an attempt to attack the suppressing effects of liberal political rule on an emerging ›religious subjectivity‹, Mahmood in fact, develops an Islamic female counter-subject. One would indeed question why these ›subjects‹ then take on the imagery and ›absolute‹ embodiments of the alterity and ›difference‹ of Islam. Mahmood, in taking ›Salafi piety‹ among women as a remake of any conventional concept of feminism, is in fact setting up a basis for strong attacks on secular feminist discourses. Here, Western feminism is featured as a decisive force in the shaping of anti-Islamic attitudes in the West. In effect, however, Mahmood radicalises, in a sort of *pars pro toto* game, Salafi (so-called reformist) fundamentalism into the absolutist privileged position of authentic Islam. The paradox is that by depending on Foucault (and Asad), Mahmood sets female piety politics (and Salafism) as a core test for modern recognition of Islam – revising claims for ›tolerance‹ into the featuring of an object for antagonism and hatred.

In connection with the minutely designed applications of Foucault in gender studies and religious anthropology, we may observe a growing trend of inquisition-like generalisations of religion and religious expression. The religious anthropologies of Islam imply that human beings in general and ›Islamic individuals‹ in specific are ›in essence‹ religious beings, and that their religiousness is grounded in authentic Islam and bound accordingly to all spheres and moments of action. In this sense, they reinvent the physical dimension of religion, interlock-

---

sons of Power in Christianity and Islam, Baltimore/London 1993; Asad, Talal: *Formations of the Secular: Christianity, Islam, Modernity*, Stanford, Ca. 2003; cf. Mahmood, Saba: *Politics of Piety: The Islamic Revival and the Feminist Subject*, Princeton 2005; Mahmood, Saba: »Secularism, Hermeneutics, and Empire: The Politics of Islamic Reformation«, in: Public Culture 18.2 (2006), pp. 323–347.

42 Mahmood: »Politics of Piety«, Princeton 2005, p. 115.

ing it with strategic geopolitics over rejection or integration of Islam. The field of social research was opened up with a new component of deciphering humanity in terms of a general religious anthropology, dividing and denoting a total specificity of the individual of a ›Muslim‹ and his political being, and generalising performed embodiment of ›piety‹ into a holistic critique of ›intolerance‹ of modern liberalism with respect to Islamic alterity.

We may well recall, in this context, that there is a certain real and factual political turn connected with Foucault's discourse on body empowerment. It is another new medium of the ›digital age‹, the Internet, through which today any local preacher, any ›real Muslim‹ – as much as, paradoxically, quite often in very similar ways any ›Anti-Muslim‹ movements – can speak out on what, according to their reading and understanding of holy scriptures, are the ›revealed‹ politics of the day, or have to be, or how ›authentic‹ Muslim ›selves‹ have to act and to appear coherently in public and private spheres. This ambiguous bond of the ›religious subject‹ and the ›net‹ was – in practice as much as in study – turned into a new field of conflict and manipulation.

The modern shattering events of religion (9/11, »war on terrorism«, »clash of civilizations«, inherent presence of Islam) remain controversial. Conventional theory treats this issue as a sort of effect and mis-perceived anecdote of the global expansion of the spirit of ›Enlightenment‹ and Western ideology in the non-western world. Alternatively, it is generally believed that these contemporary events of religion relate to ›the event of an idea‹ which was so long suppressed, namely, that Islam has a civilizational power quite similar to that of other world religions. Is the event of religion really only a reaction to the insensitive language of modern secularism? In the light of a well-noticed 14th of October 2001 speech of Jürgen Habermas at the historical Paulskirche of Frankfurt, a founding place of modern liberal, secular Germany, ›we‹, the secularist modernists, should maintain our rationalism of world dominance by – as Habermas supposes – becoming more sensitive and developing an integrative language that combines the awareness of religious traditions with that of modern science. Habermas argued that we should attempt to diminish, however, the normative social effects of relentless religious truths by way of »salvaging deconstruction«, i.e. reducing the power of religious institutions to a capability of public language and representation, and work for the transposition of religious visions into the context of the inner civil theology of the individual subject. If this – more or less – is the tenor of Habermas' October 2001 speech at the Paulskirche in Frankfurt, then this is, I believe, through its submission to strategic and hegemonic dimensions of contemporary »religious language« (or even by consciously propagating this submission), a disappointing document and the end of critical philosophy.

The question arises as to what – quite in continuity to the axial discourse set out by Jaspers – Habermas contributes to the actual purport of religion, as opposed to denouncing the ever more sublime forms of political manipulation and instrumentalisation of ›religion‹, reducing the types of ›communication‹ they have in mind to the absurd. Habermas rather neglects the realpolitik of body and mind in modern mass societies to which the anthropologists point (even if they do so in the more or less ideological, however no less powerful sense of ›embodied piety‹). The reality of embodiment politics has already overturned the vicious circle between elitist liberal secularism – now acknowledging religion as a fact –, public suppression of religion, and radical religious alterity. Habermas – quite implicitly depending on Jaspers – seems to attempt to transform the »*Pastorenkirche*«, the Church of the priest, into the civil religion of priestly actors in order to re-enact a basis for liberal communicative action. He misreads the invisible hands (or even ever less invisible hands) which have turned ›religion‹ into micro-issues of ›piety power‹ and at the same time into the very strategic tool in the ›net‹ of hegemonic power which is necessarily just the other side of the coin of global governance that depends on invoking radical religious alterity, when needed. Today ›piety politics‹ are at work to provoke a disastrous performative polarisation of religious difference in order to manipulate culturally ›industrialised‹ believers and spiritualised mass-individuals – here and there – in a game of antagonisms between global orthodoxies and heterodox religious protest cultures: a new »dispositif«, to use this concept of Foucault again. One is compelled to ask: How does »rational theology« matter as a force for ›self-critique‹ and ›differentiation‹, or even as a field of symbolic representation, in dealing with the irrationality relating to this new ›net‹ of modernity, where religion (›other‹ and ›theirs‹) as a whole is recognised as one of the most effective forms of mediating global hegemonic power? In this sense, we may claim that the ›return of political theology‹ as a major issue in the American Social Sciences is indeed a shattering event, which coincides with the outspoken militarisation of

American Foreign Policy in the aftermath of the Revolution in Iran and gradually leads to the respective undermining of liberal alternatives.

In this context, Axial Age Theory remains a sort of helpless footing for conventional European and Western elites. With respect to Jaspers and Habermas, indeed, »*Wissenschaftlichkeit und Humanität suchen sich gegenseitig*«.[43] However, when it comes to communication and power it should be noted that axial theory itself entails a certain ›communicative deficit‹ in the selection and empowering of the essentials of universalism. Furthermore, recent applications of Axial Age Theory fail in the way they have largely neglected Jaspers' quest for humanism and understanding humanity as a whole, focusing on specificities and differences rather than on the actual ›common grounds‹ of communication. Indeed, the debate has suited the enhancement of disciplinary research on spiritual and intellectual events and movements that changed the interpretation of tradition. However, it also led to the perception of ›civilizations‹ as a sort of inner essentialism with core traditions, and as the ›continuity‹ of religious visions and moral principles for modern reconstruction. This, in the first place, shows that the assumptions and essentials of Axial authentication of Western modernity as well as their parameters of cultural comparison were placed at the centre of any interactive perspective, and certainly also at the centre of the discourse of reconstruction in the modern world and among all cultures it contacts.

The ›event of Islam‹ – as Foucault indeed signified – brought new patterns of communication into existence. This is beyond the rational administration of »revelation«. With regard to only the communicative aspects of »*Auflösung der Werte* (dissolution of values)«, and the axial achievement of re-instituting their continuity in applying self-affirmative mechanisms of cultural reconstruction, this no longer serves a purpose. It rather points to a deadlock with respect to universalism. Jaspers, in fact, re-invokes axial processes in order to produce and perpetuating social values and principles which were constitutive in the formative process of the Western world and in defending it in the post-World War II era against Marxism and Nihilism.[44] Certainly in his time he could not figure out the ontological questions with respect to

43 Jaspers: »Erneuerung der Universität«, p. 144.

44 Jaspers: »Vom Ursprung und Ziel der Geschichte«, p. 167ff.

the inner and recursive techniques and principles which are at work in the world of Islam, which also include the subtle anti-secular and anti-liberal reconstructions today. The question of whether there exist today ›different‹ forms and strategies of subjectification evolving in originally ›non-Western‹ contexts remains of comparative importance. For example, the world importance of Sufism, both in its traditional forms as well as a New Age religion, relates to modern universal dimensions of individualism.[45] Furthermore, there are in the case of Islam these ›inner‹ relationships to axiality and the West – monotheism, revelation, as well as ›late‹ (i.e. reflective) axiality – which form a specific dimension of its modern reconstruction.

It may be possible that the intensive inner encounter with Western modernity produces more than one form of an Islamic subject striving for self-determination combined with a certain Muslim touch. Beyond ›inner‹ dimensions of self-thematization and self-knowledge arising in encounter with the genealogy of occidental development of culture, other forms are obvious. Here, certainly, what Foucault later named the »technologies of the self« actualising the ›costs of ascetic rationalism‹ come to the forth. More specifically the question of how ›low‹ folk traditions become ›high‹, depending on education, mass media, tourism etc. and on encounters with modern middle class culture, seems important not only for migrants to Europe. Quite similarly, folk traditions of the poorer strata in Islamic heartlands are entering the ›net‹ of mass-society and consumerism.

6. FUTURE OF EUROPE, FACTS AND IDEAS

The broader effect of Foucault's Iran on research and debate with respect to modern Islam and related geopolitical strategies is the way it re-maps patterns of comparison. Following the paradigms of Max Weber, axial age theory focuses on rationalistic components, structures and principles. It seems to involve only one aspect of the current range of inter-religious communication and is certainly of declining importance (even though always renewed when it comes to repression

45 Cf. Stauth, Georg: »Introduction: Muslim Saints and Modernity«, in: On Archaeology of Sainthood in Islam, Yearbook of the Sociology of Islam 5 (2004), pp. 7–23.

and anti-liberalism). In contrast, the debate on ›Orientalism‹ stimulated by Edward Said's application of Foucault has already mapped a specific dimension of modern cross-culture communication: the ›knowledge‹ problem related to perceptions and encounters of colonizing modes. In a reversive application of this critique of Western rationalist hegemony, Islamic political activism took part in the recent ›real‹ history of Islamic reconstruction. This is where the growing intensification and acceleration of cross-cultural communication came into play: It implies ever more sophisticated and multiplied, as well as hardened, forms of cultural and subsequently social differentiation.

If the Islamic turn of the Iranian revolution's shattering events led to the eradication of a powerful Western-supported government, as described by Foucault, it was the event of an embodied idea. Following this ›turn‹, it was ›post-Iran‹ in Western theory which developed ›religion‹ into a post-colonial ›dispositive‹ for holistic combinations of state and religion or profane and sacred spheres, on the one side, and of differentiated spheres of religion and liberalism, science, legal regulation and administrative institutions on the other.

On the other hand, the actualisation of Jaspers' theory in recent years was fruitful in raising questions about the interpretation of historical facts and experiences of transformation in early civilizations. At the same time, however, interpretations of historical realities took on a sort of radicalisation that appeared largely due to the program of enacting new hegemonic reinterpretations of World History. The parametric comparisons that developed with reference to the Axial Age have engaged – and continue to engage – in a strategic discourse about repositioning »civilizations« within the framework of the modern world.[46]

»*Der Einzelne ist er selbst nur, wenn auch der andere er selbst ist. Freiheit ist nur in dem Maße, als alle frei sind*«. Jaspers' concept of recognition includes the liberty of revealed otherness, and certainly also a common open discourse about what that means in terms of social order and the shared worlds of material, moral, spiritual and intellectual existence. Today the strategic gain seems minimal when we insist – with Jaspers' humanism in mind – that the West, together with Islam, shares ›revelation‹ as a common ground in biblical traditions; an interactive platform of ritual, symbolic and medial social integration; and the Mediterranean cultural core: communication.

46 E.g. Eisenstadt: »Culture and Power«, pp. 3–16.

It is interesting to note that both Jaspers and Foucault see the strategic gains linked to communication; both, however, were also aware of the potential loss of autonomy which relates to it. Quite paradoxically, the communicative interchanges based on ›revelation‹, ›spirituality‹ and ›piety‹ at the same time served on different levels – as I wished to show – as mediating modes of empowerment of ›difference‹ and conflict and, furthermore, leading to the inauguration of new and radical projects of world and global order based on various options of the silent or absolute invocation of the ›otherness‹ of Islam.

In the last instance, for Jaspers the Axial Age meant a transitional process from ›revelation to communication‹. By contrast, Foucault's ›Iran‹ signified a series of discursive steps from ›political spirituality of Islam‹ to the effects of ›piety politics‹. Both, in contrary to their own intentions, signify instances and different stages of the unfolding modes of interlocking ›religion‹ into the ›net‹ of global governance. These transitions, which we actually take as examples of the new global ›dispositif‹ of religion, seem to indicate a silent communication theory of its own: From ›great monumental projects‹ (communication and ›revelation‹) and stressing the ›Museum of Modernity‹, the geostrategic importance of ›*Musealisierung*‹ for cultural reconstruction, as with Jaspers on the one hand, and on the other, the sublime reinventions of everyday strategies governed by »piety politics« (focusing in Foucault's spiritual actualisation of Islam). These in fact also are complementary forms of transitions in civilizational change: the decline from ›value‹ and ›structure‹ to new sublime expressions of individualism. Correspondingly, by departing from Jaspers and Foucault, we might be able to trace decisive acts of moulding ›history‹ and ›religion‹ into the material of connected ›subjective‹ regulations in terms of geo-political interest. Where Jaspers' »humanism« turns out to be transformed into new apologetics of hegemonic power, it is Foucault's anticipation of »what is to come« that fits »Islam« into the »subjective« heterodoxies of insisting on a quest for origin and authentication within the premises of modern mass industrialised culture and consumerist needs. All this points to a loss of, rather than a future for, ›humanism‹: the devaluation of universalism in terms of what ›real freedom‹ could mean.

Foucault's »inner motive« regarding »Iran« derived in the first place from his »French« perspective on revolution rather than from a natural interest in religion, Islam or Iran. For him this perspective was represented the French historian Maurice Furet,[47] who renewed the issue of »break« in that he showed that the revolutionary want for change among the masses reflected in achievements already reached under the ›ancient regime‹, and in this sense incorporated »continuity« with the ideology for change. In this context, for Foucault, from the limited view of events in Iran at the time, »Islam« stood for ›real tradition‹ as opposed to the ›false tradition‹ of the Shah. With respect to »history«, Foucault's interest in Iran meshes with that of Jaspers: the study of a revaluation of the past in terms of an »axial break«. Certainly, there is an ambiguous tension between ›break‹ as the advent of a new form of strategic »*Musealisierung*« and »break« as the reality of an »event«, actualising an inner care for history. For Foucault this actualisation attained its peak with the embodiment of »Islam« as an idea, and subsequently, as an embodiment of power. In this embodiment, »communication« and »spirituality« coincide as »dispositif« and thus as discursive forces of history, as a process of transposing historical »structure« into a »idea« in a moment of »continuity« and of the »self«. Certainly, when taking Foucault in this way, we might include a critical stand against ›communication as humanism‹. From this impetus of ›political spirituality‹, civilizational analysis should include the dialectics of ›dispositif‹, which reflects the tenuous relations between the ›net‹ and the ›bio-techniques‹ of the self, and co-inciting with it the analysis of various antagonising forms of incorporating ›history‹ into the ›present‹.

BIBLIOGRAPHY

Al-Attas, Syed Muhammad al-Naguib: *Islam, Secularism and the Philosophy of the Future*, London 1985.

Arnason, Johann P./Eisenstadt, Shmuel N./Wittrock, Björn (Eds.): *Axial Civilizations and World History*, Leiden 2005.

Arnason, Johann P./Salvatore, Armando/Stauth, Georg (Eds.): *Islam in Process. Historical and Civilizational Perspectives*, Bielefeld 2006 (= Yearbook of the Sociology of Islam 7).

Asad, Talal: *Formations of the Secular: Christianity, Islam, Modernity*, Stanford, Ca. 2003.

47 Furet, Maurice: *Penser la Révolution Française*, Paris 1978.

Asad, Talal: *Genealogies of Religion: Discipline and Reasons of Power in Christianity and Islam*, Baltimore/London 1993.

Asad, Talal: *The Idea of an Islamic Anthropology of Islam*, Washington D. C. 1986.

Assmann, Jan: »Axial ›Breakthroughs‹ and Semantic ›Relocations‹ in Ancient Egypt and Israel«, in: Arnason, Johann P./Eisenstadt, Shmuel N./Wittrock, Björn (Eds.): *Axial Civilizations and World History*, Leiden 2005, pp. 133–156.

Aysha, Emad El-Din: »Foucault's Iran and Islamic Identity Politics Beyond Civilizational Clashes, External and Internal«, in: International Studies Perspectives 7 (2006), pp. 377–394..

Breuer, Stefan: *Ästhetischer Fundamentalismus: George und der deutsche Antimodernismus*, Darmstadt 1996.

Daedalus. Special Issue 104.2 (1974): Karl Jaspers, *Wisdom, Revelation and Doubt: Perspectives on the First Millenium B.C.*

Eisenstadt, Shmuel N.: »Allgemeine Einleitung: die Bedingungen für die Entstehung und Institutionalisierung der Kulturen der Achsenzeit«, in: Eisenstadt, Shmuel N. (Ed.): *Kulturen der Achsenzeit I*, Frankfurt/Main, 1987, p. 10–40.

Eisenstadt, Shmuel N.: *Die Antinomien der Moderne: Die jakobinischen Grundzüge der Moderne und des Fundamentalismus. Heterodoxien, Utopismus und Jakobinismus in der Konstitution fundamentalistischer Bewegungen*, Frankfurt/Main 1998.

Ess, Josef van: »Islam and the Axial Age«, in: Arnason, Johann P./Salvatore, Armando/Stauth, Georg (Eds.): *Islam in Process: Historical and Civilizational Perspectives*, Bielefeld 2006 (= Yearbook of the Sociology of Islam 7), pp. 220–240.

Foucault, Michel: »Réponse à une lectrice Iranienne«, (reply to an Iranian Female Reader), in: Le Nouvel Observateur 731 (1978), 13.–19.11.1978, p. 26.

Foucault, Michel: »Réponse à une lectrice Iranienne«, in: *Dites et Ecrits. Schriften*, vol. III (1976–1979), Frankfurt/Main 2003, p. 887.

Foucault, Michel: *Dites et Ecrits. Schriften*, vol. III (1976–1979), Frankfurt/Main 2003.

Foucault, Michel: »Das Spiel des Michel Foucault«, in: Foucault, Michel: *Dites et Ecrits. Schriften*, vol. III (1976–1979), Frankfurt/Main 2003, pp. 391–429.

Foucault, Michel: *Politics, Philosophy, Culture: Interviews and Other Writings (1977–1984)*, transl. by A. Sheridan et al., ed. and introd. L. D. Kritzmann, New York/London 1988.

Furet, Maurice: *Penser la Révolution Française*, Paris 1978.

Gellner, Ernest: *Muslim Society*, Cambridge 1981.

Gießmann, Sebastian: »Canalize is to Colonize. The Saint-Simonians Invent Modernity« (http//www.atopia.tk).

Henrich, Dieter: »Karl Jaspers: Thinking with Max Weber in Mind«, in: Mommsen, Wolfgang J./Osterhammel, Jürgen (Eds.): *Max Weber and his Contemporaries: The German Historical Institute*, London 1987, pp. 528–544.

Iqbal, Mohammad: *The Reconstruction of Religious Thought in Islam*, Lahore 1954 (reprint of 1927 edition).

Jaspers, Karl: »Die Achsenzeit der Weltgeschichte«, in: Der Monat 1.6 (1949), pp. 3–9.

Jaspers, Karl: »Die Schuldfrage«, in: Jaspers, Karl: *Erneuerung der Universität: Reden und Schriften (1945/46)*, ed. Renato de Rosa, Heidelberg 1986, pp. 113–213.

Jaspers, Karl: »Schema der Weltgeschichte«, in: Jaspers, Karl: *Vom Ursprung und Ziel der Geschichte*, Munich 1949, pp. 43–48.

Jaspers, Karl: »Über Bedingungen und Möglichkeiten eines neuen Humanismus«, in: Jaspers, Karl: *Rechenschaft und Ausblick: Reden und Aufsätze*, Munich 1951, pp. 265–292.

Jaspers, Karl: »Über meine Philosophie«, in: Jaspers, Karl: *Rechenschaft und Ausblick: Reden und Aufsätze*, Munich 1951, pp. 333–365.

Jaspers, Karl: »Von der biblischen Religion«, in: Die Wandlung I.1 (1945/46), pp. 406–413.

Jaspers, Karl: »Was ist Europa?«, in: Jaspers, Karl: *Erneuerung der Universität: Reden und Schriften (1945/46)*, ed. Renato de Rosa, Heidelberg 1986, pp. 245–274.

Jaspers, Karl: »Wisdom, Revelation and Doubt: Perspectives on the First Millenium B.C.«, in: Daedalus 104.2 (1974).

Jaspers, Karl: *Erneuerung der Universität. Reden und Schriften* (1945/46), ed. Renato de Rosa, Heidelberg 1986.

Jaspers, Karl: *Europa der Gegenwart*, Vienna 1947.

Jaspers, Karl: *Nietzsche und das Christentum*, Hameln 1938.

Jaspers, Karl: *Rechenschaft und Ausblick: Reden und Aufsätze*, Munich 1951.

Jaspers, Karl: *Vom Ursprung und Ziel der Geschichte*, Munich 1949.

Landry, Jean-Michel: »Confession, Obedience and Subjects. Michel Foucault's Unpublished Lectures on the Government of the Living«, in: Telos 146 (2009), pp. 11–123.

Mahmood, Saba: »Secularism, Hermeneutics, and Empire: The Politics of Islamic Reformation«, in: Public Culture 18.2 (2006), pp. 323–347.

Mahmood, Saba: *Politics of Piety: The Islamic Revival and the Feminist Subject*, Princeton 2005.

Manasse, Ernst Moritz: »Jaspers' Relation to Max Weber«, in: *The Philosophy of Karl Jaspers*, New York o. J., pp. 369–391.

Peter, Frank/Arigita, E.: »Authorising Islam in Europe«, in: Muslim World 96.4 (2006), pp. 537–737.

Polletta, Francesca: »Free Spaces in Collective Action«, in: Theory and Society 28 (1999), pp. 1–38.

Rodinson, Maxim: *Islam und Kapitalismus*, Frankfurt/Main 1971.

Sedgwick, Mark: *Against the Modern World*, Oxford 2004.

Sennelart, Michel: »Situierung der Vorlesungen«, in: Foucault, Michel: *Geschichte der Gouvernmentalität I: Sicherheit, Terriorium, Bevölkerung*, Frankfurt/Main 2004, pp. 527–57.

Sennelart, Michel: »Situierung der Vorlesungen«, in: *Geschichte der Gouvernmentalität II: Die Geburt der Biopolitik*, Frankfurt/Main 2004, pp. 445–489.

Stauth, Georg/Turner, Bryan S.: »The Priest is a Beefsteak Eater – Rationalisation and Cultural Control«, in: Stauth, Georg/Turner, Bryan S.: *Nietzsche's Dance*, Oxford 1988, pp. 99–122.

Stauth, Georg: »Foucault und Islam«, in: Stauth, Georg: *Protestantisierung des Islams* (2006) (http://www.ifeas.uni-mainz.de/working papers/AP70.pdf), pp. 7–12.

Stauth, Georg: »Nietzsche, Weber, and the affirmative sociology of culture«, in: European Journal of Sociology 23 (1992), pp. 219–247.

Stauth, Georg: »Revolution in Spiritless Times. An Essay on Michel Foucault's Enquiries into the Iranian Revolution«, in: International Sociology 6.3 (1991), pp. 259–280.

Stauth, Georg: Protestantisierung des Islams (2006) (http://www.ifeas.uni-mainz.de/workingpapers/AP70.pdf).

Stauth, Georg: »Introduction. Muslim Saints and Modernity«, in: On Archaeology of Sainthood in Islam, Yearbook of the Sociology of Islam 5 (2004), pp. 7–23.

Sternberger, Dolf: »Jaspers und der Staat«, in: Frankfurter Allgemeine Zeitung, 22.02.1963, p. 2.

Taubes, Jacob: *Ad Karl Schmitt: Gegenstrebige Fügung*. Berlin 1987.

Taubes, Jacob: *Der Preis des Messianismus: Briefe von Jacob Taubes an Gershom Scholem und andere Materialien*, ed. Elettra Stimilli, Würzburg 2006.

Taubes, Jacob: *Die politische Theologie des Paulus*, ed. Aleida and Jan Assmann, Munich 1993.

Telos. Special Issue: *Carl Schmitt, Enemy or Foe?* 72 (1987).

Turner, Bryan S.: *Weber and Islam. A Critical Study*, London 1974.

Yavuz, Hakan: »Is there a Turkish Islam? The Emergence of Convergence and Consensus«, in: Journal of Muslim Minority Affairs 24.2 (2004), pp. 213–232.

II.3 The Theory of the Axial Age Revisited from a Theological Perspective

Georg Essen

In view of the topic of our conference I will refrain from a comprehensive reconstruction of the idea of the axial age. Instead, I will restrict myself to emphasizing some aspects that are essential for my theological disciplinary approach to our topic. If I develop in the following some aspects usually connected with axial age theory, I refer both to Karl Jaspers as well as to Shmuel Eisenstadt, without wanting to blur any differences between them.[1] In doing so, I will neither address the issue of the historical periodization of the axial age, nor the issue of which cultures belong to the so-called cultures of the axial age. Methodologically, I use the axial age as a temporal term – used with comparative intent, it can help to construe temporal structures of order, which can, with practical intent, also function as concepts of meaning for historical thinking.

Firstly I focus on some aspects of contents which are, according to Jaspers as well as to Eisenstadt, constitutive of axial cultures. Following their fundamental definition, cultures of the axial age are marked by specific differentiations. According to Eisenstadt, those ideas that aim at an ontologically and cosmologically relevant differentiation be-

1 Cf. Eisenstadt, Shmuel N.: (Ed.): *The Origins and Diversity of Axial Age Civilizations*, Albany 1986; Arnason, Eisenstadt, Wittrock (Eds.): *Axial Civilization and World History*, Leiden 2005; Jaspers, Karl: *Vom Ursprung und Ziel der Geschichte*, Munich 1949.

tween a »transcendent« and »worldly« order are fundamental. A new relation of the human being with himself and the world is connected with this distinction. This relation could be called »the invention of the inner human«, because the abovementioned ontological differentiation is connected with the discovery of the difference between »inside« and »outside«[2]. The axial-cultural differentiation enables humans to conceive of themselves in a twofold manner. On the one hand, a human being can perceive of himself as singular compared to the whole world. Through that singularity he correlates with himself and with reality as such. Here one can find the beginnings of a form of relation with oneself, leading to the term »subject« in the tradition of Western philosophy. This self-perception has a correlate in the monotheistic religions of Judaism, Christianity and Islam, insofar as the human being learns to say »I« by means of the individuating gaze of God, who is discerned and believed as a person.[3] This anthropological breakthrough is usually associated with Jewish prophecy, in which an amazing subjectifying of the human relation with God as well as an internalisation of belief takes place. On the other hand, the axial-cultural differentiation leads to an alternative form of the relation of the human being with himself and the world, in which the axial-cultural processes of distinction are bridged in a specific way. These are ways of understanding in which the realities of humans and the world are attempted to be grasped as a comprehensive, and in the end consistent, whole. This leads to humans' understanding of themselves as worldly beings in this world. The most reflective and incisive expression of such an understanding of the world can be found in East Asian thinking, in far Eastern religions. Those religions can be called monism insofar as they try to apprehend the comprehensive entity and entirety of reality. Thus, my question: does the idea of the axial age, by referring to axial-cultural differentiation, offer an opportunity for the theory of religion

---

2 Assmann, Jan (Ed.): *Die Erfindung des inneren Menschen. Studien zur religiösen Anthropologie*, Gütersloh 1993 (= Studien zum Verstehen fremder Religionen, 6).

3 Essen, Georg: »Ethical Monotheism and Human Freedom: Theological Convergences with the Pluralism of the Modern Age«, in: Hintersteiner, Norbert (Ed.): *Naming and Thinking God in Europe Today: Theology in Global Dialogue (Currents of Encounter)*, Amsterdam/New York 2007, pp. 265–283.

to quasi-return to an axial-cultural common ground »behind« the relevant differences of monotheistic and monistic ways of understanding the world? In doing so, the theory of the axial age would offer an opportunity for the hermeneutics of religion to claim an inclusivistic universalism by referring to an axial-cultural syndrome. This universalism could once again enclose the two great cultural and religious models of understanding the world. I mainly raise this question because the theory of the axial age seeks to connect two fundamental religious alternatives with each other: on the one hand, theistic religious ideas; on the other hand, monistic conceptions that do not have a personified idea of god. This consideration could be important because the idea of the axial age obviously offers an alternative to Ernst Troeltsch[4]. He argued that mosaic monotheism and far-eastern monism both lead to worldviews that are hermeneutically incompatible.

In the second place, the assumption of a reality which reaches beyond that currently given makes it possible to look at the world as an entirety from a transcendent standpoint. This has far-reaching consequences for the practical relation humans have with the world: A frame of reference, which orientates and stipulates the acting of humans, is constituted from an external standpoint. In this way questions of morality and meaning are articulated. But not only this! This increased reflexivity leads to the perspective systems theory calls the observation of a »second order«. It does not only allow for reflexive reference to differences between the transcendent and the worldly order, but to the fundamental premises of both spheres as well. These processes lead to a new culture of reflection. Jaspers, especially, outlines a rationalisation of the worldview, which goes along with that. This rationalisation destroys the causal nexus of a magical-mystical understanding of the self and the world. Thus, in the perspective of a cognitive development from myth to logos, a world of discourse is established, later called philosophy. This itself is – also in view of our topic – interesting for other reasons. A superficial look at the theory of the axial age primarily understands the axial syndromes as a starting-point of the great world religions that are present until today. Howev-

4 Troeltsch, Ernst: *Die Absolutheit des Christentums und die Religionsgeschichte (1902/1912).* Mit den Thesen von 1901 und den handschriftlichen Zusätzen, ed. Trutz Rendtorff in coop. with Stefan Pautler, Berlin u. a.1998.

er, this view of the axial age from the perspective of the history of religion is one-sided. In my opinion, Jürgen Habermas was right in pointing out that not only mosaic monotheism, but also occidental philosophy, are heirs of the axial-cultural revolution of world-views.[5] Differentiations connected with it do not only lead to monotheistic religion, but also to Greek metaphysics. The world-transcendent authority of judgement was not only interpreted religiously; it led to a philosophical morality of principles as well. Furthermore, the position of the individual in the entirety of the world unfolds in a semantic field which was not only connoted religiously: soul, subject, person etc. Habermas refers to »complementary figures of the intellect« which are due to the abovementioned development of the axial age. The culture of reflection, initiated by the axial-cultural differentiations, actually led to the fact that the mentioned axial-cultural distinctions of transcendent and worldly order became reflexive. This offers an opportunity for understanding the profane world as an independent realm and ascribing it a place next to the transcendent, sacral world. According to Eisenstadt, but also to Jaspers, this has far-reaching socio-cultural consequences, because the identified differentiation goes along with the establishment of institutional elites that become supporters of the axial-cultural worldview. Furthermore, in both spheres elaborated worlds of discourse develop, in which »secular knowledge« finds a place next to »revealed knowledge«. The theory of the axial age offers an opportunity to correlate both forms of understanding the world, namely, as outcomes of the axial-cultural revolution of worldviews. This consideration seems to be relevant in light of our theoretical reflections about the idea of humanism. The equality of origin of a human way of understanding of the world, one which is not bound to religion, can in that way not only be assumed due to rationally autonomous reasons, but also by means of a historical recourse to the axial age.

5 Cf. Habermas, Jürgen: »Ein Bewußtsein vom dem, was fehlt. Über Glauben und Wissen und den Defaitismus der modernen Vernunft« 10.2.2007 (www.nzz.ch); Essen, Georg: »›... allerlei unlautere Religionsideen‹. Zur aktuellen Bedeutung der Religionsphilosophie Kants«, in: Danz, Christian/Hermanni, Friedrich (Eds.): *Wahrheitsansprüche der Weltreligionen: Konturen gegenwärtiger Religionstheologie*, Neukirchen-Vluyn 2006, pp. 133–147.

There is one further point: Jaspers, as much as Eisenstadt, ascribes the differentiation between the religious and the worldly sphere to the axial age. On the one hand, this means that religion increasingly confronts political authority and cultural order as a different, independent and autonomous realm. This comes along with an increased independence of the religious culture of reflection, in the wake of which attempts of a professionalisation of religious self-descriptions develop. The arising self-reflexivity of religious systems in principle enables a religion to inscribe the difference of system and environment into its own structure, making way for a reflected self-understanding via the detour of an environmental relation. Axial-cultural religions thereby have the possibility to overcome the different varieties of a religious exclusivism.[6] This discloses an epistemic attitude to determine personal convictions of truth that generate identity, while relations with one's environment are included. Insofar as the term »axial age« functions in this context as a critically and normatively ideal term, the axial-cultural syndrome would be the pool of common grounds, without which an understanding aiming at reciprocal recognition cannot exist. There is a further point: the culture of reflection of the axial age leads to a rationalisation of worldview. In the wake of this a de-mythologizing was promoted that comprised the relation of humans with the world as much as with religion. What is especially interesting from the perspective of religious studies is Jaspers' observation that cognitive development also led to an »ethical interpretation of religion«. This sheds a different light on the phenomenon of religiously motivated violence, insofar as an axial-cultural religion of worldview makes an ethically motivated criticism of religion possible. On the other hand, the complex processes of profane systems of order for politics, authority and law, which are independent of religion, can be ascribed to the axial-cultural revolution of worldview. The orientating reference to

6 Essen, Georg: »›Nature‹ as a humanistic principle of universal communication. A European historical case study regarding natural law«, in: The Journal for Transdisciplinary Research in South Africa 2 (2006), pp. 277–288.; Essen, Georg: *Sinnstiftende Unruhe im System des Rechts: Religion im Beziehungsgeflecht von modernem Verfassungsstaat und säkularer Zivilgesellschaft*, Göttingen 2004; Essen, Georg: »Who Observes Religions? Negotiating Faith, Reason and the Ideas of Humanism in an ›Era of Terrorism‹« (under preparation).

the axial age would also enable axial-cultural religions to internally convert certain cognitive dissonances. This is requested from all religions and worldviews by the already rudimentarily given constitution of international law: the premises of modern international law rest, on the one hand, on a disentanglement of religion and politics, and on the other, on the condition that law and ethos can be justified on the grounds of a profane morality.

A third consideration is concerned with consequences for a theory of modernity that Jaspers and Eisenstadt connect with the concept of the axial age. According to Jaspers, the revolution of the worldview of the axial age belongs to the context of discovery of modernity. In this regard the idea of science, the rationalisation of ›lifeworlds‹ and the self-perception of mankind as world history are essential. Beyond this, it is interesting that the genesis of modernity and its execution is for Jaspers the first intellectually and materially completely new incident since the axial age. Furthermore, it is worth mentioning that Jaspers considers the coming up of a new – for us, still far away and invisible – second axial age of the very act of becoming human as possible. He justifies this vision by referring to the completely new constellation brought about after the Second World War, in which scientific, technical and civilising processes come to the fore. Jaspers identifies these processes with the coming up of a world history that comprises all cultures and the whole of mankind. Eisenstadt also does not doubt the correlation between axial cultures and modernity assumed by Jaspers. However, out of fundamental methodological considerations, and in view of the historical material, he expounds the problem of the alleged inevitability with which modernity arose from the potential of axial cultures. Instead, he correlates »the multiplicity of axial cultures« with his concept of »multiple modernities«.[7] In this context he takes the axial-cultural syndrome as the effective formation of ideas, which might more strongly distinguish Max Weber's theses on the particularity of the occidental processes of rationalisation in the context of an intercultural hermeneutics that is determined in an axial way. In the background, there is the assumption of a polycentrism among the economical, cultural und civilising realms. These realms interdigitate with accelerated technical-scientific developments and develop towards a

7 Cf. Eisenstadt, Shmuel N.: »Multiple Modernities«, in: Daedalus 129 (2000), pp 1–29.

genesis of the polycentric globalisation processes that had already begun by the late 18th century. This theory corresponds with the considerations of Christopher A. Bayly, who outlines a period of 134 years as the axial age of the history of mankind in his study »The Birth of the Modern World, 1780-1914: Global Connections and Comparisons«[8].

If we look at the three highly divergent conceptions of Jaspers, Eisenstadt and Bayly, we might conclude that the generations at the turn of the 20th to the 21st century participate in a new axial-cultural syndrome, because the complex processes of globalisation determine our realm of experiences and shape our horizon of expectations. On the one hand, the analyses undertaken by Bayly and Eisenstadt point towards the necessity of understanding the current situation within a historical perspective. It is obviously necessary to inscribe the idea of the axial age into a critical theory of modernity, which likewise includes economical, sociological and cultural questions. What is actually new, which has taken place in the last 10 to 20 years, is the reflection on processes of globalisation that start to connect with general consciousness, which is based on the lifeworld.

The leading categories of the axial-cultural realm of theory are obviously »polycentrism«, »multicausality« and »plurality«, with which the special development of modernity in Europe is again put into perspective and a re-evaluation of the roles of India and China is undertaken.[9] In this context it is interesting that a return to »world history« or »global history« starts to emerge in these hermeneutical processes of decentralisation. This return seems to be a counter movement, which is by no means incidental. A couple of related projects are currently being undertaken. They seek a normative basis for the actual processes of globalisation, which are endowed with meaning as well. Furthermore, they inquire into a possible foundation of an intercultural understanding. The »world ethos« project, initiated by Hans Küng, is probably the most well-known among them. However, our humanism project is also among them. The idea of the axial age is inscribed into these projects as a theoretical and at the same time practice-oriented approach. This serves our purpose of pointing out interculturally rec-

8 Cf. Bayly, Christopher A.: *The Birth of the Modern World, 1780–1914: Global Connections and Comparisons*, Malden u. a. 2007.

9 Dittmer, Jörg: »Jaspers' ›Achsenzeit‹ und das interkulturelle Gespräch« (http://www.chairete.de/Beitrag/TA/jaspers_achsenzeit.pdf).

ognizable »overlapping and reference structures« of religion and culture, which could be universalized without disrespect for one's own cultural difference. This can already be observed in Jaspers, whose theory of the axial age is supposed to offer heuristic, but also normatively leading categories, in order to compose a comprehensive universal or world history that goes beyond the particular occidental history. Jaspers explicitly breaks with the occidental tradition that the Christian date of the incarnation of God as Jesus of Nazareth is understood as the »axis of world history«. He connects the inscription of Christianity into an axial-cultural world history with the demand for a universalistic disentanglement which liberates from the particularity of Christianity. This is the hermeneutical condition for the universalisability of his »axis of world history«, which can cope with the cultural and historical plurality.

A fourth and last consideration tries to put the rule to the test and submits the proposal: what kind of consequences could an axial-cultural orientation have for Christianity? The most important function could be a critical examination of the Christian patterns of interpretation that generate culture. Based on these results, Christianity may present its normatively leading proposals for a meaningful life to a public discourse on the prerequisites and forms of globalized cultures and multicultural societies. By doing so, Christianity refers among other things to the following axial-culturally recognisable leading categories. The Christian belief in the revealed God, whose individuating gaze is directed at each human face, allows for a concrete idea of human nature that becomes a categorical imperative for Christians. This includes respect for the dignity of a human being as an individual that cannot be replaced. Furthermore, it comprises the unconditional recognition of subjective freedom, which only has its actual identity in the cultural forms of communication of community and society. These principles oblige Christianity to take a firm stand concerning the question of universal validity of human rights. Belief in creation opens up a certain understanding of reality, insofar as the idea of a positive release of the world into independence seems to make possible the secularity of a free formation of the world. This consideration is hermeneutically leading for the self-definition of Christianity »within« a culture, insofar as the difference of creation leads to a theological understanding of culture, conceiving it as a possible field of practical action for humans. Furthermore, this is also a way to approach reconciliation with the profanity of (mainly) Western cultures. This insight is of great intercultural importance for at least two reasons: on the one hand, it allows for a qualification of a claim for integration into a system, which is made by a religion having become a cultural sub-area a long time ago. According to this claim, religion would have to be the substantial centre of culture. On the other hand, only the confession of representing normativity within a culture, which is marked by decentralisation, enables a religion to recognise the internal and external plurality of culture and to demonstrate respect for different ways of living. Theological affirmations of decentralisation as well as of pluralisation are both crucial. Only in this way can religions be prevented from foisting their own universalistic claims towards meaning upon the unifying trends in a homogeneous global culture. By turning the cultural plurality of the world into its own immanent problem, Christianity mainly contradicts fundamentalist urges to associate with anti-globalist tendencies of re-particularisation in the »Clash of Cultures«.

BIBLIOGRAPHY

Arnason, Johann P./Eisenstadt, Shmuel N./ Wittrock, Björn (Eds.): *Axial Civilizations and World History*, Leiden 2005.

Assmann, Jan (Ed.): *Die Erfindung des inneren Menschen. Studien zur religiösen Anthropologie*, Gütersloh 1993 (Studien zum Verstehen fremder Religionen, 6).

Bayly, Christopher A.: *The Birth of the Modern World, 1780–1914: Global Connections and Comparisons*, Malden u. a. 2007.

Dittmer, Jörg: »Jaspers' ›Achsenzeit‹ und das interkulturelle Gespräch«. http://www.chairete.de/Beitrag/TA/jaspers_achsenzeit.pdf

Eisenstadt, Shmuel N.: (Ed.): *The Origins and Diversity of Axial Age Civilizations*, Albany 1986.

Eisenstadt, Shmuel N.: »Multiple Modernities«, in: Daedalus 129 (2000), pp 1–29.

Essen, Georg: »Ethical Monotheism and Human Freedom: Theological Convergences with the Pluralism of the Modern Age«, in: Hintersteiner, Norbert (Ed.): *Naming and Thinking God in Europe Today: Theology in Global Dialogue (Currents of Encounter)*, Amsterdam/New York 2007, pp. 265–283.

Essen, Georg: »›... allerlei unlautere Religionsideen‹. Zur aktuellen Bedeutung der Religionsphilosophie Kants«, in: Danz, Christian/ Hermanni, Friedrich (Eds.): *Wahrheitsansprüche der Weltreligionen: Konturen gegenwärtiger Religionstheologie*, Neukirchen-Vluyn 2006, pp. 133–147.

Essen, Georg: »›Nature‹ as a humanistic principle of universal communication. A European historical case study regarding natural law«, in: The Journal for Transdisciplinary Research in South Africa 2 (2006), pp. 277–288.

Essen, Georg: *Sinnstiftende Unruhe im System des Rechts: Religion im Beziehungsgeflecht von modernem Verfassungsstaat und säkularer Zivilgesellschaft*, Göttingen 2004.

Essen, Georg: »Who Observes Religions? Negotiating Faith, Reason and the Ideas of Humanism in an ›Era of Terrorism‹« (under preparation).

Habermas, Jürgen: »Ein Bewußtsein vom dem, was fehlt. Über Glauben und Wissen und den Defaitismus der modernen Vernunft« 10.2.2007. (www.nzz.ch).

Jaspers, Karl: *Vom Ursprung und Ziel der Geschichte*, Munich 1949.

Troeltsch, Ernst: *Die Absolutheit des Christentums und die Religionsgeschichte (1902/1912)*. Mit den Thesen von 1901 und den handschriftlichen Zusätzen, ed. Trutz. Rendtorff in coop. with Stefan Pautler, Berlin u. a. 1998.

II.4 How Unique is East Asian Modernity?

VOLKER H. SCHMIDT

The paper examines Shmuel Eisenstadt's claim that Japan constitutes a unique modernity, one that differs fundamentally from Western modernity. Since this claim, like the multiple modernities approach founded by Eisenstadt, is directed against the convergence thesis of classical modernization theory, that thesis' meaning is first briefly reconstructed. Moreover, to stand Eisenstadt's case on a broader basis, the four tiger states of South Korea, Taiwan, Hong Kong and Singapore are added to the sample, thus extending Japanese modernity to a larger East Asian modernity. These five countries are then compared with the five largest Western countries along several dimensions that seem to be particularly salient for probing modernization theory. Surprisingly, the comparison fully confirms the theory. The paper then moves on to assess Eisenstadt's claim in light of his own conceptualization of modernity. This conceptualization renders his proposal more plausible, but at considerable cost. The conclusion is devoted to asking how Eisenstadt's substantive concerns could be met without reading too much into his empirical findings.

»The great wealth-producing nations of western Europe, North America and much of East Asia share common features that set them apart from the world of 200 years ago, and also from today's developing nations«.[1]

1 Myers, Ramon H.: »Economic Life in Mainland China and Taiwan and the Rise of a Productive Market Economy«, in: Ash, Robert/Greene, J. Megan

1.

A protracted debate in the social sciences concerns the similarity or distinctness of modern societies. The position emphasizing similarities is often inspired by some version of modernization theory, a macro-sociological approach developed in the 1950s and 60s for studying global social change, in particular the prerequisites and consequences of the spread of modernity. Scholars leaning to the opposite view come from otherwise highly diverse intellectual traditions but are united in their aversion to that theory. One of its most outspoken critics is Shmuel Eisenstadt, a former champion of modernization theory, who devised the

»multiple modernities« paradigm in an effort to pluralize the concept of modernity and to shed light on differences between modern societies. The gist of this paradigm is expressly directed against modernization theory, especially against that theory's convergence claim accentuating modern societies' commonalities. This claim, says Eisenstadt, must be rejected because »the actual developments in modernizing societies have refuted the homogenizing […] assumptions of [the] Western program of modernity«

by giving rise to multiple patterns of societal organization that are doubtless modern, yet clearly different from Western modernity[2], the reference model for most studies investigating modernization processes in non-Western locations.

Given that Japan was the first non-Western country to become fully modern, Eisenstadt has singled it out as the »most important test case« for the convergence claim. He acknowledges that the reasons behind Japan's modernization may have been similar to those of its Western forerunners, yet maintains that the *patterns* of modernity that emerged from the process are not. Modern Japan, he argues, exhibits peculiarities that are not just local variations of the Western model, but

---

(Eds.): *Taiwan in the 21st Century: Aspects and Limitations of a Developmental Model*, London 2007, pp. 10.

2 Eisenstadt, Shmuel N.: »Multiple Modernities«, in: Daedalus 129 (2000), p. 1.

distinguish it *fundamentally* from this model.[3] Hence the notion of a unique Japanese modernity.

The aim of the present paper is to scrutinize this proposition.[4] But rather than confining myself to Japan, following Tu[5] I have decided to add the four so-called tiger states of South Korea, Taiwan, Hong Kong and Singapore to the sample, which not only equal Japan in its modernization success, but also share a common cultural heritage with it, namely Confucianism.[6] Since multiple modernities is Eisenstadt's attempt at a cultural turn, an effort to argue that enduring cultural traditions have a profound effect on modern societies that prevent their convergence, he would probably find this treatment of Japanese modernity as part of a larger *East Asian* modernity agreeable, not least because it stands the comparison with Western modernity on a broader basis, thus potentially strengthening his case.[7]

---

3 Eisenstadt, Shmuel N.: *Die Vielfalt der Moderne*, Weilerswist 2000, pp. 110f.

4 Modernization theory has been criticized from many perspectives and for multiple reasons. Here, I focus exclusively on multiple modernists' criticism of the theory's convergence claim. Given this limited purpose, I cannot address other criticisms levelled at the paradigm.

5 Tu, Weiming: »Implications of the Rise of ›Confucian‹ East Asia«, in: Daedalus 129 (2000), pp. 195–218.

6 Tu (»Implications of the Rise of ›Confucian‹ East Asia«, p. 218) treats these five countries as the currently most advanced exemplars of East Asian modernity, which he characterizes as »particularly intriguing« for debates revolving around the subject of this paper.

7 Given that seven out of 10 East Asians live in China, one might wonder why China was not also included in the sample. The reason is that the main purpose of this paper is to scrutinize the plausibility of Eisenstadt's criticism of modernization theory's convergence claim, and this claim refers to societal entities of roughly similar levels of socio-economic development. China's current level of development is in many ways similar to that of Albania. But as little as the possible finding of »fundamental« differences between, say, Albania and Sweden would qualify to substantiate or refute claims about the unity or diversity of *European* modernity, it would make as litte sense to liken Japan and the four tigers to China in terms of their modernness. Hence China's exclusion.

Before proceeding with the empirical analysis, however, the pertinent premises of modernization theory must be briefly reiterated. Their reconstruction will supply us with the criteria by which we are to carry out the comparison (section 2). As it turns out, Eisenstadt's case appears rather weak when judged by these criteria, which generate little evidence for the existence of a uniquely Japanese or, for that matter, East Asian modernity (section 3).[8] Judging the proposal in light of his own conception of modernity, the case gains in plausibility, but only at the cost of trivializing the concept of modernity and other problems associated with Eisenstadt's theory (section 4). The paper closes with a few remarks on how the two approaches could cross-fertilize each other if treated as complementary rather than as opposing paradigms (section 5).

2.

As indicated above, the main point of contention between modernization theory and multiple modernists is the former's claim that modernization is a homogenizing process resulting in the convergence of the societies undergoing it: »a process of social change whereby less developed societies acquire characteristics common to more developed societies«, as Daniel Lerner,[9] one of the theory's leading advocates, put it. But what does modernization theory actually mean by »convergence«? To answer this question, it is important to keep in mind that

8 One way of reading that part of the paper is to treat it as a reminder of what it takes to criticize a theory properly. Being uncomfortable with some of its premises does not suffice. To come up with a sound criticism, we first have to try to understand these premises' intended meaning(s). Then we can subject them to conceptual or empirical criticism if we have reason to believe there is something wrong with them. But we cannot confront a theory with evidence that, given its premises, has no (or at best very little) bearing on it. As will become clear below, I try to argue that multiple modernists (Eisenstadt in particular) do precisely that. Hence their failure to come up with a potent challenge to modernization theory.

9 Lerner, Daniel: »Modernization«, in: Sills, David L./Merton, Robert K. (Eds.): *International Encyclopedia of the Social Sciences*, New York 1968, p. 386.

modernization theory is conceptually anchored in the work of Talcott Parsons. As is well known, Parsons' theory of modernity is embedded in a more encompassing theory of action systems.[10] Society, in Parsons' conceptualization, is a subsystem of the social system, which in turn is one of four subsystems of the general action system, the other three being the cultural system, the personality system, and the behavioral organism.

Modernization theory concerns itself only with social, cultural and personality systems. It argues that upon modernization the *personality system* becomes increasingly achievement oriented, aware of its own individuality, and empathetic; that modernization leads to rationalization, value generalization and the diffusion of secular norms in the *cultural system*, and that functional differentiation is the dominant trend in, as well as the foremost structural characteristic of, modern *society*, the social system that is of special interest to sociological theory.[11]

Much like other macro-sociological approaches, modernization theory places particular emphasis on developments in the economic and political subsystems of society,[12] but also on other important subsystems such as the educational system, the scientific system, the legal system and the system of mass media are also examined. In the *economy*, the most salient change from the viewpoint of modernization theory is the emergence of self-sustained growth; in *politics*, it is growing participation by the population; in *education*, the spread of mass schooling; in *science*, the establishment of the research university

10 For a brief introduction, see Turner, Jonathan H.: *The Structure of Sociological Theory*, 7th edition, Belmont, CA 2003, ch. 3.

11 Lerner, Daniel: *The Passing of Traditional Society: Modernizing the Middle East*, Glencoe 1958; Lerner: »Modernization«; Parsons, Talcott: »Evolutionary Universals in Society«, in: American Sociological Review 29 (1964), pp. 339–357; Parsons, Talcott: *The Evolution of Society*, ed. with an introduction by Jackson Toby, Englewood Cliffs 1977.

12 Lerner (»Modernization«, p. 388), for instance, views economic development as the »prime mover« of modernization, and scholars employing a broadly modernization theoretical frame of analysis have repeatedly emphasized the importance of political initiative for successful »late« modernization (see, e.g., Bendix, Reinhard: »Preconditions of Development: A Comparison of Japan and Germany«, in: Dore, Ronald (Ed.): *Aspects of Social Change in Modern Japan*, Princeton 1970, pp. 27–68.)

and other institutions engaged in systematic knowledge production; in *law*, the enunciation of universalistic, highly abstract norms and their application by professionally trained, independent judges; in the *media*, the rapid diffusion of information to mass audiences and, thus, the creation of public opinion.

The concept of functional differentiation, while highlighting a key, perhaps *the* key difference to the structure of pre-modern society whose mode of societal organization is dominated by the stratification system, is institutionally underdetermined and hence compatible with a variety of institutional forms. The main source of inspiration guiding modernization theory's understanding of the institutional make-up of modern society is, once again, Parsons' work, this time his theory of evolutionary universals. In an influential article outlining that theory, Parsons associates the progression of stages of societal evolution with critical breakthroughs in social organization that give more advanced societies an edge over less advanced ones in terms of their capacity to adapt to environmental conditions. In the case of modernity, Parsons identifies four such universals that he believes were crucial both for its breakthrough and ultimate consolidation: *money and market systems* in the economy, *democracy* in the political realm, the *rule of law* and equality before the law in the legal system, and *bureaucratic organization* of public and private institutions.[13]

This characterization obviously bears much resemblance to »the« Western model of modernity, to which it does indeed owe a lot. Note, however, that it does not reflect a consensual position shared by all modernization theorists. Samuel Huntington,[14] for instance, in his book *Political Order in Changing Societies*, offers a less demanding conceptualization of at least *political* modernity by arguing that the most important political distinction in the modern age is not that between democracies and dictatorships but that between governments which

13 Parsons: »Evolutionary Universals in Society«, p. 357. On the last page of his article, Parsons identifies the institutionalization of research and development (»scientific investigation and technological application of science«) as what he might well have called a fifth evolutionary universal, arguing that this structural complex has come to assume the same significance as the other four in the 20th century.

14 Huntington, Samuel P.: *Political Order in Changing Societies*, New Haven 1968.

really govern the country under their formal jurisdiction and those that do not. A modern political order, on his conceptualization, is a system of rationalized authority wherein office holders are expected to serve the public (rather than primarily their own) interest and have the capacity to execute chosen policies based on control of a well-functioning state apparatus. This leaves room for political alternatives beyond (what is now widely viewed as) the Western model,[15] for instance for authoritarian regimes that, if they manage to garner a modicum of support, can serve as functional equivalents – during the early stages of transition to modernity, even as promising alternatives – to democratic systems in Huntington's view.

Parsons too allowed for more than one route to modernity and for differential institutionalization of its »program«, as can be seen from his treatment of the Soviet Union as a near equal to the United States with respect to the depth and levels of modernization it had achieved by the second half of the 20th century.[16] He was, however, skeptical as to the long-term stability of Soviet-style political systems because of their inbuilt legitimacy deficits.[17] History seems to have proven him right on this point.

But be this as it may, Parsons explicitly stated his belief that there could be »[great] variations within the modern type of society«[18] and

---

15 In the 1950s and 60s, when modernization theory was most influential, few consolidated democracies existed even in (Western) Europe. The Iberian peninsula was governed by dictatorial regimes; Greece, after a long period of political instability, experienced a military coup in 1967; Italy continued to be divided into a »civic« north and a south dominated by hierarchical patron-client relations (on the Italian case, see Putnam, Robert D.: *Making Democracy Work: Civic Traditions in Modern Italy*, Princeton 1993), and West Germany, upon which democracy had in effect been imposed by the victors of the Second World War, was still struggling with a highly authoritarian legacy. The case for identifying »the« Western model with political democracy would therefore have been much weaker then than it may appear today.

16 Parsons: »The Evolution of Society«, pp. 216ff.

17 Parsons: »Evolutionary Universals in Society«, p. 126.

18 Parsons: »The Evolution of Society«, p. 228. It would therefore be wrong to equate »convergence«, as understood by modernization theory, with »identity«. No modernization theorist believed any two countries would

that many more such variations would probably emerge as a result of the global trend »toward completion« of this type of society, a development which he predicted would likely continue well into the 21st century.[19]

The notion of convergence must be understood against the backdrop of this expectation. It applies first and foremost to the *basic structure* of society, the premise being that pre-modern and modern societies differ much more from each other than do the many varieties of (the one type of) modern society that emerge as a result of successful modernization,[20] a process that Parsons viewed as far from complete. Convergence, thus understood, occurs when modernizing countries meet two main conditions. First, they must move toward establishing a set of key institutions that the theory regards as essential to modernity,[21] and second, they must succeed in making these institutions perform in line with their stated purposes, rather than being mere »façades«[22] of modernity.[23]

---

ever be exactly alike. The same is of course true of the literature suggesting the contemporary social world is best conceived of as *one* globally encompassing world society.

19 Parsons: »The Evolution of Society«, p. 241.

20 Parsons was not the only modernization theorist holding such views. See, for instance, Lerner: The Passing of Traditional Society, ch. III, and Smelser, Neil J.: »Toward a Theory of Modernization«, in: Smelser, Neil J.: *Essays in Sociological Explanation*, Englewood Cliffs 1968, pp 125–146.

21 Some of the most important of these institutions are: a growth-producing, preferably capitalist economy; a system of »good«, preferably democratic political governance; the rule of law and a legal system guaranteeing a core set of human rights; bureaucratic administrations staffed with technically competent personnel and insulated from »special« interests; a collectively run or regulated welfare system covering the entire population and securing its basic needs; mass (public) education; research and development in large science organizations; etc.

22 Meyer, John W./Boli, John/Thomas, George M./Ramirez, Francisco O.: »World Society and the Nation State«, in: American Journal of Sociology 103 (1997), pp. 144–182.

23 This qualification is necessary in view of the findings of sociological neo-institutionalism. As John Meyer and his colleagues have shown in many

Modernization theorists are aware that many obstacles have to be overcome to meet these conditions, and that the processes through which this may occur are risky, complex, painful (often traumatic and violent), and contested, with the outcomes always uncertain. They know there is no guarantee of success, but where modernization *does* succeed, they expect society to enhance its performance in virtually all spheres: in the economy, in politics, in the law, in education, in the sciences, in medicine, etc.

These expectations provide us with the criteria by which we are to determine the correctness or falsity of modernization theory's convergence claim. To refute this claim using Japanese or East Asian modernity as a test case we have to show that (1) the basic structure of society in East Asia and/or (2) the performance of its main subsystems differ profoundly from their equivalents in the West. If no evidence of such divergence can be found, then modernization theory must be deemed confirmed.

3.

Having established the requisite criteria, I now proceed with the comparison. The USA, Germany, the United Kingdom, France and Italy were chosen as representatives of Western modernity on the grounds of their being the largest Western countries. The data come from a number of sources and studies that cover both country groups or (much of) the entire globe. The Human Development Index (HDI) is a good starting point. It is a summary measure used by the United Nations to rank all member states for which sufficient information is

---

studies (Meyer/Boli/Thomas/Ramirez: »World Society and the Nation State« provides the best summary), the contemporary world exhibits a striking degree of institutional isomorphism. They also note, however, that formal institutional structures are often »decoupled« from actual institutional practice, meaning that there is a substantial mismatch between the seeming adoption of a particular model and its factual implementation and performance, an observation that gives rise to various diagnoses of institutional failure. For modernization theory, a merely symbolic adherence to shared models does not suffice to carry the notion of convergence; similarity, in this approach, means similar results too.

available by level of human development, understood as the combined effect of life expectancy, educational attainment and gross domestic product (GDP) adjusted by purchasing power parity (PPP). The index is constantly updated and published in regular Human Development Reports. The latest index (UNDP 2007) is based on data for 2005.

Since Taiwan is not a member of the United Nations, it is not included in the HDI. Therefore, the data for Taiwan (referring to 2006) draw upon the CIA World Factbook, which is only available in electronic form. Table 1 below presents the figures. Countries are listed by »group membership« and population size.

Table 1: Human Development Index (HDI)

Country	HDI Rank	GDP per capita (PPP US$)	Life Expec-tancy at birth (years)	Adult literacy rate (% age 15 and above)	Change of HDI-Index 1980-2005 (%)**	Total po pulation (millions)*
Japan	10	33,632	82.7	99.0	8	127,08
South Korea	26	24,801	79.2	99.0	23	48,51
Taiwan		31,100*	77.9*	96.1*		22,97
Hong Kong	24	42,306	82.2	94.6	17	7,05
Singapore	23	49,704	80.2	94.4	20	4,66
USA	13	45,592	79.1	99.0	7	307,21
Germany	22	34,401	80.2	99.0	8	82,33
France	8	33,674	81.0	99.0	9	62,15
UK	21	35,130	79.3	99.0	10	61,11
Italy	18	30,353	81.1	98.9	10	58,13

Sources: United Nations Development Programme: *Human Development Report* 2009

*CIA World Factbook 2009

**United Nations Development Programme: *Human Development*

All nine United Nations member countries fall into the »high human development« category. Since Taiwan's figures are between those of Singapore and South Korea on all pertinent indicators, it is safe to conjecture that the country would be placed in their immediate neighborhood if it were included in the index. A closer look at the index itself reveals that no non-Western country except Israel, which is often treated as a part of the West, is ahead of any East Asian country from the sample. The best performer outside either region is oil-rich Brunei Darussalam (rank no. 30), with Argentina and Chile (nos. 38 and 40, respectively) the highest ranked industrialized countries.

The HDI confirms Eisenstadt's point about Japan being the best test case for the convergence claim, and it also confirms my point that this case can be sensibly extended to the four tigers. But while certainly suggestive, it is too narrow a measure for settling the dispute about the similarity or diversity of Western and Japanese/East Asian *modernity*, which requires a closer look at society's main subsystems. As for their institutional design, it is well known that all ten countries resemble each other in a formal sense. Thus, politically they are all sovereign nation-states (or semi-sovereign quasi states)[24] with legal bureaucratic governments; economically, they all practice variants of what Weber calls »modern capitalism«; and all of them have established differentiated legal, educational, scientific, medical systems – precisely as modernization theory predicts. That neither Hong Kong nor Singapore are Western-style liberal democracies has no bearing on this finding; for one thing, because their combined populations represent just 5 per cent of our East Asian sample, for another, because democracy is not a prerequisite of political modernity in theoretical thought on modernization anyway.

So in terms of the basic structure of societal organization there is clearly convergence. However, since variants of the above institutions have been established almost everywhere, homologies of this sort need not be very instructive. It may be true that the whole world follows more or less the same models of development, but it is also true that huge gaps often exist between talk and action, between the official

---

24 As in the case of Hong Kong, which is actually a »special administrative region« within the Peoples' Republic of China (PRC), but is nonetheless treated as a separate unit in much of the social science literature due to its peculiar history, relative autonomy and level of development. Needless to say, the PRC also treats Taiwan as a (renegade) province, but realistically speaking it makes more sense to consider Taiwan as a separate unit because it is a nation-state in all but its recognized status.

language in which society describes itself and the actual performance of its institutions. For example, that a political organization calls itself a government need not mean that it really governs the territorial space in question, that it possesses a monopoly over the means of violence, that it collects taxes, that it channels them into the state's budget, that it provides collective goods to the people, etc., as the literature on weak and »failed states«[25] plainly demonstrates. Analogous observations have been made about other subsystems of society, such as the legal system[26], the educational system[27], or the scientific system.[28]

Modernization theory expects institutional performance to co-vary with levels of socio-economic development. Since the countries comprising our sample are all highly developed, they should resemble each other in this respect too. The HDI suggests that they do to some extent, but provides only limited information on select indicators. For instance, it says nothing about the quality of political systems, legal systems, educational systems, or scientific systems, all of which matter to our reference problem.

Luckily, a number of other indexes exist that can be drawn upon to complement the HDI. Two such indexes were chosen for making comparisons between political systems. They are the freedom index of Freedom House, an influential American think tank devoted to the promotion of freedom and democracy, and the worldwide governance indicators of Daniel Kaufmann and his co-authors from the World Bank, which rest on a much wider data basis than the Freedom House index. The rationale for choosing these two indexes is that both measure features that are widely viewed as essential for determining the quality of modern political systems, while differing in their respective biases.

---

25 See, e.g., Rotberg, Robert I.: »Failed States, Collapsed States, Weak States: Causes and Indicators«, in: Rotberg, Robert I. (Ed.): *State Failure and State Weakness in a Time of Terror*, Washington, D.C. 2003, pp. 1–25.

26 Transparency International: *Global Corruption Report 2007: Corruption in Judicial Systems*, Cambridge 2007.

27 Drèze, Jean/Sen, Amartya: *India: Development and Participation*, 2nd edition Delhi 2002; de Ferranti, David et al.: *Inequality in Latin America and the Caribbean: Breaking with History?* Washington, D.C. 2004.

28 Drori, Gili S./Meyer, John W./Ramirez, Francisco O./Schofer, Evan: *Science in the Modern World Polity: Institutionalization and Globalization*, Stanford 2003.

Freedom House ranks polities (currently 193 countries and 15 related and disputed territories) according to the degree of freedom (understood as political rights and civil liberties) they provide, the assumption being that liberal democracies are best suited to fostering freedom. Each polity is rated on a seven-point scale for both criteria, with 1 representing the most free and 7 the least free, and then classified according to three broad categories: free (F), partly free (PF) and not free (NF). To fine-tune the measurement, the concepts of political rights and civil liberties are disaggregated into three and four sub-categories, respectively,[29] with the sum-total in all sub-categories determining a polity's overall ranking. Ratings in the single sub-categories are indicated using a sixteen point-scale, with 16 representing the best and 1 the worst performance. All ratings are based on annually repeated surveys and aim to reflect real-world freedoms and rights enjoyed by the populations in question.[30] Table 2 presents the results for the overall freedom ratings plus those for one of the sub-categories, namely »rule of law«. The ratings for rule of law are included in the table, firstly, because no studies exist that compare the performance of legal systems separately on a global scale, and secondly, because the rule of law is also one of the indicators used by Kaufmann et al.[31] to assess the quality of governance, thus permitting a direct comparison between the two indexes.

---

29 They are »electoral process«, »political pluralism and participation«, and »functioning of government« for political rights, and »freedom of expression and belief«, »associational and organizational rights«, »rule of law«, and »personal autonomy and individual rights« for civil liberties.

30 Critics have raised concern though that Freedom House might not always provide an accurate picture of people's real freedoms because it measures »only the extent to which civil and political liberties are institutionalized, which does not necessarily reflect the extent to which liberties are actually respected by political elites« (Inglehart, Ronald/Welzel, Christian: *Modernization, Cultural Change, and Democracy: The Human Development Sequence*, Cambridge 2005, p. 153). Likewise, Freedom House does not sufficiently distinguish between formal and effective democracy (Inglehart/Welzel: »Modernization«, p. 158).

31 Kaufmann, Daniel/Kray, Aart/Mastruzzi, Massimo: *Governance Matters VII: Aggregate and Individual Governance Indicators 1996–2006, World*

Kaufmann et al.[32] distinguish six indicators to measure the governance performance of 212 polities: voice and accountability; political stability and absence of violence; government effectiveness; regulatory quality; rule of law; and control of corruption.[33] Ratings are based on perceptions of a large and fairly diverse set of stakeholders surveyed by numerous organizations, including Freedom House, whose data are factored into the aggregated country scores. Scores range from -2.50 to 2.50, with higher scores corresponding to better performance. Annual repetitions of the procedure aim to capture changes over time, with gradual extensions of the data basis made to improve the ratings' reliability. Table 2 presents the latest scores for four of the six indicators. Rule of law focuses on the extent to which legal rules are publicly observed, in particular the quality of contract enforcement, property rights, the police and the courts. Voice and accountability measures attributes similar to those used by Freedom House to determine degrees of freedom and democracy. Government effectiveness refers to the quality of public goods and the civil service, independence of the administration from political pressure, the quality of policy formulation and implementation, and the credibility of governments' commitment to formally adopted policies. And corruption control stands for the bureaucratic quality of government: the degree to which public offices are filled on the basis of technical skills (rather than social capital) and used to serve the public (rather than for private gain, as in the case of capture of the state by powerful elite groups).

What does table 2 show? Firstly, it shows that the rankings assigned to most countries are relatively close to each other in most respects. Secondly, Freedom House and Kaufmann et al. rate the performance of Singapore's rule of law on the one hand, and Italy's on the other, quite differently. Thirdly, both indexes concur that Singapore and Hong Kong are no liberal democracies, although Hong Kong's voice and accountability scores are only slightly lower than those of South Korea and Taiwan, the two »youngest« democracies in

---

Bank Policy Research Working Paper 4280, June 2008, Washington, D.C. 2008.

32 Kaufmann/ Kray/ Mastruzzi: »Governance Matters VII«.

33 This index could be charged with being slightly economistic, as the effects of institutions on economic performance seem to weigh heaviest in their overall judgment.

Table 2: Political and legal systems: democracy, rule of law, governance, corruption

Country	Freedom House			Kaufmann et al.			
	Freedom/ Democracy		Rule of Law (1-16 points)	Rule of Law (score range: -2.50 - 2.50)	Voice/ Accountability (range: -2.50 - 2.50)	Government Effectiveness (range: -2.50 - 2.50)	Corruption Control (range: -2.50 - 2.50)
	(F/PF/NF)	1-7 points					
Japan	F	1.5	15	1.39	0.93	1.32	1.20
South Korea	F	1.5	13	0.82	0.66	1.26	0.36
Taiwan	F	1.5	15	0.67	0.74	1.05	0.41
Hong Kong	PF	3.5	15	1.40	0.59	1.80	1.61
Singapore	PF	4.5	7	1.79	-0,43	2.41	2.20
USA	F	1.0	14	1.59	1.09	1.62	1.44
Germany	F	1.0	15	1.78	1.40	1.68	1.80
France	F	1.0	15	1.32	1.27	1.30	1.32
UK	F	1.0	14	1.75	1.38	1.77	1.89
Italy	F	1.5	12	0.43	1.12	0.33	0.45

Sources: Freedom House*: Freedom in the World* 2009; Daniel Kaufmann/Aart Kray/Massimo Mastruzzi: *Governance Matters VII, World Bank Policy Research Working Paper 4554*, 2008.

the region. At the same time, Singapore outperforms all other countries in terms of governmental effectiveness and corruption control, while Italy is a relative underperformer in most dimensions of governance except the extent to which citizens are free to select the legislature, to express their views and ideas, and to form political interest groups – a dimension in which Western countries are generally, if mostly moderately, ahead of their East Asian counterparts. But as telling as the variation in some dimensions of *political modernity* may be, it is too small to support the notion of »fundamental« differences between East and West,[34] especially between Japan (Eisenstadt's test case) and the West.

Findings on *economic modernity* corroborate this assessment. Table 3 compares the two regions' economic performance, based on United Nations/World Factbook GDP per capita data and the annual growth rates for nine out of the ten countries over a 30-year period, as well as the global competitiveness index developed by the World Economic Forum. That index gauges the competitiveness of 134 national economies around the world. Because of space restrictions, only three of the altogether 12 »pillars of competiveness« examined by the forum are included in the table, namely institutions, infrastructure and innovation (all of which are considered highly important in the pertinent

34 Too small, that is, in terms of this paper's reference problem: the refutation (or confirmation) of modernization theory's convergence claim. Critics of this assessment might object in two ways. (1) They could say my reconstruction of that claim is problematic (faulty, not in line with modernization theory's »true« spirit, etc.), in which case criteria other than the ones listed at the end of section II would be needed to »test« the claim, or (2) they could say convergence thus understood is ill-conceived, in which case a different conceptualization of the term would be needed. Note, however, that criticism of the second type would miss the paper's point, namely to probe Eisenstadt's criticism of modernization theory, for which we have to take *that* theory's conceptualization as our point of departure, regardless of what we make of it. And in terms of that theory's premises, some variation in the way the »executive leaders« of the state administration, as Weber (Weber, Max: *Economy and Society*, ed. by Guenther Roth and Claus Wittich, Berkeley 1978, p. 985) called the ruling elites of a modern polity, are selected is indeed a relatively minor affair – at least when compared with the conditions prevailing in a patrimonial state, to which both modernization theory and Weber contrast it.

literature),[35] together with the overall ratings of the economies in question.

Table 3: Economic systems

Country	UNDP		World Economic Forum		
	GDP per capita PPP US$	GDP per capita annual growth rate (% 1990-2007)	Global Competitiveness (Rank)	Institutions (Rank)	Innovation (Rank)
Japan	33,632	1.0	8	28	13
South Korea	24,801	4.5	19	53	17
Taiwan	31,100*	n.a.	12	37	26
Hong Kong	42,306	2.4	11	11	2
Singapore	49,704	3.8	3	1	4
USA	45,592	2.0	2	34	8
Germany	34,401	1.4	7	16	1
France	33,674	1.6	16	26	3
UK	35,130	2.4	13	21	20
Italy	30,353	1.2	48	97	59

Sources: United Nations Development Programme: *Human Development Report 2009*; World Economic Forum: *Global Competitiveness Report 2009-2010*
*CIA World Factbook 2009

As the table shows, all ten countries are amongst the globally leading economies, with the partial exception of Italy, which, as in the political field, falls behind in several dimensions, especially in those indicative of future prospects. Other than that one finds more commonalities than differences or markers of East Asian exceptionalism. The higher growth rates exhibited by the less mature »tiger« economies are in ac-

35 The other nine pillars are: macroeconomic stability, health and primary education, higher education and training, goods market efficiency, labor market efficiency, financial market sophistication, technological readiness, market size, and business sophistication.

cordance with economic growth theory, which (can be viewed as an economic »offshoot« of modernization theory and) claims that late developers can grow faster until they catch up with earlier developers[36] if they manage to create the conditions for sustained growth, as East Asia doubtless has. Other than the West, East Asia is in fact the only world region whose economy has grown consistently during the past half century.[37]

Educational modernity is a field in which East Asia seems to be at the forefront of global developments. Table 3 presents select findings from various studies analyzing the performance of educational and scientific institutions around the word, as well as expenditures on research and development (R&D), the number of scientists employed per million people, and the number of patents granted per million residents. The PISA study of 2006[38] ranks 57 countries according to the knowledge and skills of 15-year-old secondary science students; the TIMMS student achievement studies[39] present results for fourth and eighth grade students from over 40 countries in mathematics, science and reading. Neither study includes all countries from our sample, but comparing the results of both across educational fields and age groups, East Asian countries clearly emerge as top of the global league. The Western countries of our sample mostly come in a good second, although several East European countries such as Russia, Kazakhstan, Latvia and Hungary outperform them in some dimensions. Still, globally speaking, the differences between East Asian and Western educational institutions are negligible; far more significant differences are discernible between the two groups as a whole and the rest of the world: virtually all of Africa, Latin America, South Asia, and the Middle East.

---

36 See, e.g., Abramovitz, Moses: »Catching Up, Forging Ahead, and Falling Behind«, in: Journal of Economic History 46 (1986), pp. 386–405.

37 Maddison, Angus: *The World Economy: A Millennial Perspective*, Paris 2001.

38 OECD: *PISA 2006: Science Competencies for Tomorrow's World*, Paris 2007.

39 Martin, Michael O./Mullis, Ina V.S./Foy, Pierre: *TIMMS 2007 International Science Report*, Boston 2008; Martin, Michael O./Mullis, Ina V.S./Foy, Pierre: *TIMMS 2007 International Mathematics Report*, Boston 2008.

Table 4: Education, science, research and development

Country	OECD	Martin et al.	Jiao Tong University	UNDP		
	Science competence, secondary students (Rank)	Math achievements, fourth grade students (Rank)	Universities ranked among World Top 500 (Number)	R&D expenditures (as % of GDP)	Researchers in R&D (per million people)	Patents granted to residents (per million people)
Japan	6	4	31	3.1	5,287	285**
South Korea	11	n.a.	9	2.6	3,187	87**
Taiwan	4	3	7	2.5*	–	301**
Hong Kong	2	1	5	0.6	1,564	93**
Singapore	n.a.	2	2	2.3	4,999	99**
USA	29	11	152	2.7	4,605	335**
Germany	13	12	40	2.5	3,261	158
France	25	n.a.	23	2.2	3,213	155
UK	14	7***	40	1.9	2,706	62
Italy	36	16	21	1.1	1,213	71

Sources: OECD: PISA 2007; Martin et al.: *TIMMS International Mathematics Report 2007*, 2008; Jiao Tong University: *Academic Ranking of World Universities 2009*; UNDP: *Human Development Report 2007/2008*; *Bertelsmann Transformation Index 2006 **Indermit Gill and Homi Kharas, *An East Asian Renaissance, World Bank 2007*; ***Data refer to England

The same picture emerges in tertiary education, a field in which the West is still ahead of the East – both in terms of the total number of universities represented amongst the global top 500 and when adjusting numbers of well-performing universities by population size. However, East Asian universities are rapidly catching up with their Western role models, and East Asia is now the only non-Western region boasting a sizeable group of world class universities. This trend is likely to continue since much of East Asia has only just begun to build up its university sector and is massively investing in it. Expenditures in R&D show the same trend, with the two »deviant« cases (Italy and Hong Kong) signaling greater intra- than inter-regional divergence. The same holds for numbers of researchers and patents. And even though it is true that East Asia displays a certain bias toward the hard sciences while placing less emphasis on arts and social science disciplines than do Western universities and research organizations, *scientific modernity* in both regions too has clearly moved in common directions during the past few decades.[40]

Adding qualitative analyses to the quantitative performance indicators presented above, as well as studies covering further institutional sectors of society, such as health care[41] or social welfare,[42] yields the same picture. There are differences – within the West, within East Asia, and between the two regions – but none of them are *truly substantial.*

That means the convergence claim is also confirmed on our second criterion, the performance of society's subsystems. No evidence of Japanese or East Asian »uniqueness« can be detected in the central features of societal modernity as understood by modernization theo-

---

40 More recently, East Asia has also begun to expand »the socially relevant sciences«, thus relatively decreasing the focus on engineering and the natural sciences (Drori/Meyer/Ramirez/Schofer: »Science in the Modern World Polity«, p. 247).

41 WHO: *World Health Report 2000: Health Systems: Improving Performance*, Geneva 2000.

42 Schmidt, Volker H.: »Convergence with a Twist: East Asian Welfare Capitalism in Comparative Perspective«, in: Fee, Lian Kwen/Kiong, Tong Chee (Eds.): *Social Policy in Post-Industrial Singapore*, Leiden 2008, pp. 309–331.

ry.[43] Adding further aspects of development – levels of urbanization,[44] GDP by sector of the economy,[45] composition of the labor force by occupation and sex,[46] demographic change and fertility,[47] the status and role of women in society,[48] marriage, divorce rates and lifestyles,[49] everyday values[50] – once again reveals more commonalities than differences and, given the lesser progression of developmental time in East Asia, even more importantly, remarkably similar *trends*.

Common trends of social change and development are also visible in other world regions[51]. However, once we extend the scope of our analysis to the entire globe, we also find something else, namely (1)

---

43 Needless to say, the observation also holds the other way around, i.e. with regards to »Western« or »European« modernity if we look at it from the vantage point of East Asian modernity.

44 UNDP: *Human Development Report 2007/2008*, New York 2007.

45 Gill, Indermit/Kharas, Homi: *An East Asian Renaissance: Ideas For Economic Growth*, Washington, D.C. 2007.

46 CIA: The World Factbook 2007 (https://www.cia.gov/library/publications/the-world-factbook/ [accessed January 2007]).

47 Jones, Gavin W./Straughan, Paulin Tay/Chan,Angelieque (Eds.): *Ultra-Low Fertility in Pacific Asia: Trends, Causes and Policy Issues*, London 2008.

48 Peng, Ito: »Gender, Demography, and Welfare State Restructuring in Japan«, in: Marshall, Katherine/Butzbach, Oliver (Eds.): *New Social Policy Agendas for Europe and Asia. Challenges, Experience, and Lessons*, Washington, D.C. 2003, pp. 215–234; Bulbeck, Chilla: »›The Mighty Pillar of the Family‹: Young People's Vocabularies on Household Gender Arrangements in the Asia-Pacific Region«, in: Gender, Work and Organization 12 (2005), pp. 14–31.

49 Jones, Gavin W.: »The ›Flight from Marriage‹ in South-East and East Asia«, in: Journal of Comparative Family Studies 36 (2005), pp. 93–119; Quah, Stella R.: *Families in Asia: Home and Kin*, 2nd edition, London 2008.

50 Inglehart/Welzel: »Modernization, Cultural Change, and Democracy«.

51 See, e.g., Hobsbawm, Eric: *The Age of Extremes. A History of the World, 1914–1991*, New York 1994; Easterlin, Richard A: »The Worldwide Standard of Living Since 1800«, in: Journal of Economic Perspectives 14 (2000), pp. 7–26; UNDP: *Human Development Report 2010*, New York 2010, ch. 2.

that the countries comprising our sample share features that set them more apart from the rest of the world than from each other, and (2) that performance differences seem to follow a coherent pattern across societal subsystems, such that countries showing weak performance in one dimension typically do so in other dimensions as well and vice versa.[52] There are, to be sure, exceptions. Not all countries confirm the expectations derived from level of socio-economic development in all fields, but when considering the world as a whole, modernization clearly appears as a »systemic« process, with »changes in one factor [...] related to and affect[ed by] changes in other factors«[53] – just as modernization theory predicts.

4.

To the extent that Eisenstadt wants to refute modernization theory using Japan (or East Asia) as a test case, his attempt is a failure. For if we judge our sample in light of that theory's premises, as we must if we want to disprove it, then we find no evidence questioning its validity. Quite the contrary; the reality accords remarkably well with its premises. However, failure to discredit modernization theory does not necessarily invalidate his case *for* multiple modernities and *for* the uniqueness of Japanese (or East Asian) modernity because, as will become clear presently, that case rests on propositions and evidence that might merit conceptual attention even if it had no direct bearing on other schools of social thought, including modernization theory. This possibility shall now be explored. I will first review the evidence, this time restricting myself to Japan, since that is the only East Asian country Eisenstadt has dealt with at some length, and then ask whether that evidence can carry the notion of a unique modernity.

---

52 See tables 5 and 6 in the appendix for partial validation of this claim using select South Asian, Latin American and sub-Saharan cases for the purposes of illustration. The tables integrate the HDI data with those on political and economic performance (as presented in tables 2 and 3). Due to space restrictions, they contain no data on educational and scientific performance, but where such data exist, they confirm the overall picture.

53 Huntington, Samuel P.: »The Change to Change. Modernization, Development, and Politics«, in: Comparative Politics 3 (1971), pp. 288.

Empirically, Eisenstadt illustrates his case with various examples. The first example concerns the goals and effects of social movements in contemporary Japan. Generally, such movements have tended to be less radical and confrontational than their Western counterparts according to Eisenstadt, and while successful in instigating some reform, they fell short of inducing major change in the political center. This center is also not the main steering body of society, with collectively binding decisions often taken by diverse networks of bureaucrats,[54] politicians and members of powerful interest groups, rather than the government or parliament. Other features said to be unique to Japan's political system are the low weight accorded fixed principles or ideologies, which are mostly overridden by pragmatic considerations, and the relative weakness of the state vis-à-vis society that constrains the scope for coercive measures and promotes a consensual style of governance.[55]

Eisenstadt gives further examples of Japanese distinctiveness, but none of a substantially different nature. Assuming that his account is factually correct (in the sense of adequately mirroring Japanese reali-

54 The locus classicus for this observation is of course Johnson 1982. However, when claiming that bureaucratic control of a country's governance marks a significant difference from »the« West, much depends on the units of analysis compared with Japan. Reading between the lines of Eisenstadt's account, one cannot help suspecting that he often »really« means the United States when speaking of the »West«. If, however, we included countries like Germany and France, then the differences would seem less profound. Especially in Germany, the ministerial bureaucracy enjoys considerable political leeway, with parliament (and to a certain extent also the cabinet) sometimes reduced to little more than ratifying agents. This applies especially to less controversial administrative issues that form the basis of much everyday politics, but it can also hold for big issues such as choosing the right policies for containing the consequences of the meltdown of financial markets in 2008, which required a great deal of technical expertise that ordinary politicians simply did not possess. Moreover, a former adviser to the president notes that the even the US bureaucracy regularly shields problems considered to be *truly* important against unwanted interference by those who are formally in charge (see Stiglitz, Joseph: *Globalization and its Discontents*, London 2002, p. 171).

55 Eisenstadt: »Die Vielfalt der Moderne«, ch. 3.

ties), is the evidence he cites significant enough to warrant conceptualization as a unique modernity, one that differs »fundamentally« from Western modernity? That depends on the conception of modernity employed. Viewing them through the lenses of modernization theory, Eisenstadt's observations reflect only minor variations of a basic structure of society that Japan, like other East Asian modernizers, shares with the West,[56] making them rather insignificant. How about Eisenstadt's *own* theory, then? Does this theory render them more meaningful?

Answering this question is more difficult than one might expect. For, as even sympathetic observers have had occasion to note[57], Eisenstadt does not really propound a sufficiently worked-out theory of modernity, and whatever theory he draws upon remains mostly implicit rather than being systematically explicated in his writings. Reading them carefully, a vague conceptualization is nevertheless discernible. In line with what was indicated in the introduction, Eisenstadt pleads for a *cultural* conceptualization of modernity, one that is concerned about showing how »a multiplicity of cultural programs« rooted in the so-called axial civilizations gives rise to »multiple institutional and ideological patterns«.[58] As the common core underlying this multi-

56 Given that Eisenstadt knows that modernization theory's claims are restricted to this subject matter, he might arguably arrive at the same conclusion. Summarizing theoretical scholarship on modernization in the 1970s, he says it »stressed that the more modern or developed different societies become, the more similar they will become in their *basic, central, institutional aspects*« (Eisenstadt, Shmuel N.: »Convergence and Divergence of Modern and Modernizing Societies: Indications from the Analysis of the Structuring of Social Hierarchies in Middle Eastern Societies«, in: International Journal of Middle East Studies 8 (1977), p. 1; emphasis added). Note: more similar does not mean identical, and convergence of basic institutional aspects does not mean convergence in *every conceivable respect*.

57 Allardt, Erik: »Europe's Multiple Modernity«, in: Ben-Rafael, Eliezer/ Sternberg Yitzhak (Eds.): *Comparing Modernities. Pluralism versus Homogeneity*, Leiden 2005, pp. 483–499.

58 Eisenstadt: »Multiple Modernities«, p. 2.

plicity he identifies »a mode or modes of interpretation of the world«[59] that, by radicalizing the reflexivity which first crystallized in the axial age, question(s) the givenness of social and political orders, thus raising awareness of their malleability and undermining traditional forms of legitimation. Structurally, Eisenstadt's conceptualization focuses on the nation state, and combining this focus with the observation that nation states have different political systems with different socio-historical legacies, one gets the notion of multiple modernities. Multiple modernities stands for »unique expressions of modernity«,[60] for the idea that globally shared »scripts« of modernization[61] are thoroughly indigenized when locally »enacted«.

Thus understood, every case, and so by implication also Japan's case, is of course a special case – hence unique almost by definition. One may still wonder what makes the differences between Japan and the West as »fundamental« as Eisenstadt says they are, but once we accept the maxim, to quote Wolfgang Streeck's phrasing, that »each social configuration is a ›historical individual‹ that must ultimately be understood in its own terms«,[62] this question becomes relatively unimportant. All that matters is that *some* difference be detected, and that is easy, because no two units of social analysis are exactly alike.

Eisenstadt might object to this interpretation and still insist on the profoundness of the differences between Japanese (or East Asian) and Western modernity, but on what basis? If reflexivity on the part of political elites is all that it takes to be modern,[63] then the whole world is

---

59 Eisenstadt, Shmuel N.: »Modernity in Socio-Historical Perspective«, in: Ben-Rafael, Eliezer/Sternberg, Yitzhak (Eds.): *Comparing Modernities. Pluralism versus Homogeneity*, Leiden 2005, p. 31.

60 Eisenstadt: »Multiple Modernities«, p. 2.

61 Meyer/Boli/Thomas/Ramirez: »World Society and the Nation State«:

62 Streeck, Wolfgang/Yamamura, Kozo (Eds.): *The Origins of Nonliberal Capitalism. Germany and Japan in Comparison*, Ithaca 2001, p. 5.

63 Eisenstadt's analysis of culture clearly focuses on high and elite culture (see also Joas and Knöbl [Joas, Hans/Knöbl, Wolfgang: *Sozialtheorie. Zwanzig einführende Vorlesungen*, Frankfurt/Main 2004, p. 461], who like Allardt sympathize with his approach); the everyday culture of the »masses« is largely absent from his analyses. To the extent that non-elite groups figure at all in these analyses, they appear mainly in the form of social movements.

equally modern now, vast differences in the structuring of society, in levels of development, in institutional performance, in cultural continuity/change notwithstanding. And if differences such as *these* do not matter in analyses of modernity,[64] then other differences automatically gain weight. However, not just *any* differences will do to justify the notion of multiple modernities. To play the role Eisenstadt assigns them, the respective differences *must* be fundamental, for if they were not, the very rationale for pluralizing the concept of modernity would collapse. Yet Eisenstadt nowhere provides criteria for determining the relative weight of different types of difference. Instead, he simply *asserts* that some differences are fundamental. Fundamental in what sense, by what standards, and compared to what? Eisenstadt does not answer any of these questions, and he *cannot* answer them because his theory of modernity is far too vague to generate meaningful answers.

A related problem with this theory concerns the boundaries demarcating different modernities. If we have reason to believe there is more than one modernity, then we obviously want to know how many of them there are and how we can tell them apart. Eisenstadt oscillates between two options. The first, rooted in some version of methodological nationalism, equates societies with nation states, with each society constituting a separate modernity. However, if all that Eisenstadt wants to say is that countries differ from each other in certain (more or less important) respects, and if it is already established that they do *not* differ in their modernness, then why use the language of modernity in the first place? What *analytic gain* is to be derived from an academic exercise that elevates known nation states to obscure modernities? The writings of Eisenstadt and other culturalists provide no answer to this question. The second option is to aggregate groups of countries to larger, civilization-based categories, such as Western modernity, East Asian (or Confucian) modernity, Arabic modernity, etc. This option might enrich our conceptualizations of modernity with a dose of culture, but faces the problem that it assumes both greater intra-civilizational homogeneity and inter-civilizational heterogeneity than

64 For a critical discussion of this aspect, see Schmidt, Volker H.: »One World, One Modernity«, in: Schmidt, Volker H. (Ed.): *Modernity at the Beginning of the 21st Century*, Newcastle 2007, pp. 205–228; Schmidt, Volker H.: »Modernity and Diversity«, in: Social Science Information 49 (2010), pp. 511–538.

seems to be empirically verifiable[65] – which is precisely the reason why some multiple modernists, including Eisenstadt himself, are somewhat uneasy about it and repeatedly resort to methodological nationalism.[66]

Yet another possibility arises if we take seriously the stipulation that only fundamental differences qualify a social system for designation as a separate modernity. For to find fundamental differences, however we define them, one need not always cross national or civilizational boundaries. In India, for instance, enormous differences in virtually all aspects of social life exist not only between urban and rural areas, but also at the state and district levels[67] – differences that are arguably much bigger than those between, say, Denmark and Sweden[68] on the one hand, and Shanghai and New York on the other.[69] Follow-

65 Tiryakian, Edward A.: »The Meshing of Civilizations: Soft Power and the Renewal of the Civilization of Modernity«, in: Schmidt, Volker H. (Ed.): *Modernity at the Beginning of the 21st Century*, Newcastle 2007, pp. 89–113.

66 See, e.g., Wittrock, Björn: »Modernity: One, None, or Many? European Origins and Modernity as a Global Condition«, in: Daedalus 129 (2000), pp. 31–60.

67 Drèze/Sen: »India. Development and Participation«.

68 In a special issue of the journal Thesis Eleven (2004, no. 77), all Scandinavian countries are treated as separate modernities.

69 One issue that is repeatedly invoked in support of a multiple modernities perspective is that of contextually varying experiences of modernity. As I see it, this issue has two dimensions. Firstly, we have to ask whose experience we actually mean. Multiple modernists tend to focus on the experience of intellectuals, i.e. of tiny minorities that often cultivate rather peculiar sentiments and whose experience is rarely, if ever, representative of the population in general. Secondly, we have to specify the units of analysis we compare, as well as the time horizon we employ. Thus, if we compare the everyday experience of two city dwellers living in, say, present day Rome and Tokyo, then my guess would be that these two people's experience may indeed have more in common with each other than that of each of them with their respective ancestors living in 15th century Italy or Japan (for an instructive discussion of Japan's premodern conditions, see Ferris, William Wayne: *Japan to 1600: A Social and Economic History*, Honolulu 2009). It would also not surprise me if a computer programmer living in

ing this consideration would help overcome some of the limitations and problems associated with the first two options, but result in uncontrolled inflation of modernities, rendering the concept practically useless.

In short, the multiple modernities paradigm *does* allow us to treat Japanese (or East Asian) modernity as unique, but only at the price of considerable confusion and of trivialization of the concept of modernity itself. Classical sociology devised this concept to make sense of the huge social transformations that were ushered in by a series of revolutions (the commercial revolution, the scientific revolution, the industrial revolution, the political revolution, the educational revolution, etc.) that, beginning roughly around the 15th century, first shook Europe and then the world. A paradigm that dates modernity's origins back to the epistemological transformations of the axial age some 2,500 years ago (i.e., to the breakthrough of reflexivity) is bound to downplay the impact of these structural transformations (i.e., the breakthrough of an entirely new societal formation).[70] Ironically, in so doing, it also trivializes a sense in which Japan and East Asia *are* truly unique, namely that to the present time no other non-Western location has travelled the road to modernity farther than this one. Eisenstadt is

---

contemporary Mumbai had more in common with the above urbanites than with a Dalit peasant living in contemporary Bihar. Ultimately, this is of course an empirical question, and the answer will depend a lot on how the notion of experience is operationalized. So far, multiple modernists have shown little interest in the kind of evidence needed for purposes of empirical validation.

70 A particularly telling example is Peter Wagner's (Wagner, Peter: *Modernity as Experience and Interpretation: A New Sociology of Modernity*, Cambridge 2008, p. vii) treatment of Greek antiquity as »an early manifestation of modernity«. If we follow this categorization of ancient Greece, then the changes brought about by the above revolutions cannot really have been very fundamental, certainly not as profound as claimed by classical sociology and modernization theory. So who is right? While answering that question is beyond the scope of the present paper, it is perhaps worth noting that Wagner's analysis consists mainly of discourse analysis (modernity is what European and non-European scholars say it is), whereas authors subscribing to the other view identify modernity primarily with certain social structural and institutional characteristics.

of course aware of the region's level of development – which is in fact the reason he cites for contrasting Western and Japanese modernity. But a purely culturalist conceptualization of modernity lacks the conceptual means needed to appraise the significance of a transformation whose pace is historically unprecedented. For modernization, as modernization theorists knew all too well, is a multi-dimensional process that affects all spheres of life and hence cannot be reduced to cultural aspects alone.

5.

How do we proceed from here? To prevent misunderstandings, I should perhaps begin with a disclaimer. The aim of the present paper is not to vindicate modernization theory in its classical form. Like any theory, modernization theory has its weaknesses and needs to be revised in light of valid criticisms if it is to be upheld as a useful approach for studying global social change. Nor is it my intention to question the instructiveness of social scientific approaches focusing on cultural phenomena and their impact. Quite the contrary. The pertinent research, including the research inspired by the multiple modernities school, has doubtless generated useful insights. The main shortcoming of this particular school, as I see it, is that it overstates the epistemological status of its findings by failing to determine their weight for different reference problems, i.e. for a theory of modernity as against other research questions for which they might be more relevant.

Analyses of modernity target relatively high levels of abstraction, because modernity is a condition that, while initially confined to »the« West, has now spread across the whole world, albeit with different levels of operational penetration in different locations. Given the world's cultural and socio-historical diversity, this condition is bound to express itself in multiple forms. The task of sociological theory, however, is to uncover »the regularities underlying the variety«, as Daniel Lerner aptly put it.[71] If we want to know what is peculiar to modernity, then we need to focus on these regularities. Whether past efforts at conceptualizing modernity's central features have succeeded is debatable. But regardless of how one thinks about this, it makes no

71 Lerner: »The Passing of Traditional Society«, p. 78.

sense to confront that work with findings addressing completely different reference problems.

The findings of multiple modernists are a case in point. They certainly contribute to our understanding of how contextual parameters shape the construction, functioning and local »coloring« of given institutions, and if it can be shown that this occurs in a coherent manner across institutional realms – not just in the polity, but also in the economy, in law, in the educational and scientific systems, etc. –, then we might ponder conceptualizing them in terms of a »varieties of modernity« approach.[72] But the varieties that such an approach might capture would still be sub-categories of a common, shared modernity, allowing us to distinguish them both from their »peers« and from pre-modern or less modern social systems.[73] Moreover, knowledge about these varieties would not compete with the more abstract propositions of general theories of modernity, which it could, nonetheless, flesh out to a certain extent.

Of course, a varieties of modernity approach would face the same problems of boundary drawing as the multiple modernities approach, and this problem alone should be formidable enough to discourage more than occasional experimentation with it, as indicated by the varieties of capitalism literature[74] that, while shedding light on important differences between the political economies of a few leading countries, falls far short of covering the whole world of modern capitalism.[75] An

---

72 Schmidt, Volker H.: »Multiple Modernities or Varieties of Modernity?«.

73 Eisenstadt (»Multiple Modernities«, p. 3) admits as much: »In acknowledging a multiplicity of continually evolving modernities«, he writes, »one confronts the problem of just what constitutes the common core of modernity«. As this core, he identifies the »modes of interpretation of the world« (Eisenstadt: »Modernity in Socio-Historical Perspective«, p. 31) already alluded to. As demonstrated by the work of Ingelhart and others, modernization theorists would not object to a conceptualization of modernity that includes cultural aspects. They would, however, reject a purely culturalist conceptualization as too narrow.

74 See, e.g., Hall, Peter/Soskice, David (Eds.): *Varieties of Capitalism: The Institutional Foundations of Comparative Advantage*, Oxford 2001; Streeck/Yamamura: »The Origins of Nonliberal Capitalism«.

75 Becker (Becker, Uwe: *Open Varieties of Capitalism. Continuity, Change and Performances*, Basingstoke 2009) is a partial exception as the author,

alternative avoiding these difficulties, yet addressing the substantive concerns of the multiple modernities school, would consist in cross-country comparisons of the ways in which local culture »impregnates« modern institutions in different nation states. Richard Münch's[76] work provides a useful model. This work is quite informative, but since the author is a highly proficient social theorist, he does not even pretend to supplant structural theories of modernity. Instead, Münch merely aims to complement them, as indeed he should, thus tempering his ambitions as to what he can actually deliver. Multiple modernists might benefit from considering this alternative.

BIBLIOGRAPHY

Abramovitz, Moses: »Catching Up, Forging Ahead, and Falling Behind«, in: Journal of Economic History 46 (1986), pp. 386–405.

Allardt, Erik: »Europe's Multiple Modernity«, in: Ben-Rafael, Eliezer/Sternberg Yitzhak (Eds.): *Comparing Modernities: Pluralism Versus Homogeneity*, Leiden 2005, pp. 483–499.

Becker, Uwe: *Open Varieties of Capitalism. Continuity, Change and Performances*, Basingstoke 2009.

Bendix, Reinhard: »Preconditions of Development: A Comparison of Japan and Germany«, in: Dore, Ronald (Ed.): *Aspects of Social Change in Modern Japan*, Princeton 1970, pp. 27–68.

Bertelsmann: *Bertelsmann Transformation Index 2006: Political Management in International Comparison*, Gütersloh 2005.

---

while still focusing on North America and Western Europe, makes a conscious effort to address this problem and to review some of the pertinent literature on other world regions. Interestingly, his own conceptualization and findings, like those of virtually all other advocates of the varieties of capitalism approach covering at least *some* parts of East Asia (Japan; Japan and the four tigers; or Japan plus South Korea and Taiwan), undermine the juxtaposion of East Asia and »the« West by dissolving the West into a variety of discrete categories, some of which are *more different from each other* than from their East Asian counterparts.

76 Münch, Richard: *Die Kultur der Moderne*, 2 volumes, Frankfurt/Main 1986.

Bulbeck, Chilla: »›The Mighty Pillar of the Family‹: Young People's Vocabularies on Household Gender Arrangements in the Asia-Pacific Region«, in: Gender, Work and Organization 12 (2005), pp. 14–31.

CIA: *The World Factbook 2007* (https://www.cia.gov/library/publica tions/the-world-factbook/ [accessed January 2007]).

de Ferranti, David et al.: *Inequality in Latin America and the Caribbean: Breaking with History?*, Washington, D.C. 2004.

Drèze, Jean/ Sen, Amartya: *India: Development and Participation*, 2nd edition, Delhi 2002.

Drori, Gili S./Meyer, John W./Ramirez, Francisco O./Schofer, Evan: *Science in the Modern World Polity: Institutionalization and Globalization*, Stanford 2003.

Easterlin, Richard A: »The Worldwide Standard of Living Since 1800«, in: Journal of Economic Perspectives 14 (2000), pp. 7–26.

Eisenstadt, Shmuel N.: »Convergence and Divergence of Modern and Modernizing Societies: Indications from the Analysis of the Structuring of Social Hierarchies in Middle Eastern Societies«, in: International Journal of Middle East Studies 8 (1977), pp. 1–27.

Eisenstadt, Shmuel N.: »Modernity in Socio-Historical Perspective«, in: Ben-Rafael, Eliezer/Sternberg, Yitzhak (Eds.): *Comparing Modernities: Pluralism versus Homogeneity*, Leiden 2005, pp. 31–56.

Eisenstadt, Shmuel N.: »Multiple Modernities«, in: Daedalus 129 (2000), pp. 1–29.

Eisenstadt, Shmuel N.: *Die Vielfalt der Moderne*, Weilerswist 2000.

Ferris, William Wayne: *Japan to 1600: A Social and Economic History*, Honolulu 2009.

Freedom House: *Freedom in the World 2008* (http://www.freedom house.org/template.cfm?page=363&year=2008).

Gill, Indermit/Kharas, Homi: *An East Asian Renaissance: Ideas For Economic Growth*, Washington, D.C. 2007.

Hall, Peter/Soskice, David (Eds.): *Varieties of Capitalism: The Institutional Foundations of Comparative Advantage*, Oxford 2001.

Hobsbawm, Eric: *The Age of Extremes: A History of the World, 1914–1991*, New York 1994.

Huntington, Samuel P.: »The Change to Change. Modernization, Development, and Politics«, in: Comparative Politics 3 (1971), pp. 283–322.

Huntington, Samuel P.: *Political Order in Changing Societies*, New Haven 1968.

Inglehart, Ronald/Welzel, Christian: *Modernization, Cultural Change, and Democracy: The Human Development Sequence*, Cambridge 2005.

Joas, Hans/Knöbl, Wolfgang: *Sozialtheorie: Zwanzig einführende Vorlesungen*, Frankfurt/Main 2004.

Johnson, Chalmers: *Miti and the Japanese Miracle: The Growth of Industrial Policy, 1925–1975*, Stanford 1982.

Jones, Gavin W./Straughan, Paulin Tay/Chan, Angelique (Eds.): *Ultra-Low Fertility in Pacific Asia: Trends, Causes and Policy Issues*, London 2008.

Jones, Gavin W.: »The ›Flight from Marriage‹ in South-East and East Asia«, in: Journal of Comparative Family Studies 36 (2005), pp. 93–119.

Kaufmann, Daniel/Kray, Aart/Mastruzzi, Massimo: *Governance Matters VII: Aggregate and Individual Governance Indicators 1996–2006*.

Lerner, Daniel: »Modernization«, in: Sills, David L./Merton, Robert K. (Eds.): *International Encyclopedia of the Social Sciences*, New York 1968, pp. 386–395.

Lerner, Daniel: *The Passing of Traditional Society. Modernizing the Middle East*, Glencoe 1958.

Maddison, Angus: *The World Economy: A Millennial Perspective*, Paris 2001.

Martin, Michael O./Mullis, Ina V.S./Foy, Pierre: *TIMMS 2007 International Science Report*, Boston: TIMSS & PIRLS International Study Center, Lynch School of Education, Boston College 2008.

Martin, Michael O./Mullis, Ina V.S./Foy, Pierre: *TIMMS 2007 International Mathematics Report*. Boston: TIMSS & PIRLS International Study Center, Lynch School of Education, Boston College 2008.

Meyer, John W./Boli, John/Thomas, George M./Ramirez, Francisco O.: »World Society and the Nation State«, in: American Journal of Sociology 103 (1997), pp. 144–182.

Münch, Richard: *Die Kultur der Moderne*, 2 volumes, Frankfurt/Main 1986.

Myers, Ramon H.: »Economic Life in Mainland China and Taiwan and the Rise of a Productive Market Economy«, in: Ash, Robert/Greene, J. Megan (Eds.): *Taiwan in the 21st Century: Aspects and Limitations of a Developmental Model*, London 2007, pp. 10–35.

OECD: *PISA 2006: Science Competencies for Tomorrow's World*, Paris 2007.

Parsons, Talcott: »Evolutionary Universals in Society«, in: American Sociological Review 29 (1964), pp. 339–357.

Parsons, Talcott: *The Evolution of Society*, ed. with an introduction by Jackson Toby, Englewood Cliffs 1977.

Peng, Ito: »Gender, Demography, and Welfare State Restructuring in Japan«, in: Marshall, Katherine/Butzbach, Oliver (Eds.): *New Social Policy Agendas for Europe and Asia: Challenges, Experience, and Lessons*, Washington, D.C. 2003, pp. 215–234.

Putnam, Robert D.: *Making Democracy Work: Civic Traditions in Modern Italy*, Princeton 1993.

Quah, Stella R.: *Families in Asia: Home and Kin*, 2nd edition, London 2008.

Rotberg, Robert I.: »Failed States, Collapsed States, Weak States: Causes and Indicators«, in: Rotberg, Robert I. (Ed.): *State Failure and State Weakness in a Time of Terror*, Washington, D.C. 2003, pp. 1–25.

Schmidt, Volker H.: »Convergence with a Twist: East Asian Welfare Capitalism in Comparative Perspective«, in: Fee, Lian Kwen/Kiong, Tong Chee (Eds.): *Social Policy in Post-Industrial Singapore*, Leiden 2008, pp. 309–331.

Schmidt, Volker H.: »Modernity and Diversity«, in: Social Science Information 49 (2010), pp. 511–538.

Schmidt, Volker H.: »Multiple Modernities or Varieties of Modernity?«, in: Current Sociology 54 (2006), pp. 77–97.

Schmidt, Volker H.: »One World, One Modernity«, in: Schmidt, Volker H. (Ed.): *Modernity at the Beginning of the 21st Century*, Newcastle 2007, pp. 205–228.

Shanghai Jiao Tong University: *Academic Ranking of World Universities – 2008*. (http://www.arwu.org/rank2008/Top500_EN(by%20rank).pdf).

Smelser, Neil J.: »Toward a Theory of Modernization«, in: Smelser, Neil J.: *Essays in Sociological Explanation*, Englewood Cliffs 1968, pp. 125–146.

Stiglitz, Joseph: *Globalization and its Discontents*, London 2002.

Streeck, Wolfgang/Yamamura, Kozo (Eds.): *The Origins of Nonliberal Capitalism. Germany and Japan in Comparison*, Ithaca 2001.

Streeck, Wolfgang: »Introduction: Explorations into the Origins of Nonliberal Capitalism in Germany and Japan«, in: Streeck, Wolfgang/Yamamura, Kozo (Eds.): *The Origins of Nonliberal Capitalism. Germany and Japan in Comparison*, Ithaca 2001, pp. 1–38.

Thesis Eleven 77 (2004)

Tiryakian, Edward A.: »The Meshing of Civilizations: Soft Power and the Renewal of the Civilization of Modernity«, in: Schmidt, Volker H. (Ed.): *Modernity at the Beginning of the 21st Century*, Newcastle 2007, pp. 89–113.

Transparency International: *Global Corruption Report 2007: Corruption in Judicial Systems*, Cambridge 2007.

Tu, Weiming: »Implications of the Rise of ›Confucian‹ East Asia«, in: Daedalus 129 (2000), pp. 195–218.

Turner, Jonathan H.: *The Structure of Sociological Theory*, 7th edition, Belmont, CA 2003.

UNDP: *Human Development Report 2007/2008*, New York 2007.

UNDP: *Human Development Report 2010*, New York 2010.

Wagner, Peter: *Modernity as Experience and Interpretation: A New Sociology of Modernity*, Cambridge 2008.

Weber, Max: *Economy and Society*, ed. by Guenther Roth and Claus Wittich, Berkeley 1978.

World Bank: *World Bank Policy Research Working Paper 4280*, June 2008, Washington, D.C. 2008.

WHO: *World Health Report 2000: Health Systems: Improving Performance*, Geneva 2000.

Wittrock, Björn: »Modernity: One, None, or Many? European Origins and Modernity as a Global Condition«, in: Daedalus 129 (2000), pp. 31–60.

World Economic Forum: Global Competitiveness Report 2008–2009, Geneva 2008.

Appendix: Tables 5 and 6

Table 5: Select South Asian and Latin American Countries

Country	UNDP				Freedom House			Kaufmann et al.				World Economic Forum			
	HDI Rank	GDP	LE	Liter-acy	Freedom/ Democ-racy		Rule of Law	Rule of Law	Voice/ Ac-count	Gov. Ef-fectiv	Corrupt Control	Global Comp	Inst	Infra	Innov
India	134	2,753	63.4	66.0	F	2.5	9	0.10	0.38	0.03	-0.39	49	54	76	30
Pakistan	141	2,496	66.2	54.2	PF	4.5	2	-0.93	-1.05	-0.62	-0.83	101	104	89	79
Bangladesh	146	1,241	65.7	53.5	PF	4.0	5	0.81	-0.63	-0.81	-1.05	116	122	126	122
Argentinia	49	13,238	75.2	97.6	F	2.0	10	-0.52	0.33	-0.14	-0.45	85	126	88	86
Brazil	75	9,567	72.2	90.0	F	2.0	8	-0.44	0.41	-0.12	-0.24	56	93	74	43
Colombia	77	8,587	72.7	92.7	PF	3.0	7	-0.57	-0.28	0.03	-0.28	69	101	83	63
Peru	78	7,836	73.0	89.6	F	2.5	8	-0.71	-0.38	-0.44	-0.38	78	90	97	109
Bolivia	113	4,206	65.4	90.7	PF	3.0	7	-0.96	-0.49	-0.83	-0.49	120	132	122	132

Sources: UNDP: *Human Development Report 2009*
Freedom House: *Freedom in the World 2009*
Daniel Kaufmann,/Aart Kray/Massimo Mastruzzi 2008: *Governance Matters VII, World Bank Policy Research Working Paper 4554*
World Economic Forum: *Global Competitiveness Report 2009-2010*

Table 6: Select countries from Sub-Saharan Africa

Country	UNDP				Freedom House			Kaufmann et al.				World Economic Forum			
	HDI Rank	GDP	LE	Liter-acy	Freedom/ Democ-racy		Rule of Law	Rule of Law	Voice/ Ac-count	Gov. Effec-tiv	Corrupt Control	Global Comp	Inst	Infra	Innov
Botswana	125	13,604	53.4	82.9	F	2.0	13	0.67	0.49	0.70	0.90	66	29	61	71
Tanzania	151	1,208	55.0	72.3	PF	3.5	10	-0.45	-0.15	-0.42	-0.45	100	74	123	93
Nigeria	158	1,969	47.7	72.0	PF	4.5	5	-1.20	-0.54	-0.93	-1.01	99	102	126	73
Zambia	164	1,358	44.5	70.6	PF	3.0	9	-0.64	-0.26	-0.59	-0.60	112	61	111	90
Ethopia	171	779	54.7	35.9	PF	5.0	4	-0.54	-1.19	-0.45	0.70	118	75	96	112
Mosambique	172	802	47.8	44.4	PF	3.5	8	-0.68	-0.06	-0.41	0.59	129	105	116	105

Sources: UNDP: *Human Development Report 2009*
Freedom House: *Freedom in the World* 2009
Daniel Kaufmann/Aart Kray/Massimo Mastruzzi: *Governance Matters VII, World Bank Policy Research Working Paper 4554*, 2008
World Economic Forum: *Global Competitiveness Report 2009-2010*

III. Challenges and Paradigms of Humanity

III.1 Humanisms, the Still Unfulfilled Promise of the ›Axial Age‹ of Modernity

Oliver Kozlarek

The concepts ›Axial Age‹ and ›Axial Age‹ go back to the German philosopher Karl Jaspers. The contemporary debate – which refers to the same terminology, and finds one of its most prominent representatives in the Israeli sociologist Shmuel N. Eisenstadt – translates the term into the language of contemporary historical sociology. In my paper I will discuss the possibilities and limits of such an enterprise.

I will argue that although Eisenstadt and his followers did indeed enter a very interesting terrain that promised to come to grips with some of the major problems of modernization theory, they did not follow the normative motives of Jaspers' original thesis. Instead of spelling out a normative commitment to Humanism they forwarded a research program that limits itself to the recognition of cultural differences between modern societies.

At the end of my paper I will take a look at the Brasilian anthropologist Darcy Ribeiro, who already articulated in the 1960s an interesting civilization theory that was not only rooted in Latin American experience with and within modernity, but that could have provided a very interesting starting point for both: a substantial critique of modernization theory and an invincible argument for the need for a humanist project.

But let me begin by recovering some of the main elements of Jaspers' ›Axial Ages‹ hypothesis.

1. JASPERS: THE ›AXIAL AGE‹ AS A CONCEPT OF A HUMANIST FOUNDATION OF MEANING

The ›Axial Age‹ is a concept used by Jaspers in his philosophy of history. It features as the central idea in his book *Ursprung und Ziel der Geschichte* (*Origin and Goal of History*), a book that was first published in 1949. The time of publication is crucial, since it explains that the book must be read as a reaction to the experiences of two devastating wars. Jaspers' book is above all an outcry for humanism[1] that was quite common for many European intellectuals during and after World War One. Many condemned the Great War by activating argumentations that aimed to prove that the fate of humanity lies in its unity, and that therefore a war that only fosters fragmentation simply does not make any sense at all. A very prominent example is Ernst Cassirer. Although he did not play the role of a public intellectual, he presented his first piece of practical philosophy in a book called *Freiheit und Form* (*Freedom and Form*) that was published in 1918 and that tried to demonstrate that the intellectual history of Europe is intimately integrated. Cassirer's book can be seen as an attempt to prove how absurd a war is in which Europeans fight Europeans. Another example is Max Scheler. His ideas are influenced by Catholicism, but more important than the authority of the church for Scheler is the commitment to the unity of all human beings.

I think that Jaspers too has to be read as a continuation of this ›tradition‹. His philosophy of history is thus much more than an attempt to explain some logic of becoming; it is first of all an argument for the unity of the human race, without neglecting its differences.

It is in the present – more than ever – that we have to *believe* in humanity's common fate. Jaspers expresses this conviction in the discursive realm of philosophy of history not because he was concerned with the reconstruction of the past, but because he finds here a narrative framework in which he feels competent to pronounce it. Admittedly, one can find theological undertones in his language. For instance where he wrote:

»My design is supported by the thesis of believe (*Glaubensthese*) that human beings have a common origin and goal. We do not know their origin and goal.

1 This point is also made by Georg Stauth's article in this book.

> It can only be sensed by the glowing of symbols that can be interpreted in different ways. Our existence (*Dasein*) moves between them; through philosophical acknowledgment we probably try to get close to both, origin and goal […]«[2]

»*Glaubensthese*« can also be read in a non-theological way. First of all, it contains a certain declaration of ignorance. We cannot know either the origin or the goal of history. Both will always be veiled by the past, dispersed by contingency. So the reference to the ›Axial Age‹ is *not* a reference to some empirical historical origin; it is rather a possibility that allows us today to believe in the unity of humanity. To put it differently: the reference to the ›Axial Age‹ belongs to the present and to the need to remember what makes us all human in and for the present. That already shows the second meaning of Jaspers' *Glaubensthese* (his thesis of belief): it is not so much a passive rendering of some higher authority or force – at least other than humanity – that Jaspers refers to, but it expresses, on the contrary, a *decision*. What ever else Jaspers might have thought of, he also takes this decision in favor of the unity of humanity.

Therefore he claims:

> »It is all symbols, no realities. Universal history that is empirically accessible can only be captured by us in their meaning through the idea of unity of history – no matter whether it really has this meaning or if we humans have put it there. The empirical facts are being questioned if they correspond to this idea of unity or in how far they oppose to it«.[3]

The task of philosophy is not discovering historical facts in the past, but making sense of the present. Again: for Jaspers the most important challenge must have been to restore the belief in the unity of humanity. Jaspers' *Glaubensthese* (his thesis of belief) is thus a humanist thesis! It expresses the belief and the hope that human beings can live peacefully together.

The ›Axial Age‹ is the most convenient reference point for the humanist project that Jaspers brings along. More than an »empirical necessity«, the convergence of human civilizations is an »empirical

---

2 Jaspers, Karl: *Vom Ursprung und Ziel der Geschichte*, Munich 1949, p. 17. Translations: Oliver Kozlarek.

3 Jaspers: »Vom Ursprung und Ziel der Geschichte«, p. 18.

possibility«. More important than its historical factuality is the need to take a decision in favor of humanity in our contemporary world:

> »An axis of world history, if it exists, could be found *empirically* as a fact, which would be valid for all human beings, Christians included. This axis would exist where that which has ever since been called human was born, where the overwhelming fertility of the creation of the human being happened in such a manner; that is, if not empirically necessary, at least understandable for the occident and Asia and for all human beings.«[4]

It is »convincing«, not »empirically necessary«, and it is because of this that it could be »the common framework that all peoples can refer to when it comes to their ›historical self-understanding‹«.[5]

2. The Sociological Actualization of the ›Axial Age‹ Thesis

Whoever today talks about ›Axial Times‹ and the ›Axial Age‹ cannot ignore the debate that was set in motion by Shmuel N. Eisenstadt. His appropriation of the ›Axial Age‹ thesis has a different context: Motivating impulses come from problems that are rooted deeply in the tradition of post-WWII sociological theory. Eisenstadt's ›Axial-Time‹ theory is steered by theoretical ambitions to resolve technical problems of former theories. Especially, the theory of modernization – of which Eisenstadt has been an early architect – is an important point of departure.

Eisenstadt understood very early on that one of the most problematic aspects of modernization theory was its ›temporal logic‹ that was characterizing the *form* of that theory. Modernization theory reproduced the idea of modernization being a universal process, one that will sooner or later happen to all human societies unless they were resisting it. This ›sooner-or-later-dichotomy‹ was then translated into the language of social theory. Because of the strong influence of modernization theory, a world view emerged – to be sure, on a global scale – according to which the world was divided into basically two kinds of

4 Jaspers: »Vom Ursprung und Ziel der Geschichte«, p.19.

5 Jaspers: »Vom Ursprung und Ziel der Geschichte«, p.19.

societies: those that were *already* modern – first of all the US – and those that were *still* on the way, or – to use the language of modernization theory: *traditional.*

Now, this highly politically biased world-view has been discussed many times, and I don't want to get into this here. But what is important for our context is that Eisenstadt understood this problem that was intrinsic to modernization theory very clearly. Already in the 1970s he wrote:

»Although the different societies or civilizations react in specific ways to the development of ›modernity‹ – at least in so far as these differ from former historical situations concerning the problems which they try to resolve – the reaction to modernity contains also many similarities with processes of social change of earlier historical periods. Therefore a change of the perspective leads to the recognition that many similarities and continuities between the contemporary and the traditional ways of social change might be possible. This insight is determining for the understanding of the different posttraditional modern civilizations which are about to be constituted in the contemporary world.«[6]

Eisenstadt was not shy about expressing the consequences that this would have for the whole theoretical project of modernization theory. As the following lines show, he must have been convinced that modernization theory was no longer an option:

»It […] would be wrong to presuppose that the forces [of modernization] – once they make themselves felt in a society– would push this society in the direction of a predetermined end. Rather, they provoke different reactions in different societies, which depend on the internal conditions but also on the international system and the international relations in which these societies are involved.«[7]

If this is so, then a whole different way of theorizing and consequently understanding modernity was required. Instead of following the much too simple ›temporal logic‹ according to which any society has to pass through the transformation from »tradition« to »modernity« in the same way, a theory was needed that had the capacity to account for

6 Eisenstadt, Shmuel N.: *Tradition, Wandel und Modernität*, Frankfurt/Main 1973, p. 32.

7 Eisenstadt: »Tradition, Wandel und Modernität«, p. 371.

differences where they existed. Eisenstadt was certainly still interested in processes of social change and consequently in temporal sequences, but these were no longer understood as directed towards a universal *telos* of societal processes or even ›the‹ process of human civilization as such. Modernity was no longer seen as something that was achieved by a few societies, but which remained still hardly more than a wish for many others. Modernity was understood as a more or less global reality with regional and local differences. Eisenstadt gave up, at least partly, the normative orientation of modernization theory and adopted an analytical one; the exclusion which was provoked by temporal logic – the negation of ›coevalness‹[8] – was exchanged for an integral view of a global but not homogenous modernity. To put it differently: one of the theoretical cornerstones of modernization theory – its convergence thesis – was being questioned.[9]

The idea of ›synchronicity‹, that is, the fact that different modernities coexist at the same time, condensed during the 1980s and the 1990s into one of the most popular contemporary sociological ideas that is being discussed more and more even outside of the realm of sociological theory: I mean the idea of the existence, in fact the *co-existence*, of *multiple modernities*. In what is today already widely quoted as some sort of manifesto of the multiple-modernities approach, Eisenstadt explains:

»The notion of ›multiple modernities‹ denotes a certain view of the contemporary world – indeed of the history and characteristics of the modern era – that goes against the views long prevalent in scholarly and general discourse. It goes against the view of the ›classic‹ theories of modernization and of the convergence of industrial societies prevalent in the 1950s, and indeed against the classical sociological analyses of Marx, Durkheim, and (to a large extent) even of Weber, at least in one reading of his work. They all assumed, even if only implicitly, that the cultural program of modernity as it developed in modern Europe and the basic institutional constellations that emerged there would ultimately take over in all modernizing and modern societies; with the expansion of modernity they would prevail throughout the world.«[10]

8 See Fabian, Johannes: *Time and the Other*, Columbia 2002.

9 About this point see Volker Schmidt's discussion in this book.

10 Eisenstadt, Shmuel N.: »Multiple Modernities«, in: Daedalus 129.1 (2000), p. 1.

But not only does Eisenstadt want to account for the many different modernites, he also wants to *explain* the differences. Now, in order to do that, he adopts Jaspers' ›Axial Age‹ theory. Different modernities, thus his thesis, do follow different civilizational paths. Or: the different modernities that can be accounted for in our contemporary world are stemming from a particular kind of civilization that had the potential for producing modern societies. This particular kinds of civilizations are the so-called Axial Age civilizations. They are seen as predecessors of modernity or modernities. Let me try a brief assessment of the approach of the Axial Age Civilizations-multiple modernity approach that Eisenstadt has come up with:

(1) On a definitely positive end of an evaluation scale is the fact that the Axial Age theorem allows to articulate a theory of modernity that is not limited to only one model of modernity. To put it differently: Eisenstadt's approach is a promising tool to overcome Eurocentrism.
(2) Another positive point is that the awareness of differences and multiplicities of modernities does not conflate with what has been termed in recent years as ›methodological nationalism‹.[11] Civilizations are definitely not limited to the borders of nation states. They provide an analytical unit that stretches beyond national borders.
(3) Finally, the Civilization-theoretical approach helps to develop an integral model of societies in which culture and institutional characteristics are viewed as intrinsically interwoven. However, there are of course also a few problems to which I will briefly turn now:

1. The first problem could be named a ›misplaced concreteness‹, and it refers directly to Eisenstadt's use of the ›Axial Age‹ hypothesis: A few years ago a conference that was held in Florence on the topic was evaluated by Eisenstadt, Johann Arnason and Björn Wittrock with the following statement:

»[…] a stronger emphasis should be placed on the diversity of developments in different regions during the Axial Age, and of the resultant traditions; more comparative analysis is needed, and the idea of a shared problematic of order,

11 See Beck, Ulrich: *Macht und Gegenmacht im globalen Zeitalter*, Frankfurt/Main 2002.

common to Greek, Jewish and Chinese traditions may have to be relativized or reformulated; the interpretation of Axial Age might have to move towards a model of ›multiple axialities‹ (analogous to the emerging paradigm of ›multiple modernities‹).«[12]

What becomes very clear here is the problem that I would refer to as ›misplaced concreteness‹. Sociological research seems to get lost in the study of ancient civilizations if it really understands the Axial Age as providing clues for the understanding of our contemporary modernities. On the other hand, it loses sight of the problems that all human beings are sharing in our present *global modernity*. Especially compared to Jaspers the problem of the sociological appropriation of the ›Axial Age‹ approach seems to be the emphasis on empirical historical details.

2. Another problem has been highlighted by Gerard Delanty: The focus on Axial Age breakthroughs could lead to the fact that other transformations and changes that occur later on are not registered. They tend to be considered as less important or even errant. Delanty explains:

»Aside from the difficulty that it is not at all clear how the various historical elaborations are connected or driven by the original impetus, the result of this exercise is that non-western modernities are ultimately failed modernities.«[13]

3. That brings me to my next point. Gurminder K. Bhambra sees the fundamental problem with the civilizational analysis in the fact that civilizations do appear basically as reified entities that develop quite independently from each other.[14] Her conclusion is:

---

12 Arnason, Johann P./Eisenstadt, Shmuel N./Wittrock, Björn (Eds.): *Axial Civilizations and World History*, Leiden/Boston 2005, p. 4.

13 This could be thought of Islam (see Georg Stauth in this book); Delanty, Gerard: »The Exhaustion of Axial Age? Remarks on Eisenstadt's Civilizational Theory of Modernity«, in: Erwägen – Wissen – Ethik 17 (2006), pp. 26–28.

14 Bhambra, Gurminder K.: »From Civilisational Analysis to Connected Histories and Cosmopolitanisms: a Response to Professor Eisenstadt's ›Culture and Power‹«, in: Erwägen – Wissen – Ethik 17 (2006), pp. 20–22.

»This methodology serves rather only to reinforce the differences between societies (and civilizations) and the separateness of their trajectories, rather than facilitating an examination of their interconnections.«[15]

The problem I would add to this is that it fails to understand how modernity brings all these different civilizations together, how they get »connected« and »entangled« in what might be called today a »global modernity« with many different faces despite all their affinities.

Let me sum up: Through »misplaced concreteness«, that is: much too strong a focus on the empirical development of axial civilizations, Eisenstadt's theory loses sight of its initial goal: that is, modernity. His effort to explain differences between modern societies paradoxically drifts away from a comprehensive explanation of what makes modernity still a legitimate reference point despite all the differences. Compared to Jaspers, the normative commitment that – in the case of the German philosopher – was rooted in humanism, is given up.

3. A Different Civilization Theory

A somehow different civilization theory comes from Latin America. It was articulated by the Brazilian anthropologist Darcy Ribeiro who presented his theory in the 1960s as a response to modernization theory. The starting point for his own reflection is thus the same that Eisenstadt uses as his entry point for his civilization theory, as we just heard.[16] I will briefly sketch some ideas of Ribeiro's theory that have the potential to respond to the abovementioned shortcomings of Eisenstadt's Civilization theory:

1. Ribeiro avoids the problem that I called ›misplaced concreteness‹ because he distinguishes clearly between theory and theoretical decisions, on the one hand, and the imperatives of historico-empirical re-

15 Bhambra: »From Civilisational Analysis to Connected Histories«, p. 21.

16 At one point in an interview with Heinz Rudolf Sonntag, Ribeiro refers directly to Eisenstadt. See Ribeiro, Darcy: *Der zivilisatorische Prozeß*, Frankfurt/Main 1971, p. 281. It becomes clear though that he refers to Eisenstadt as a representative, not a critic of modernization theory.

ality on the other. Heinz Rudolf Sonntag sums this up in the following sentence:

»Ribeiro insists that his evolutionary sequence is not a historical but a theoretical one. By doing so he manifests a different concept of history: the overall historical process represents the raw material that gets its structure only by putting it into a concept«.[17]

Essential for this ›work on concepts‹ (*Begriffsarbeit*) are the *experiences* that Latin Americans have accumulated over the past 500 years and that nourish many Latin American ideas and thoughts.[18] I am talking about the experience of counter-running processes of evolution and civilization in general, but very clearly about the experience (or experiences) of coloniality in more concrete terms. How does Ribeiro account for these experiences in his theoretical structure? This brings me to my second point:

2. He basically distinguishes between what he calls »evolutionary acceleration« and »historical integration«. »Evolutionary acceleration« refers to the civilizational process that a specific civilization goes through without any major influences from the outside. On the other hand, the concept of »historical integration« refers to the fact that one civilization starts to dominate others and tries to incorporate them. Very clearly, what this refers to is the European civilization that started to dominate over most other civilizations some 500 years ago.

3. Modernity is the outcome of this ›encounter‹ of different civilizations. Only an incomplete image of modernity would neglect coloniality as one of the major characteristics of modernity. It is one of its most important mechanisms of ›historical integration‹. It was this ›historical integration‹ that produced the global modernity we are all sharing today. This also means that modernity actually is a historical era in its own right that is not explainable simply by referring to Axial Age civilizations. But although modernity is not reducible to this first Axial Age that Jaspers and Eisenstadt had in mind, it could be understood as

17 Sonntag, Heinz Rudolf: »Nachwort«, in: Darcy Ribeiro: *Der zivilisatorische Prozeß*, Frankfurt/Main 1971, p. 254.

18 See Ribeiro, Darcy: *Unterentwicklung, Kultur und Zivilisation: Ungewöhnliche Versuche*, Frankfurt/Main 1980, p. 38.

a new, a second Axial Age that starts to form a new civilization: the first truly global civilization in human history that challenges basically all former civilizations – even the strongest of the Axial Civilizations, like the European.

4. Finally, the new Axial Age ›Modernity‹ resets the normative agenda: It is the Axial Age of modernity that brings into perspective for the first time in human history a humanism that responds to the challenge to include *all* human beings regardless of where they are living or what their ethnic, cultural or religious backgrounds may be. Modernity puts on the agenda an inclusive humanism that does not suppress differences, but at the same time does not give up the belief in the unity of humanity. Today all human beings do not only share a common *conditio humana*, but also the *condition moderne*, *i.e.*: a common world they have to build together. For Ribeiro it was clear that this is a task that has to be assumed by those who have made the experience of having been excluded. It is up to them to inaugurate this new humanism that is no longer exclusive. At the same time, it is also up to them to vindicate the unfulfilled promises of Modernity.

4. Civilization, Modernity and Humanism as Reference Points for a Human World

Darcy Ribeiro's assessment of Civilizations, Modernity and Humanism is very typical of post-colonial writers. They do not reject these concepts radically. But neither do they accept in an uncritical fashion the ideas that Western thinkers have put into them. Modernity has constituted a common world that all human beings are sharing today. But the experiences gathered in this process of »growing together«, for which colonialism has been an important factor, are different. Post-colonial thinkers remember the experiences that colonial and post-colonial societies have created.

Excavating the forgotten or neglected experiences of those who were not allowed to participate actively in the construction of the new world, is an important step towards a construction of a common world. The task of our contemporary Modernity, understood as a second Axial Age, is to provide a space where all these different experiences can be exchanged. Such a space of dialogue and communication would be already a humanist achievement. This must also have been the understanding of Edward Said, who wrote:

> »Humanism, I strongly believe, must excavate the silences, the world of memory, of itinerant, barely surviving groups, the places of exclusion and invisibility, the kind of testimony that doesn't make it onto the reports but which more and more is about whether an overexploited environment, sustainable small economies and small nations, and marginalized peoples outside as well as inside the maw of the metropolitan center can survive the grinding down and flattening out and displacement that are such prominent features of globalization«.[19]

Needless to say, the social and the cultural sciences play an important role in this deeply humanist enterprise.

But it is not enough to remember the hardship and suffering that colonialism and other atrocities have inflicted on so many human beings in this bitter process of becoming one humanity and one world. It would be just as important to look for directions. What shall this common world of and for all human beings look like? To be sure, an answer to this question is not something the social sciences and the humanities have to *invent*. But they possess the methodological and conceptual tools to extract and expose possibilities from different discursive realms. Their hermeneutical and translational skills have to be mentioned here. They will be indispensable for the sense generation that a common world of all human beings has to come to terms with. Hopefully, these skills may enable the social and cultural sciences to listen to the multiplicity of voices forming a meaning- and sense-generating polyphony before they burst into cacophony.

On a conceptual level, concepts like ›Civilization‹, ›Modernity‹ and ›Humanism‹ may still provide important normative reference points for this ›unfinished project‹ of the construction of a common world. That does not mean that new concepts can or should not emerge. But we have good reasons to believe that for now, these concepts have helped people everywhere of the world to imagine themselves in this common world of all human beings.

---

19 Said, Edward W.: *Humanism and Democratic Criticism*, New York a.o. 2004, 81-82.

BIBLIOGRAPHY

Arnason, Johann P./Eisenstadt, Shmuel N./Wittrock, Björn (Eds.): *Axial Civilizations and World History*, Leiden/Boston 2005.

Beck, Ulrich: *Macht und Gegenmacht im globalen Zeitalter*, Frankfurt/Main 2002.

Bhambra, Gurminder K.: »From Civilisational Analysis to Connected Histories and Cosmopolitanisms: a Response to Professor Eisenstadt's ›Culture and Power‹«, in: Erwägen – Wissen – Ethik 17 (2006), pp. 20–22.

Delanty, Gerard: »The Exhaustion of Axial Age? Remarks on Eisenstadt's Civilizational Theory of Modernity«, in: Erwägen – Wissen – Ethik 17 (2006), pp. 26–28.

Eisenstadt, Shmuel N.: »Multiple Modernities«, in: Daedalus 129.1 (2000), p. 1–29.

Eisenstadt, Shmuel N.: *Tradition, Wandel und Modernität*, Frankfurt/Main 1973.

Fabian, Johannes: *Time and the Other*, Columbia 2002.

Jaspers, Karl: *Vom Ursprung und Ziel der Geschichte*, Munich 1949.

Ribeiro, Darcy: *Der zivilisatorische Prozeß*, Frankfurt/Main 1971.

Ribeiro, Darcy: *Unterentwicklung, Kultur und Zivilisation: Ungewöhnliche Versuche*, Frankfurt/Main 1980.

Said, Edward W.: *Humanism and Democratic Criticism*, New York a.o. 2004.

Sonntag, Heinz Rudolf: »Nachwort«, in: Darcy Ribeiro: *Der zivilisatorische Prozeß*, Frankfurt/Main 1971, p. 234–285.

III.2 The Arena Games in the Roman Empire

A Contribution to the Explanation of the History of Morals and Humanity

GEORG W. OESTERDIEKHOFF

> »The main attractiveness of the games was lying in their horrific character. The pleasure of the Romans into this kind of sports was tremendously brutal and perverse«.[1]

Roman arena games essentially consisted of gladiator fights to life or death, cruel executions of delinquents, and chases with wild animals. Millions of humans and millions of animals were killed in the arenas during the Imperial period. This article shows that the aforesaid elements of the games are found in most pre-modern societies around the globe since the oldest times, both in ancient civilizations and tribal societies. The rise of animal protection, the abolishment of duel cultures and sadistic punishment systems belong to cultural transformations that arise as late as the era of enlightenment and modernization. It can be shown that psychic-cognitive structures account for the ubiquity of the cruel practices in pre-modern societies and for their abolishment during the processes of modernization. Cross-cultural psychology is able to link these historical cognitive structures and transformations to empirical results detected among different contemporary cultures around the globe in the past 70 years.

1 Grant, Michael: *Die Gladiatoren*, Stuttgart 1982, p. 82, transl. by Georg W. Oesterdiekhoff (*The Gladiators*, New York 1971).

1. INTRODUCTION

This article applies the scientific tools of developmental psychology in order to explain some relevant aspects of the history of morals and customs. The article is based on »Structure-Genetic Sociology«[2], an approach stemming from Piagetian Cross-Cultural Psychology, using its empirical results for the reconstruction of the history of mankind, especially the history of science, world-view, religion, law, morals, customs, behaviour and other issues. This article focuses on the development of social cognitions (empathy, sympathy, taking over perspectives), moral judgments (human rights, justice) and peacefulness (cruelty, sadism), understanding these several parts of social cognition as different dimensions of the ontogenetic psychic-cognitive development. The historical development of psychic-cognitive and socio-mo ral abilities will be demonstrated by analyzing the Roman games, where deadly combat both between humans and between humans and animals, agonizing chases with animals and sadistic executions took place in the arenas. This article shows that these relevant elements that constitute the arena games are not tied to Roman antiquity but are found in all ancient and pre-modern societies. The systemic cause for the ubiquity of these three forms of cruelty across all pre-modern cultures is found in the elemental psychic-cognitive stage of pre-modern populations. The decline of these three forms of primitive cruelty in modern societies during the past few centuries is essentially the consequence of the rise of intelligence and cognitive operations of the populations, a cognitive growth implying mental, social and moral dimensions. Thus, both the ubiquity of these forms of primitive cruelty across all pre-modern societies and their abolishment since the age of enlightenment and early modernization must be referred to basic structures of psychic-cognitive development. This is the reason why mod-

---

2 Oesterdiekhoff, Georg W.: *Kulturelle Bedingungen kognitiver Entwicklung: Der strukturgenetische Ansatz in der Soziologie,* Frankfurt/Main 1997; Oesterdiekhoff, Georg W.: *Zivilisation und Strukturgenese: Norbert Elias und Jean Piaget im Vergleich,* Frankfurt/Main 2000; Oesterdiekhoff, Georg W.: *Archaische Kultur und moderne Zivilisation,* Hamburg/Münster/London 2006; Oesterdiekhoff, Georg W.: *Kulturelle Evolution des Geistes: Die historische Wechselwirkung von Psyche und Gesellschaft,* Hamburg/Münster/London 2006.

ern mankind looks upon the antique Roman games with awe while the old Romans were horrified by cannibalistic cultures. Developmental psychology can demonstrate that this historical development of moral sentiment and sensibility is rooted in the ontogenetic path of cognitive development.

2. THEORETICAL APPROACHES

2.1 Norbert Elias' Civilization Theory

Among the classical sociological, ethnological and psychological approaches, Norbert Elias' Civilization Theory (1976), known as the last classical sociologist, is the only one to have the necessary equipment to explain the essential structures of the history of violence and cruelty in a sufficient and encompassing way. Civilization Theory consists of an assumption of a dialectical relationship between psycho- and sociogenesis, between psycho-cognitive and institutional structures. Elias describes the lower, elementally childlike level of the development of personality, psyche, cognition, emotion, and behaviour as the usual and normal traits of adult humans in pre-modern societies. Thus, Civilization Theory is based on concepts stemming from developmental psychology, outlined in the frame of Freudian concepts of drives and personality. Personality and behaviour both of children of all societies and adults of pre-modern societies are, compared to modern adults, more dominated by drives (›Id‹), while the ›Ego‹ is less differentiated and the ›Super-Ego‹ is more weakly developed. Thresholds of shame and embarrassment are less developed, so that pre-modern humans live and act more directly, spontaneously, emotionally, at lower levels of considering consequences and circumstances. The ability for thinking in logical and abstract ways is not as strongly developed as it is among modern, educated persons.[3]

It is useful to apply the concepts of Civilization Theory to the explanation of both pre-modern practices of cruelty, sadistic punishment law systems, arena combats and chases, and its abolishment for the

3 Elias, Norbert: *Über den Prozess der Zivilisation*, 2 vols., vol. 1, Frankfurt/Main 1976, pp. 312–454. (*The Civilizing Process*, Williston, Vermont 1994).

past 250 years. The extent of naïvety, recklessness, and shamelessness characterizing the behaviour of both the spectators in the arena and the arena games in general can only be explained by considering that the personality structures of pre-modern populations were shaped by more simple and elemental psychic stages. Elias' thesis, referring to the psychic maturation of European mankind at the eve of the modern world, delivers a convincing explanation for the abolishment and disappearance of these brutal forms of entertainment and punishment.

2.2 Structure-Genetic Sociology as Successor of Civilization Theory

Developmental psychology has been showing for more than 100 years that the development from suckling to adult is a continuous process characterized by the steady maturation of personality, thinking, interests, morals, and abilities. This ontogenetic development is basically a biologically rooted process, although it is affected by social influences which shape the content of the ontogenetic structures only a little but influence the timetable of passing the stages and the summit of the final stage of maturation adults can attain. The proof of this fact is immediately evident by considering that across all cultures babies cannot speak, children are not able to think in formal-operational ways, and only adolescents can acquire the capacity of constructing theories.

Jean Piaget delivered the biggest and most influential contribution to the foundations of developmental psychology. It is useful to interpret his approach not as one which is opposite to other theories and ideas but as an encompassing work that better expresses the common insights and general assumptions of developmental psychology. According to his stage theory, the *sensory-motor* stage of the suckling is succeeded by the *pre-operational* stage of the child where thinking processes and representations are established. Only in the third stage of *concrete operations* can the logic of actions be formed when visually given objects can be logically structured and co-ordinated. After the tenth year of age thinking attains the fourth stage of *formal operations* that implies the thinking processes gaining experimental, hypothetical-deductive, abstract-logical and systemic capacities.

These various cognitive structures are the key for the understanding of the development of personality, emotion, thinking, world-view, morals, and behaviour. At every higher stage the human being acquires new possibilities of thinking and behaviour and surpasses primitive forms of thinking and behaviour.[4]

Piagetian theory has been applied and tested across pre-modern societies for more than 70 years. More than 1000 enquiries in more than 100 cultures have been carried out in this time span. All humans across all cultures develop the characteristics of sensory-motor and pre-operational stages in the same way. But the concrete operational stage is not developed by all adults in pre-modern cultures – only by varying percentages, and if it is developed, then not in all areas of experience but only in several areas, depending on specific interests prevailing in certain cultures and depending on individual capacities and experiences. Formal-operational thinking is either not at all or only little and sparsely developed among adults of pre-modern societies. While the development of pre-modern adults stops at an earlier level, modern adults attain comparatively higher levels of cognition. Pre-modern adults differ from children by their major life experience but not by their cognitive, qualitative structures.

Cross-Cultural Psychology found out that cultural factors account for these divergent development paths. Divergent cultural *chances* and *forces* cause the different final stages adults can attain. Primary and secondary socialisation practices, especially the quality and amount of school education, are the relevant factors which compel or constrain the final stages of adults, a fact that is valid across all races, nations, and cultures.[5]

---

4 Piaget, Jean/Inhelder, Bärbel: *Psychologie des Kindes*, Frankfurt/Main 1980 (*The Psychology of the Child*, New York 1969); Piaget, Jean: *Psychologie der Intelligenz*, Stuttgart 1984 (*Psychology of Intelligence*, Totowa, New Jersey 1968); Werner, Heinz: *Einführung in die Entwicklungspsychologie*, Leipzig 1959 (*The Comparative Psychology of Mental Development*, New York 1964).

5 Lurija, Alexander: *Die historische Bedingtheit individueller Erkenntnisprozesse*, Weinheim 1986 (*Cognitive Development*, Harvard, Mass. 1982); Hallpike, Christopher: *The Evolution of Moral Understanding*, Alton, England 2004; Dasen, Pierre/Berry, John W. (Eds.): *Culture and Cognition: Readings in Cross-Cultural Psychology*, London 2004; Dasen, Pierre (Ed.): *Piagetian Psychology: Cross-Cultural Contributions*, New York 1977; Mogdil, Celia/Mogdil, Sohan: *Piagetian Research*, vols. 1–8, London 1976; Freitag, Barbara: *Der Aufbau kindlicher Bewusstseinsstrukturen*

If illiterate humans of contemporary developmental regions (village residents, socially weak city dwellers) do not attain the formal operational stage, then it is quite clear that the mental development of humans from pre-modern cultures 200, 2000 or 20000 years ago was tied to pre-formal levels, too. Only modern educational and cultural ideas and institutions provided the incentive to force the psychic-cognitive development above the pre-formal level, while humans of pre-modern cultures were normally characterized by lower levels of cognition.[6]

Against these facts, developmental psychology gains the status of the most fundamental Historical Psychology, respectively Historical Anthropology. Developmental psychology provides the essential key for the understanding of personality, psyche, thinking and behaviour of pre-modern (and modern) humans. Structure-Genetic Sociology has given evidence to the fact that the reconstruction of the history of science, religion, law, customs, morals, and behaviour can be worked out on the basis of Piagetian stage theory.[7]

This Piagetian result is confirmed by the other branch of intelligence research, the psychometric approach. Thousands of empirical studies have proven that pre-modern populations across all races and nations develop IQ scores between 50 and 75, compared to British IQ scores of today (100). For more than 120 years scores have been rising, especially in industrialized countries, but more and more in devel-

---

im gesellschaftlichen Kontext, Munich 1983; Poortinga, Ype (Ed.): *Basis Problems in Cross-Cultural Psychology*, Amsterdam 1977; Schoefthaler, Traugott/Goldschmidt, Dietrich (Eds.): *Soziale Struktur und Vernunft*, Frankfurt/Main 1984; Oesterdiekhoff: »Kulturelle Bedingungen kognitiver Entwicklung«; Oesterdiekhoff: »Zivilisation und Strukturgenese«; Oesterdiekhoff: »Archaische Kultur und moderne Zivilisation«; Oesterdiekhoff: »Kulturelle Evolution des Geistes«.

6 Oesterdiekhoff: »Kulturelle Bedingungen kognitiver Entwicklung«; idem: »Zivilisation und Strukturgenese«; idem: »Kulturelle Evolution des Geistes«; Hallpike, Christopher: *Grundlagen primitiven Denkens*, Munich 1994 (= Foundations of Primitive Thought, Oxford 1978); Lurija: »Die historische Bedingtheit individueller Erkenntnisprozesse«.

7 Oesterdiekhoff: »Kulturelle Bedingungen kognitiver Entwicklung«; idem »Zivilisation und Strukturgenese«; idem: »Kulturelle Evolution des Geistes«; idem: »Archaische Kultur und moderne Zivilisation«.

oping countries, too. The rise of intelligence is called the »Flynn effect« and corresponds to the rise of the abovementioned cognitive operations. Both branches of intelligence research come out with the same empirical observations and theoretical conclusions.[8]

2.3 The Contribution of Lawrence Kohlberg's Developmental Psychology of Morals

Cognitive maturation manifests through different steps of moral thinking and behaviour. Jean Piaget (1973) called the lower stages of moral thinking moral realism, while the higher stages, called the autonomous morals, unfold not before early adolescence. Piaget himself realized that the moral structures of children correspond to the morals of premodern societies. The »objective responsibility« of children is similar to the »Erfolgshaftung« of ancient law, »immanent justice« fits the ordeals, and the general understanding of law matches the idea of »ordo« (the good, old law). The transformation of sadistic to humane punishment law and further law developments can be reduced and referred to ontogenetic developmental concepts.[9]

Lawrence Kohlberg's theory of moral development is based on the Piagetian approach. Kohlberg was able to show that the developmental

---

8 Bayley, N.: »On the Growth of Intelligence«, in: American Journal of Psychology 10 (1955), pp. 808–815; Raven, J./Raven, J.C./Court, J. H.: *Manual for Raven's Progressive Matrices and Vocabulary Scales*, Oxford 1993; Flynn, James R.: »Massive IQ-Gains in 14 Nations: What IQ-Tests Really Measure«, in: Psychological Bulletin 101.2 (1987), pp. 171–191; Neisser, Ulric (Ed.): *The Rising Curve: Long-Term Gains in IQ and Related Measures*, Washington 1998; Irvine, S./Berry, John W. (Eds.): *Human Abilities in Cultural Context*, two vols., Cambridge 1988; Oesterdiekhoff: »Kulturelle Evolution des Geistes«.

9 Piaget, Jean: *Das moralische Urteil beim Kinde*, Frankfurt/Main 1973 (*The Moral Judgment of the Child*, Harmondsworth 1977); Oesterdiekhoff: »Kulturelle Evolution des Geistes«, pp. 328–426; Hallpike: »The Evolution of Moral Understanding«; Raddings, Christopher: »Evolution of Medieval Mentalities«, in: American Historical Review 83 (1978), 577–597.

stages of moral judgment and acting depend on the different levels of general logical structures according to the theory of Piaget.[10]

Kohlberg found six stages of moral development, classifiable in three phases: the pre-conventional (stages 1, 2), the conventional (3, 4) and the post-conventional phase (5, 6). The pre-conventional phase is characterized by a naïve egoism which can only be limited by strong counter-actors. Stage 3 describes a moral behaviour stemming from the concern to please familiar persons (»house-wife morals«). Stage 4 expresses a moral understanding that identifies moral behaviour with the obeying of laws and rules, norms and conventions. The post-conventional phase contains general and abstract moral principles that are more important and dominating than public conventions (phase 2) or egoistic interests (phase 1).[11]

The pre-conventional phase is identical with the moral thinking of all children up to their tenth year of age and corresponds to thinking processes below the level of formal operations. The two succeeding phases correspond to different levels within the stage of formal operations.[12] Around 80% of all persons of 24 years of age or older in industrial societies are distributed at stages 3, 4, and 5. 20% of them achieve stage 5, only a few of them 6. This result refers to all populations of industrial or industrializing societies around the globe.[13]

All enquiries among populations in pre-modern and pre-industrialized cultures have proven that adults there cannot surpass stage 3 but are distributed at stages 1, 2, and 3, whereby only the responsible lead-

---

10 Kohlberg, Lawrence: *Die Psychologie der Moralentwicklung*, Frankfurt/Main 1996 (*The Psychology of Moral Development*, New York 1993), pp. 123ff, 217ff.; Selman, Robert: *Entwicklung des sozialen Verstehens*, Frankfurt/Main 1984 (*The Growth of Personal Understanding*, San Diego 1980); Snarey, J. R.: *Cross-Cultural Universality of Social-Moral Development: A Critical Review of Kohlbergian Research*, in: *Psychological Bulletin* 97 (1985), pp. 202–232.

11 Kohlberg: »Die Psychologie der Moralentwicklung«, pp. 126–132; Kohlberg, Lawrence/Turiel, Elliot: »Moralische Entwicklung und Erziehung«, in: Portele, Gerhard (Ed.): *Sozialisation und Moral*, Weinheim 1978, pp. 13–80.

12 Kohlberg: »Die Psychologie der Moralentwicklung«, pp. 124f.

13 Kohlberg: »Die Psychologie der Moralentwicklung«, pp. 34,98,106; Kohlberg/Turiel: »Moralische Entwicklung und Erziehung«, p. 45.

ers and chiefs attain stage 3[14] offer an overview of these cross-cultural researches in remote societies. »Moral judgment states 4, 5 and 6 are not generally found in interviews with traditional adults who live in small scale societies such as isolated tribal communities [...] rather only stages 1 to 3 seem to dominate among such groups of people.«[15]

According to this always replicated fact one must draw the clear conclusion that the moral psychology of children is identical with the general moral history of mankind. As late as the beginning of modern society, major parts of the population have started to develop stage 4, while the moral thinking of more than 90% of humans of pre-industrial societies were tied to stages 1 and 2. This fact implies that the history of law, customs, interactions and morals can be decoded only by the knowledge of the structures of pre-conventional thinking.

I want to present the moral concept »value of life« in order to show the ways in which humans at different moral stages use to judge and act. Kohlberg and his co-workers presented the following story in innumerable enquiries carried out in different cultures: A woman is suffering from cancer. A pharmacist has developed a medicine that could save the woman's life. He invested 200 USD to develop the medicine

---

14 Kohlberg/Turiel: »Moralische Entwicklung und Erziehung«, p. 46; Tietjen, A./Walker L. J.: »Moral Reasoning and Leadership among Men in a Papua New-Guinea Society«, in: Developmental Psychology 21.6 (1985), pp. 982–992; Edwards, Carol P.: *The Effect of Experience on Moral Developments: Results from Kenya*, Harvard University 1974 (unpublished dissertation); Edwards, Carol P.: »Societal Complexity and Moral Development«, in: Ethos 3 (1975), pp. 505–527; Kohlberg: »Die Psychologie der Moralentwicklung«, p. 58; Nisan, M./Kohlberg, L.: »Universality and Variation in Moral Judgement: A Longitudinal and Cross-Sectional Study in Turkey«, in: Child Development 53 (1982), pp. 865–876; Gorsuch, R. J./Barnes, M. L.: »Stages of Ethical Reasoning and Moral Norms of Carib Youths«, in: Journal of Cross-Cultural Psychology 4 (1973), pp. 283–301; Oesterdiekhoff: »Kulturelle Evolution des Geistes, pp. 302–306«; Snarey: »Cross-Cultural Universality of Social-Moral Development«, pp. 202–232; Hallpike: »The Evolution of Moral Understanding«, pp. 202–232.

15 Edwards, Carol P.: »The Comparative Study of the Development of Moral Judgment and Reasoning«, in: Wagner, D. A./Stevenson, H. W. (Eds.): *Handbook of Cross-Cultural Human Development*, San Francisco 1981, pp. 268.

and now demands 2000 USD from the sick woman's husband. The husband cannot pay this amount and has the choice between seeing his wife dying or stealing the medicine. Actually he steals the medicine. Was this theft justified, and if it was, why?

The pre-conventional and conventional answers very often imply that the husband should only save the woman´s life if he loves her and even if he loves her, as many people say, obedience to the laws which forbid theft is more obliging and justifiably prevents the husband from stealing. Here a pre-conventional answer that is typical for all children from industrialized countries and for adults of pre-modern societies: Jimmy, 10 years old, US-city:

»It depends on how much he loves his woman. If he loves her, than he should steal. – Question: And if he does not love her? – Answer: If he wants that she dies then he should not save her life, this is my personal opinion. – Question: Would it be right to steal? – Answer: It would be right because he knows that his wife has to die if he does not steal the medicine. – Question: Has the pharmacist the right to claim so much if no law forbids this high claim? – Answer: Yes, it is his medicine; consider his investments into its development. – Question: Should the judge convict the husband? – Answer: He should imprison him for the theft and the pharmacist too, because he has claimed so much.«

Kohlberg[16] figured out numbers typical for industrial populations:

Table 1:

stage	percentage of those who support the theft and say it is justified	the judge should not sentence the husband for imprisonment
1/2	42	33
2	64	12
2/3	67	52
3	62	46
3/4	74	40
4	63	42
4/5	90	100

16 Kohlberg: »Die Psychologie der Moralentwicklung«, p. 416.

Not before stage 4 the clear acknowledgment breaks through that the judge should not convict the theft and that this theft is an obligation for everybody to save the wife. But even a large proportion of those who realize that it is right to save the woman's life do not feel obliged to do so. Helkama[17], like some others, figured out that only 17% of those who were at stage 3 believed that the husband would be responsible for the death of the woman if he refused to steal. The corresponding rates at stage 4 are 28% and at stage 5 53%. The other group of persons, however, would not feel guilty if they did not intervene by stealing, although appreciating the general idea of doing so. The higher the stage of moral judgment, the higher the probability of moral practice; with the rising insight into the right the obligation to put the right into practice is climbing at the same rate.[18]

The readiness to torture humans and the achieved level of mental development are empirically correlated. The famous Milgram experiment[19] tested the readiness of humans to torture other humans. The tested persons should mediate electric shocks to persons who gave wrong answers. The tested persons were asked to increase stepwise the electric shocks, even up to the deadly dose of 450 volts, although the victims feigned their pain by screaming and crying. 65% of the tested persons »killed« their victims when they were not in the same room. The »killing rate« sunk to 40% when the victim was in the same room, and to 30% when the victim had body contact with the tested person. But 75% of those who attain the post-conventional phase of moral judgment refused to give electric shocks, compared to only 13% of those persons who are in the pre-conventional and conventional moral phases.[20] This fact implies that humans at the lower stages are in most

17 Helkama, K.: *The Development of the Attribution of Responsibility: A Critical Survey of Empirical Research and a Theoretical Outline*, Helsinki 1979.

18 McNamee, S.: »Moral Behaviour, Moral Development, and Motivation«, in: Journal of Moral Education 7 (1977), pp. 27–31; Kohlberg: »Die Psychologie der Moralentwicklung«, pp. 285, 447; Piaget: »Das moralische Urteil beim Kinde«.

19 Milgram, Stanley: *Das Milgram-Experiment. Zur Gehorsamsbereitschaft gegenüber Autorität*, Reinbek 1997 (transl. of *Obedience to Authority*, New York 1975).

20 Kohlberg: »Die Psychologie der Moralentwicklung«, pp. 16, 286.

cases always ready to torture and kill other persons when authorities ask them, while the rate of refusals climbs with the reached stage of cognitive and moral judgment. The rise of the higher stages 4, 5, and 6 is a historical process lasting for the last 100–200 years as a consequence of modernization, steadily penetrating the ideas of humans more and more during the past decades and generations. This fact implies that the readiness for sadistic tortures was greater in pre-modern societies than in modern ones; and this readiness will be weakened continuously when the post-conventional stage will further spread and increase due to rising levels of culture and education.

2.4 Developmental Psychology of Morals as the Theory of the Moral History of Mankind

These results of cross-cultural psychology of morals must be put into the context of »Structure-Genetic Sociology« which demonstrated the prevalence of pre-formal structures of cognition not only for traditional concepts of morals but also for all other topics, for social, logical and physical issues. By using the developmental psychology of morals to explain the historical phenomena of morals, for example to explain pre-modern violence practices such as gladiator fights, sadistic punishment law, cruelty practices etc., it is always necessary to consider that pre-conventional moral thinking does not alone account for pre-modern violence practices, but rather it is always in coherence with all other pre-formal psychic-cognitive phenomena that constitute the primitive psyche.[21]

Pre-formal thinking is defined by cognitive egocentrism, comparative weakness and narrowness of mind, attention and apperception. The pre-formal mind regularly concentrates, depending on the amount of difficulty of the task that is to be processed, on one central aspect of the phenomenon and fails with co-ordinating and considering several aspects that constitute a phenomenon. To give a famous example: just like all little children, a large number of pre-modern adults believes that the pouring of water from one wide glass to a tall and narrow glass magically raises the amount of water, as hundreds of cross-cultural experiments have astonishingly found out in all pre-modern cultures around the globe. This experiment controls the ability to co-ordinate

21 Oesterdiekhoff: »Zivilisation und Strukturgenese«, pp. 285–314.

the logical structures of objects given to the senses; therefore it is an experiment to identify the existence of concrete operations. This non-preservation of dimensions and aspects is found across all physical, logical, social, and moral dimensions of experience. This failure is also detected in the difficulty of understanding perspectives or the internal states of other persons etc.[22]

This cognitive egocentrism is an essential basis for ancient cruelty practices such as gladiator fights or sadistic punishment customs. The spectators identify with the victorious killers, not with their dying victims. They feel strong and powerful by identifying with the killers and victors. The spectators live out an egocentric feeling of power and combat when the victors, with whom they identify, bring their victims to their knees. The victorious manslaughter reveals feelings of pleasure; empathy for the victims is totally absent. It brings pleasure, as all ancient reports show, to observe how the tortures can be extended. How many times does the leopard need to kill and eat the human? Where can the girl find a place to delay the time when the lion will see and attack her? Whoever loves to see such things, like ancient people, is characterized by lower levels of psychic development, lower levels of taking over perspectives, empathy, sympathy, moral attitudes. Ancient man concentrates on his own feelings of power by identifying with the victor, and neglects the perspective of the victim. He is unable to take over all perspectives in a sufficient way, just as he is unable to preserve masses, volumes, lengths etc., due to his pre-formal inability to consider several dimensions at the same time. He is obsessed by his cruel passions to an extent which suppresses all feelings of sympathy and empathy. This explains the naïvety, lack of inhibition, and shamelessness of ancient spectators, as it is reported in historical and ethnographic sources (see the reports below).

The rise of the »higher psychic functions« (Vygotski, Lurija, Leontjew) in modernity, of formal operations (Piaget), accounts for the fact that modern populations cannot enjoy such scenes, why they deny

22 Hallpike: »Grundlagen primitiven Denkens«; Poortinga: »Basis Problems in Cross-Cultural Psychology«; Dasen: »Piagetian Psychology; Dasen/Berry: »Culture and Cognition«; Schoefthaler/Goldschmidt: »Soziale Struktur und Vernunft; Oesterdiekhoff: »Kulturelle Bedingungen kognitiver Entwicklung«; idem: »Zivilisation und Strukturgenese«; idem: »Kulturelle Evolution des Geistes«.

them completely and why such cruelty practices have vanished in the past centuries. Formal operations raise the ability levels of taking over perspectives, empathy, sympathy, sensibility, moral judgment, the tendency not to torture but to support other people, to engage in human affairs etc.,[23] to an extent that makes it impossible to tolerate sadistic punishment practices and executions, cruel chases and gladiator fights, carried out in the context of arena and public festivities.[24] Formal-operationally structured modern people cannot avoid taking over the perspective of the victims immediately and sufficiently, and that is why these arena spectacles would be completely denied and prevented if anybody were to try to re-establish them.

The thousands of cross-cultural experiments which have given evidence for the pre-operational or pre-formal ways of thinking of pre-modern populations, for example the non-preservation of volumes or social perspectives, must be connected to the social and moral deficits that constitute and characterize the primitive behaviour of ancient spectators. The abovementioned pre-conventional answers referring to the case of the sick woman must be put into this context, too. In the context of the pre-conventional mind, in the context of the primitive psyche, the life of a person has no absolute value in itself but can be computed and qualified to material interests and needs. The pre-conventional husband can easily accept the death of his wife if he does not love her or if he wants to avoid conviction. If he is not strongly emotionally or materially interested in the life of his wife he feels not at all obliged to help her. This primitive attitude is well-known in ethnographic and historical reports, too.[25] As humans at the lower stages of mental and moral development, according to the Milgram-experi-

23 Selman: »Entwicklung des sozialen Verstehens«; Kohlberg: »Die Psychologie der Moralentwicklung«; Snarey: »Cross-Cultural Universality«; Hallpike: »The Evolution of Moral Understanding«.

24 Oesterdiekhoff: »Zivilisation und Strukturgenese«; idem: »Archaische Kultur und moderne Zivilisation«.

25 Hallpike: »The Evolution of Moral Understanding«; pp. 209, 240; Staewen, Christoph: *Kulturelle und psychologische Bedingungen der Zusammenarbeit mit Afrikanern*, Munich 1991, p. 212; Staewen, Christoph/ Schoenberg, Fritz: *Kulturwandel und Angstentwicklung bei den Yorubas Westafrikas*, Munich 1970, pp. 301,304,367; Schweitzer, Albert: *Selbstzeugnisse*, Stuttgart 1960.

ment interpreted in the light of developmental psychology, see no problems in killing other persons with electric shocks, so too could the populations of pre-modern societies observe and enjoy, without shame and embarrassment but with lust and pleasure, how women and children were slaughtered, burnt or voraciously eaten by beasts.

The *lack of moral inhibitions* is one dimension of cognitive deficits and psychic primitiveness underlying these phenomena. But the archaic violence phenomena cannot not only be explained in terms of missing inhibitions but also by the *prevalence of special needs* that are nowadays lowered in the subconscious but are no longer identifiable as conscious wishes. The humans of today would not ecstatically cheer and scream with pleasure when victims were burnt, slaughtered or eaten, as ancient people used to do; thus it is quite clear that aggressive-sadistic drive tendencies[26] are more restricted and limited in the formal-operational psyche and personality than they were in the ancient psyche. Only mentally disordered individuals of today would love such scenes; in antiquity, however, emperor, senators and the people enjoyed these brutal events. Sadistic drive tendencies can overwhelm and dominate the primitive psyche more easily than the psyche characterized by the »higher psychic functions«. The civilized psyche, according to N. Elias (1976), levers the thresholds of aggressive acts and is more successful in suppressing sadistic impulses. That is the reason for the decline of these sadistic violence practices over the course of the past centuries.

3. Historical and Ethnographic Data on Violence and Cruelty

3.1 The Ubiquity of Certain Sadistic Practices in Pre-modern Societies

The core of the ancient arena games consisted of gladiator fights, sadistic executions of delinquents, chases with animals and sea battles. The Roman games put these sadistic elements in a splendid context of festivities and ceremonies. The arenas were visited by tens of thou-

26 Eibl-Eibesfeldt, Irenaeus: *Der vorprogrammierte Mensch: Das Ererbte als bestimmender Faktor im menschlichen Verhalten*, Vienna 1973.

sands of visitors, among them the state elite of the emperor, senators, and knights, so that the Roman games got the status of a unique trait of the Roman culture. But the uniqueness of this trait can only relate to the tremendous expense and the enormous frame, not the individual elements that constitute the games. With the exception of the sea battles (*naumachiae*), all the other three elements of the Roman games are found world-wide, more or less in all pre-modern societies, but not at all in modern ones. The ubiquity of these cruel practices in all pre-modern societies hints at the fact that they must be deduced from the universality of the pre-formal, primitive psyche, while the abolishment of these practices in the modern world during the past centuries has been caused by the rise of the »higher psychic functions«, a rise that is proven by the empirical facts of cross-cultural psychology.

This universality of these three forms of violence practice can be shown with a short overview.

The fighting of gladiators corresponds to the fight between men in front of the tribe, village or people that is found in every pre-modern society. An adult man in a pre-modern society must face such combats, either against neighbours or against strangers, perhaps once or several times in his lifetime. Men, women, children living among Native Americans, in a tribal society in Australia, in a state society in Africa or in medieval Europe are used to watching such dangerous or deadly combats between hostile men. In tribal societies, the death rates caused by manslaughter within the group are similar to those caused by intertribal fights. About one third of the humans living in pre-modern societies over the past thousands of years died in such violence.[27]

---

27 Keegan, John: *Die Kultur des Krieges*, Reinbek 1996 (transl. of *A History of Warfare,* New York 1993); Keeley, Lawrence H.: *War Before Civilization*, Oxford 1996; Hallpike: »The Evolution of Moral Understanding«; Oesterdiekhoff: »Zivilisation und Strukturgenese«, pp. 258–314; Lafiteau, Joseph-Francois: *Die Sitten der amerikanischen Wilden im Verhältnis zu den Sitten der Frühzeit*, Weinheim 1987. (Transl. of *Les moeurs des savages ameriquaines comparée aux premiers temps*, Paris 1724); *Post, Albert Hermann: Bausteine für eine allgemeine Rechtswissenschaft auf vergleichend-ethnologischer Grundlage*, Oldenburg 1880.

Duel culture stems from the stone ages, is found in every pre-modern society, and stops as late as in the middle of modernization.[28] Duels were a part of popular culture, following folkloristic traditions and norms. Knight tournaments consist of both knights' duels and combat groups of horsemen, often including deadly outcomes, carried out in front of the elite and people and thereby comparable to the Roman games.[29] All around the world, duels were parts of juridical ordeals.[30] Against this background the gladiator fights in the Roman Empire are easier to understand. Brutal duels were a normal trait in Roman culture, so its people did not have to get accustomed to these phenomena. Celtic, Greek or Egyptian people who visited the Colosseum or another amphitheatre were not surprised by such combats because they probably had known such things since their childhood.

The second part of arena games, the sadistic execution of delinquents, is not only typical for Roman culture but for all pre-modern cultures. Roman society used, among other venues, the arena games in particular for the execution of delinquents. Executions in pre-modern societies are usually held in front of the people to entertain them in the context of a festival. The people enjoyed the execution of delinquents, carried out on marketplaces or in arenas, as an amusing ceremony and as an entertaining event.

»First of all the judgment on the ancient punishment law is necessary: It can only be named as deeply inhumane. Humans were torn to pieces and slaughtered like by butchers, their remainders were nailed to gallows, burnt or boiled; they were torn by beasts or killed by gluing pliers. Their bones were destroyed [...] How could people watch, with pleasant excitement in the context of a festival, how humans were burnt or hung half-coaled?«[31]

---

28 Oesterdiekhoff: »Zivilisation und Strukturgenese«, pp. 296–307; Elias: »Über den Prozess der Zivilisation«; Hallpike: »The Evolution of Moral Understanding«, pp. 187–218.

29 Bumke, Joachim: *Höfische Kultur,* two vols., Munich 1986, vol. 1, pp. 342–378.

30 Schild, Wolfgang: *Alte Gerichtsbarkeit*, Munich 1980; Post: »Bausteine für eine allgemeine Rechtswissenschaft«; Seagle, William: *Weltgeschichte des Rechts*, Berlin 1967 (transl. of *The History of Law*, New York: Tudor Publishing 1946).

31 Schild: »Alte Gerichtsbarkeit«, p. 93 (transl. by Georg W. Oesterdiekhoff).

These medieval practices, including the full participation of the entire people, are found in all pre-modern societies, among Native Americans, Australian Aborigines, in ancient China and India, Black Africa and ancient Europe as a continuous and permanent phenomenon.[32] Present-day reports on lynch-mob justice in developmental regions can reveal the mental background of these practices:

> »A boy is lying on his back, fixed by a crowd, screaming in horror [...] An old, smiling man is ready to cut the boy's hand with a single stroke [...] All the people were laughing and smiling. And I asked myself what happens in the brains of these people? How can a human stand by and laugh facing such a torture? How can a human enjoy the torture of a small boy? [...] And this was Nairobi, one of the most modern capitals in Black-Africa«.[33]

This report is not exotic but typical of the usual behaviour of people in pre-modern social structures when practising self-justice. This primitive and sadistic cruelty underlies both the observation and practice of lynch-mob justice, execution and punishment practices, gladiator fights and chases in arenas. This kind of ethnographic report illuminates the public atmosphere and the naïve, brutal and sadistic excitement ancient people enjoyed in arenas when humans were slaughtered and murdered. A pre-formally structured mind, a stone-hearted, narrow-minded and egocentric psyche account for this mentality which underlies ancient cruelty practices.

Not only are deadly combat between gladiators and the execution of delinquents, found as typical phenomena in pre-modern societies,

---

32 van Dülmen, Richard: *Theater des Schreckens*, Munich 1988, pp. 163, 172; Wrede, Richard: *Die Körperstrafen: Von der Urzeit bis ins 20. Jahrhundert*, Wiesbaden 2004; Oesterdiekhoff: »Zivilisation und Strukturgenese«, pp. 307ff.; Staewen/Schoenberg: »Kulturwandel und Angstentwicklung«, p. 285; Post: »Bausteine für eine allgemeine Rechtswissenschaft«; Seagle: »Weltgeschichte des Rechts«; Schild: »Alte Gerichtsbarkeit«; Lafiteau: »Die Sitten der amerikanischen Wilden«, pp. 400–410; Kiefer, Otto: *Kulturgeschichte Roms*, Berlin 1933, pp. 77–95; Huizinga, Johann: *Herbst des Mittelalters*, Stuttgart 1975, p. 25.

33 Richburg, Keith B.: *Jenseits von Amerika: Eine Konfrontation mit Afrika, dem Land meiner Vorfahren*, Berlin 1999, p. 288 (transl. by Georg W. Oesterdiekhoff) (*Out of America*, New York 1997).

but also chases with beasts, the third element of the Roman games. Chases with beasts which fought against other beasts or against humans are found in ancient China, ancient and medieval Europe, and other parts of the world. Fights between cocks or dogs are a beloved leisure time practice in all three developed continents of today. Fights between men and bulls are known in modern Spain until today. A low level of animal protection and rough conduct with pets and cattle are related to all backward societies. Animal protection movements and the concern for their health and life have been rising since modernity. Both the brutal treatment of animals in the arenas and elsewhere in pre-modern societies and the rise of a more caring conduct must be referred to the explicated trends of cognitive development of mankind.[34]

The lower psychic-cognitive development of populations in pre-modern societies accounts for the ubiquity of sadistic practices underlying the culture of deadly combats, sadistic torture and execution, the brutal treatment of animals and related phenomena in pre-modern societies. The rise of »higher psychic functions« is the central cause for the abolishment of these brutal phenomena and for the rise of the humane punishment system and animal protection in modernizing countries in the past 200 years.

3.2 The Arena Games in the Roman Empire

Chases with animals and ritual fights are documented in Italy at least since the sixth century B. C. The building of amphitheatres spread across the whole empire from the year 80 B. C. Arena fights, also carried out in more modest contexts, took place both in small towns and major cities. The arena games became the most exciting part of Roman leisure time activities; all people enjoyed these festivities as most entertaining and fascinating for a period of 700 years throughout the whole existence of the empire. Augustus allowed 66 days per year for the games in Rome, Marcus Aurelius 135, and the number climbed to more than 175 days in the fourth century. Special games and private

---

34 Schweitzer: »Selbstzeugnisse«, pp. 82, 339; Oesterdiekhoff: »Zivilisation und Strukturgenese«, p. 299; Friedländer, Ludwig: *Sittengeschichte Roms*, Cologne 1975, pp. 474, 487, 493, 512 (*Roman Life and Manners*, New York 1965).

activities must be added to these numbers. In the games organized by Augustus during his government lasting 41 years, 10000 men fought and 3500 animals were killed.[35] In Trajan's games, 10000 men fought and 11000 animals were slaughtered in the one year, 107 A. C.[36] 700000 people were murdered in the Colosseum alone over the course of about 400 years. Millions of people and millions of animals were killed in the arenas across the whole empire over the course of 700 years.

Chases with animals (*venationes*) were carried out in a splendid, excellent and huge context. Exotic beasts from all parts of the known world were imported and slaughtered. The people enjoyed watching how bulls and lions, elephants and rhinoceroses, leopards and wolves, fought and tore each other to pieces. Sometimes some hundred soldiers, on horses or not, fought against 300 lions or 400 bears. Some fighters (*venatores*) fought alone or in small groups against a selection of beasts. *Ad bestias* was the standard conviction for delinquents who did not belong to the state elite of senators, state officials, and soldiers. The elite (*honestiores*) had the privilege to get executed by the sword. Private persons (*humiliores*) who had betrayed, stolen, raped, or seduced, people not always charged with severe crimes but more often with common or light crimes, had to face being thrown in the arenas in order to be torn and eaten by the beasts.[37] The people enjoyed seeing how humans hanging on a cross were torn and eaten by beasts or how naked girls and women, tied to a stake, were chopped to pieces. Pictures show how naked women, tied and sitting on bulls, were torn down from the bull's necks and killed by jumping leopards.[38]

The delinquents, tied to stake, could be lucky if they were quickly killed by a single stroke or bite of a beast. Sometimes they had to en-

35 Augustus: *Res gestae*, ed. Marion Giebel, Stuttgart 2004, pp. 26–28.

36 Friedländer: »Sittengeschichte Roms«, p. 488f.; Grant: »Die Gladiatoren«, p. 31.

37 Wiedemann, Thomas: *Kaiser und Gladiatoren: Die Macht der Spiele im antiken Rom*, Darmstadt 2001, p. 86 (*Emperors and Gladiators*, Florence 1995).

38 Auguet, Roland: *Cruelty and Civilization: The Roman Games*, New York 1994, p. 107; Baker, Alan: *Gladiatoren: Kampfspiele auf Leben und Tod*. Hamburg 2004, pp. 125–134 (*The Gladiator*, London 2000); Friedländer: »Sittengeschichte Roms«, pp. 488ff.

dure a long torture because the beast began its work at their extremities or lost interest for a while.[39]

Alternatively, delinquents had to kill each other without rules and without chances for survival. Often delinquents were divided into two groups who had to kill each other until the arena was filled with hundreds of corpses. The spectacle was not finished before the last delinquent, man or woman, had died. They were forced by fire and sword to start such fights and had no chance of escape. Such forms of execution of delinquents were most loved by the spectators and were regular parts of the games, carried out especially in the midday breaks.[40]

The gladiators were educated fighters usually belonging to a specific school and in the hands of editors. About 60% of the gladiators were prisoners of war or slaves, 40% were waged fighters or daring men. But from the end of the first century the majority of gladiators were not slaves but free persons.[41] Even senators, knights, emperors and many women fought in the arena. Nero, Titus, Hadrian, Caligula, Commodus and other emperors loved to fight in the arena in front of 50,000 people; Commodus fought 1,000 times in the arena.[42] Most of the gladiators were killed after several fights, within the first months or years of their career, but some of them could survive and were released after a few years of fighting.[43]

The poet Martial praised Domitian (81–96 A. C.), who organized fights between women and dwarfs, a spectacle most beloved by the masses. He understood such fights as a great pleasure, as »fun for the

---

39 Auguet: »Cruelty and Civilization«, p. 95.

40 Friedländer: »Sittengeschichte Roms«, p. 502; Baker: »Gladiatoren«, p. 150–181; Wiedemann: »Kaiser und Gladiatoren«, pp. 77–108; Grant: »Die Gladiatoren«, p. 99.

41 Junkelmann, Marcus: *Das Spiel mit dem Tod: So kämpften Roms Gladiatoren*, Mainz 2000.

42 Sueton: *Kaiserbiografien*, Essen 2004, pp. 187ff., 261 (*De Vita Caesarum*, orig.); Friedländer: »Sittengeschichte Roms«, p. 472; Grant: »Die Gladiatoren«, p. 85; Baker: »Gladiatoren«, p. 147.

43 Nyáry, Josef: *Die Gladiatoren: Zum Töten erzogen, zum Sterben bestimmt*, Düsseldorf/Vienna 1982, p. 31; Grant: »Die Gladiatoren«, p. 23–30, 42; Meijer, Fik: *Gladiatoren: Das Spiel um Leben und Tod*, Düsseldorf/Zurich 2004, p. 45 (*The Gladiators,* New York 2007); Wiedemann: »Kaiser und Gladiatoren«, p. 127.

gods who laughed about it«. Boys and girls had to repeatedly fight and kill each other because again and again the crowd demanded new stimuli and extreme variations.[44]

Sometimes two gladiators or some groups of gladiators fought. When a gladiator was not killed during the fight but lost his balance and fell down wounded and gave up the fight, the editor decided if the victorious gladiator should kill his opponent or not. A lot of editors were proud to have all inferior fighters killed who had given up the fight due to wounds or exhaustion. But usually the editor left the decision to the hands of the crowd, which by acclamation could decide the life or death of the inferior gladiator. Only hard-fighting and bold inferior fighters had a chance for the editor and crowd to reprieve them. In most cases, weak or slow fighters who gave up the fight or lost the battle had to envisage their death because the disappointed and furious crowd demanded their death. The crowd expected all gladiators to die without hesitation or refusal.[45]

3.3 The Spectators

The elite of the state sat in the first 19 rows of the Colosseum, the middle class occupied the following 19 rows, and the lower classes and the women were placed in the last rows of the theatre. This sitting order reveals that not only the lower classes but the whole society enjoyed and supported this bloody entertainment. The games were carried out because the people loved and enjoyed them most. The bloody spectacles corresponded to the needs and wishes of ancient man. Whoever refused to see the cruel executions and the agonised fights was held to be a coward and lost all respect. Lawyers compared such weakness with the weakness of men who refused to immediately kill the lovers of their wives, a legal right not only in Rome but in most pre-modern societies, a right that was requested if a man wanted to keep his honour as a bold and proud man.[46]

---

44 Friedländer: »Sittengeschichte Roms«, p. 466; Wiedemann: »Kaiser und Gladiatoren«, p. 119.

45 Baker: »Gladiatoren«, p. 104–107; Grant: »Die Gladiatoren«, p. 57; Wiedemann: »Kaiser und Gladiatoren«, pp. 109–131.

46 Wiedemann: »Kaiser und Gladiatoren«, pp. 141f.; Post: »Bausteine für eine allgemeine Rechtswissenschaft«; Seagle: »Weltgeschichte des

The crowd screamed furiously when gladiators showed weak performance

»and was insulted when a gladiator did not like to die. By whips and gluing irons cowards and slow fighters were forced to attack. The furious spectators cried: ›Kill, whip, burn‹! Why does this man refuse to be killed by the sword? Why does that gladiator hesitate to kill his opponent with one stroke? Why does this man dislike dying?«[47]

Many of reports prove that the spectators enjoyed seeing the blood and cruelties. The more the events got cruel in the arena, the higher developed the fascination and enthusiasm of the crowd. Sympathy for tortured and mutilated women, children, men, and beasts normally did not arise, as all related ancient reports and eye-witnesses reveal.[48]

The poet Prudentius scolds the behaviour of the vestal virgins who used to sit next to the family of the emperor by describing the conduct of one of these virgin priests:

»She has such a sweet and smooth mind! She jumps to every sword stroke, and whenever the victorious gladiator stuck his sword into the neck of his opponent she calls him to be her lover, and by directing her thumb downwards, the holy girl orders to tear out the chest of the defeated gladiator, while her victorious idol plunged his sword into the opponent's body.«[49]

Neither the terrible smell nor the chopped bodies, nor the death of children, women, and men nor the misery of the animals seriously affected the masses. Ancient humans loved to see how victims were chopped to pieces, eaten, burnt, speared, or trampled on. Ancient humans could not only stand to see such cruelties but loved to watch

---

Rechts«; Schild: »Alte Gerichtsbarkeit«; Oesterdiekhoff: »Zivilisation und Strukturgenese«, pp. 322–344.

47 Friedländer: »Sittengeschichte Roms«, p. 484.

48 Grant: »Die Gladiatoren«, pp. 58, 93; Wiedemann: »Kaiser und Gladiatoren«, pp. 92, 95f.; Sueton: »Kaiserbiografien«; Augustinus: *Bekenntnisse*, Stuttgart 1989, pp. 154–156; Tertullian: *Über die Spiele*, Stuttgart 2002, p. 67.

49 Cited in: Wiedemann: »Kaiser und Gladiatoren«, p. 154f., transl. by Georg W. Oesterdiekhoff.

such scenes – two psychic aspects that must be analytically differentiated. The spectator was not a passive consumer, but the most influential initiator of the cruelties, most responsible for their existence.[50] The primitive psyche of ancient humans is the sole cause of the existence of these spectacles! Whoever has stood in even the higher rows of the Colosseum knows how closely the incidents in the arena would be appear to all senses. Not one spectator could have been prevented from being totally confronted by the spectacle. Koehne[51] is right when writing: »the disgust with regard to how humans are tortured is a relatively recent progression in morals«.

»The differences of judgment on the games between ancient and modern educated persons reveal more than anything else the tremendous gap between ancient and modern modes of thinking and emotion. We scarcely encounter an expression of disgust in the whole Roman literature, a disgust indispensable for the sentiments of the modern world. In ancient society, the arena combats are usually mentioned with the biggest indifference«.[52]

Friedlaender admits that only one figure in Roman antiquity, the late Seneca, took up a moralistic and humanistic position. He denies that such positions were taken by any other ancient intellectual, including Cicero, Plutarch, Horatius, Epictet, Symmachus, Ovidius, Tacitus and all other authors and philosophers. Wiedemann[53] confirms Friedlaender's theory in a long chapter of his book, saying »that all objections by Roman and Greek philosophers against arena games cannot be classified as ›humane‹ in any modern meaning«. Wiedemann maintains that the people of antiquity never had sympathy for the victims. But Wiedemann's position is too extreme and unrealistic. We find sentences in the writings of Seneca and Tertullian[54] that clearly show the condemnation of the cruelty and reveal sympathy for the victims. It is

---

50 Grant: »Die Gladiatoren«, p. 91; Friedlaender: »Sittengeschichte Roms«, pp. 473.

51 Koehne, Eckart/Ewigleben, Cornelia (Eds.): *Gladiatoren und Caesaren: Die Macht der Unterhaltung im antiken Rom*, Hamburg 2000, p. 18.

52 Friedländer: »Sittengeschichte Roms«, p. 500, transl. by Georg W. Oesterdiekhoff.

53 Wiedemann: »Kaiser und Gladiatoren«, p. 132.

54 Tertullian: »Über die Spiele«, p. 61.

psychologically impossible that the spectators never had sympathy for some specific victims in some specific situations. The primitive psyche is absolutely not characterized by the total ignorance of sympathy and the steady desire for cruelty, but rather by the weakness of general intellectual considerations and psychic brakes, the lack of high thresholds of shame and embarrassment[55] which could sufficiently control the urge of drives and wishes. The primitive psyche is more easily overwhelmed by drives which suppress the appearance of controlling and regulating ideas and objections against living out drive tendencies. The suggestibility of the primitive psyche[56] implies a tendency for actions to develop in a way that suppresses contrary reflections. Operational thinking is more successful in the suppression of irrational or cruel-sadistic tendencies because operational thinking is characterized by the simultaneous consideration of several aspects, that is, by the self-control of ideas and wishes.[57] But the primitive psyche is more easily overwhelmed both by feelings of sympathy and emotions of cruelty. Thus, a great speaker can drive a large ancient crowd to feel guilty of things they had not really done, so that they are overwhelmed and oppressed by feelings of depression and sadness.[58] But if primitive man wants to live out and experience his cruel fantasies, like ancient man in the arenas, then he is overwhelmed by his aggressive instincts which are not suppressed by the control functions of »higher psychic functions«, including the moral instance of the »super-ego«. That accounts for his incapacity to develop general humane standards that forbid using humans as tools to entertain spectators. The desire for cruelty usually prevented the appearance of feelings of sympathy for the victims, so that usually these feelings could not arise or were totally suppressed. But it is quite clear that spectators who liked a specific defeated gladiator could feel sympathy for his sad fate. However, they did not draw the general conclusion that everybody should be saved

---

55 Elias: »Über den Prozess der Zivilisation«.

56 Carothers, John C.: *The Mind of Man in Africa*, London 1972.

57 Piaget: »Psychologie der Intelligenz«; Piaget/Inhelder: »Psychologie des Kindes«; Staewen: »Kulturelle und psychologische Bedingungen der Zusammenarbeit mit Afrikanern«.

58 Gurjewitsch, Aaron: *Das Weltbild des Mittelalters*, Munich 1980; Delumeau, Jean: *Angst im Abendland,* two vols., Reinbek 1985 (transl of *La Peur en Occident*, Paris 1978).

from this sad fate because the feelings of sympathy were bound to personal relations and specific circumstances, not to general moral and humanitarian standards. The primitive, pre-formal psyche decides depending on personal interests and specific circumstances, not according to general humanitarian standards and moral principles. This is the difference from modern standards developed in the context of formal operations, respectively »higher psychic functions«, standards which prescribe that sadistic practices to entertain people can never be justified. Ancient critics could therefore not develop intellectual clubs or unions, political movements or literary circles that tried to abolish such kinds of entertainment. In this sense, Friedlaender's and Wiedemann's thesis is right when they say that the arena games were totally accepted and justified, and were seen as absolutely normal aspects of social life.

3.4 The Cultural Gap between Modernity and Antiquity

Baker[59] puts it rightly:

»The enthusiasm of the Romans for this spectacle is a clear fact. Most of the humans of today would head off to the incidents in the arena in the utmost horror: It would be absolutely intolerable to see just once how a living woman or man would be eaten by wild beasts, or to watch such scenes for a whole day or for several days.«

He continues:[60]

»No mentally sane person of today would try to re-establish the arena festivities with gladiator fights – the spectacle of women and men who kill each other on a bloody battle field would arouse a storm of protest. But such a modern reaction would have provoked amusement and condemnation in the mind of every average citizen of ancient Rome.«

These judgments by Baker are right in every relevant respect. I am quite sure that a lot of social scientists and historians do not the capacity to sufficiently grasp these facts. Many of them might say that modern humans would like to see such things and might enjoy them in the

59 Baker: »Gladiatoren«, p. 10f.

60 Baker: »Gladiatoren«, p. 55.

same way if they had the possibility. Or they may hint at comparisons to My Lai and Auschwitz, Stalingrad and Dresden, saying that the levels of cruelty were the same. Or they naïvely point to hooligans, violent movies and terrorism in order to maintain that not the mentality and psyche but solely the forms of violence have changed.

But it is absolutely unthinkable that in modern arenas in front of 50000 spectators humans would fight to the death, naked women would be eaten by beasts and hundreds of delinquents would have to massacre each other. It is absolutely unthinkable that present-day spectators would watch such brutal scenes with enthusiasm and fascination and clap and cheer to the most horrible acts, demand the murder of cowardly fighters and watch in pleasure how beasts eat children and women. It is absolutely unthinkable that the president and the ministers of a modern country would enter the arena to fight as gladiators and kill humans, as Commodus and other emperors did. It is absolutely unthinkable that a president or chancellor would disguise themself in a beast's fur, enter the arena, and carry out sexual activities with naked women tied to stakes – like Nero did.[61] He was cheered by the masses for this extreme behaviour, while any modern politician who behaved this way would be removed from public life forever. It would be hard or impossible to find a corresponding example of such an extreme behaviour in any Western country in the past 200 years.

Cruel punishment laws and agonised fights and chases do not exist in the modern world because they are completely denied. If any politician tried to re-establish these practices, he would immediately be stopped. It would be as abstruse as the introduction of ordeals by fire and water, cannibalism and human sacrifices for the gods.

The denial of these practices has nothing to do with the development of compensates, with institutional barriers or changes in modes and customs. It would be wrong to say that the arena games have been completely replaced by violent movies or football games as mere institutional changes which do not imply psychic-cognitive transformations. On the contrary, the transformation of entertainment and leisure time practices, the transformation from arena games to violent movies or boxing matches are parts of processes of civilization and psychogenetic developments, a process of the extenuation of aggressive-sadistic drives and of the refinement of psychic-cognitive and

61 Sueton: »Kaiserbiografien«, p. 261.

moral standards. The abolishment of cruel practices is not a merely institutional process but a reflection of the psychic-cognitive progress of modern mankind.

Arena games existed because ancient man was able to watch these things *and* longed for them. The abolishment of these practices is the result of the modern psychic transformation that implies that modern man is incapable of experiencing and tolerating these things *and* has no related desire. Many modern humans would suffer from physical and psychic problems if they were forced to observe such tortures and murders. A lot or most of modern humans would never overcome the memories of such experiences for their whole lifetime and would need psychotherapeutic treatment with unclear or no success. If modern humans were to travel to antiquity with a time machine and visit the arena games, they would doubt the idea of the unity of mankind. A big difference with ancient humans who enjoyed the spectacle and cheered with pleasure; modern humans would get sick and turn crazy!

Grant[62] maintained that the Nazis' crimes and the Roman games were the worst aberrations of mankind, aberrations of the same level, quantitatively and qualitatively. First of all, his judgment can only refer to specifically European history; civil wars in China sometimes produced much higher numbers of victims. Secondly, we must differentiate between the extent of damage and the psychic-cognitive level that causes and underlies this damage. The cruelty of the world wars cannot only be explained in terms of rational game theory; it includes mentalities of the time, that is imperialistic, semi-barbarian and only half-modernized mentalities. But the cruelty of the arena games did not serve political aims; it was pointless, mere fun and was supposed to entertain and please. Emperors fighting in arenas, dwarfs who kill women, humans burning as lamps, beasts with body parts in their mouths – these cultures where the emperor, elite of the state and 50,000 people watch such scenes are more naïve, sadistic, childish, unconcerned, stubborn, precarious and insensitive. It was the heart and the centre of the Roman culture which concertedly enjoyed this, not a small group of idiots and mentally disordered persons.

62 Grant: »Die Gladiatoren«, p.8.

4. CONCLUSIONS

The empirical result of cross-cultural psychology of the pre-formal psychic stage of pre-modern mankind accounts for the history of morals and customs of mankind. The lower levels of the psyche are linked to phenomena such as cannibalism, sadistic punishment practices or arena games. Cannibalism belongs to the entire history of mankind: in Oceania and Africa up to the 20th century, in America up to the 19th century, and remnants of cannibalism could be found in the European antiquity. The reported insensitivity of cannibals when hunting their victims or holding them as cattle until they are fat enough to be eaten gives evidence to the lower psychic-cognitive level of pre-modern mankind. Cannibalism appears as much more naïve, ruthless, and childish than arena games, so that ancient civilizations had attained a higher level than cannibalistic cultures.[63]

Developmental psychology, developed in the context of »Structure-Genetic Theory«, gives independent and clear proof to the fact of the lower level of pre-modern mankind. This fact falsifies all attempts to explain ancient cruelty practices in terms of mere institutions and circumstances. The clear fact of the pre-formal psychic-cognitive stage of pre-modern mankind convincingly proves that phenomena such as cannibalism, arena games, and sadistic punishment practices must be attributed to this psychic stage and must be deduced from it. The inductive chain of arguments, basing on the analysis of ethnographic and historical facts and their inherent logic, must be linked to hypothetical-deductive argumentation, stemming from developmental psychology, inducing a systemic and coherent theory of moral development.

The incredible sadism of old punishment practices and the wild insensitivity of cannibalism can only be explained by the fact of the dominance of primitive psychic functions. A very simple-minded psyche preferring a direct path from need to satisfaction, a narrow and naïve mind missing so many sensitivities, reflections and worlds of ideas, usually believed to be anthropological universals and conditions, must be provided to explain these things. Only among peoples with childish

63 Volhard, Ewald: *Kannibalismus*, Stuttgart 1939; Oesterdiekhoff: »Archaische Kultur und moderne Zivilisation«.

IQ scores below 70, as cross-cultural intelligence research found out[64], is it possible for their emperors to jump into arenas to behave there as sadists, fighters and sexual criminals.

Therefore, pre-modern populations live in a quite different cultural reality, compared to modern standards; a culture that is characterized by ardour, warmth, emotionality, liveliness on the one hand and cruelty, infantilism, suggestibility, and insensitivity on the other hand. This psychic state resembles the relations set out in fairy tales. Johan Huizinga[65] (1975: 10f, transl. by G.O.), the great old man of the history of mentalities, excellently knew how to characterize this pre-modern psychic state:

»The insensitivity of the callousness of those times was so incredible that we do not know how to condemn it. Life was so colourful and dazzling that one breath accepted both blood and roses. The people staggered between hellish fears and childish fun, sadistic callousness and sobbing emotion like giants with a childlike mind.«

BIBLIOGRAPHY

Auguet, Roland: *Cruelty and Civilization: The Roman Games*, New York 1994.

Augustinus: *Bekenntnisse*, Stuttgart 1989.

Augustus: *Res gestae*, ed. Marion Giebel, Stuttgart 2004.

Baker, Alan: *Gladiatoren: Kampfspiele auf Leben und Tod*, Hamburg 2004 (The Gladiator, London 2000).

Bayley, N.: »On the Growth of Intelligence«, in: American Journal of Psychology 10 (1955), pp. 808–815.

Bumke, Joachim: *Höfische Kultur*, 2 vols., Munich 1986.

Carothers, John C.: *The Mind of Man in Africa*, London 1972.

64 Oesterdiekhoff: »Mental Growth of Mankind«; Bayley: »On the Growth of Intelligence«; Raven/Raven/Court: »Manual for Raven's Progressive Matrices and Vocabulary Scales«; Flynn: »Massive IQ-Gains in 14 Nations«.

65 Huizinga: »Herbst des Mittelalters«, pp. 10f., transl. by Georg W. Oesterdiekhoff; Irvine, S./Berry, John W. (Eds.): *Human Abilities in Cultural Context*, 2 vols., Cambridge 1988.

Dasen, Pierre (Ed.): *Piagetian Psychology: Cross-Cultural Contributions*, New York 1977.

Dasen, Pierre/Berry, John W. (Eds.): *Culture and Cognition: Readings in Cross-Cultural Psychology*, London 2004.

Delumeau, Jean: *Angst im Abendland*, two vols., Reinbek 1985 (*La Peur en Occident*, Paris 1978).

Edwards, Carol P.: »Societal Complexity and Moral Development«, in: Ethos 3 (1975), pp. 505–527.

Edwards, Carol P.: »The Comparative Study of the Development of Moral Judgment and Reasoning«, in: Wagner, D. A./Stevenson, H. W. (Eds.): *Handbook of Cross-Cultural Human Development*, San Francisco 1981, pp. 248–279.

Edwards, Carol P.: *The Effect of Experience on Moral Developments: Results from Kenya*, Harvard University 1974 (unpublished dissertation).

Eibl-Eibesfeldt, Irenaeus: *Der vorprogrammierte Mensch: Das Ererbte als bestimmender Faktor im menschlichen Verhalten*, Vienna 1973.

Elias, Norbert: *Über den Prozess der Zivilisation*, 2 vols., vol. 1, Frankfurt/Main 1976 (*The Civilizing Process*, Williston, Vermont 1994).

Flynn, James R.: »Massive IQ-Gains in 14 Nations: What IQ-Tests Really Measure«, in: Psychological Bulletin 101.2 (1987), pp. 171–191.

Freitag, Barbara: *Der Aufbau kindlicher Bewusstseinsstrukturen im gesellschaftlichen Kontext*, Munich 1983.

Friedländer, Ludwig: *Sittengeschichte Roms*, Cologne 1975 (Roman Life and Manners, New York 1965).

Gorsuch, R. J./Barnes, M. L.: »Stages of Ethical Reasoning and Moral Norms of Carib Youths«, in: Journal of Cross-Cultural Psychology 4 (1973), pp. 283–301.

Grant, Michael: *Die Gladiatoren*, Stuttgart 1982 (*The Gladiators*, New York 1971).

Gurjewitsch, Aaron: *Das Weltbild des Mittelalters*, Munich 1980.

Hallpike, Christopher: *Grundlagen primitiven Denkens*. Munich 1994 (*Foundations of Primitive Thought*, Oxford 1978).

Hallpike, Christopher: *The Evolution of Moral Understanding*, Alton, England 2004.

Helkama, K.: *The Development of the Attribution of Responsibility: A Critical Survey of Empirical Research and a Theoretical Outline*, Helsinki 1979.

Huizinga, Johan: *Herbst des Mittelalters*, Stuttgart 1975.

Irvine, S./Berry, John W. (Eds.): *Human Abilities in Cultural Context*, 2 vols., Cambridge 1988.

Junkelmann, Marcus: *Das Spiel mit dem Tod: So kämpften Roms Gladiatoren*, Mainz 2000.

Keegan, John: *Die Kultur des Krieges*, Reinbek 1996 (A History of Warfare, New York 1993)

Keeley, Lawrence H.: *War Before Civilization*, Oxford 1996.

Kiefer, Otto: *Kulturgeschichte Roms*, Berlin 1933.

Kohlberg, Lawrence/Turiel, Elliot: »Moralische Entwicklung und Erziehung«, in: Portele, Gerhard (Ed.): *Sozialisation und Moral*, Weinheim 1978, pp. 13–80.

Kohlberg, Lawrence: *Die Psychologie der Moralentwicklung*, Frankfurt/Main 1996 (*The Psychology of Moral Development*, New York 1993).

Köhne, Eckart/Ewigleben, Cornelia (Eds.): *Gladiatoren und Caesaren: Die Macht der Unterhaltung im antiken Rom*, Hamburg 2000.

Lafiteau, Joseph-Francois: *Die Sitten der amerikanischen Wilden im Verhältnis zu den Sitten der Frühzeit*, Weinheim 1987. (*Les moeurs des savages ameriquaines comparée aux premiers temps*, Paris 1724).

Lurija, Alexander: *Die historische Bedingtheit individueller Erkenntnisprozesse*, Weinheim 1986 (*Cognitive Development*, Harvard, Mass. 1982)

McNamee, S.: »Moral Behaviour, Moral Development, and Motivation«, in: Journal of Moral Education 7 (1977), pp. 27–31.

Meijer, Fik: *Gladiatoren: Das Spiel um Leben und Tod*, Düsseldorf/Zurich 2004 (*The Gladiators*, New York 2007).

Milgram, Stanley: *Das Milgram-Experiment: Zur Gehorsamsbereitschaft gegenüber Autorität*, Reinbek 1997 (*Obedience to Authority*, New York 1975).

Mogdil, Celia/Mogdil, Sohan: *Piagetian Research*, vols. 1–8, London 1976.

Neisser, Ulric (Ed.): *The Rising Curve: Long-Term Gains in IQ and Related Measures*, Washington 1998.

Nisan, M./Kohlberg, L.: »Universality and Variation in Moral Judgement: A Longitudinal and Cross-Sectional Study in Turkey«, in: Child Development 53 (1982), pp. 865–876.

Nyáry, Josef: *Die Gladiatoren: Zum Toten erzogen, zum Sterben bestimmt*, Düsseldorf/Vienna 1982.

Oesterdiekhoff, Georg W.: »Mental Growth of Mankind. The Psychometrical and the Cognitive-Developmental Approach in Comparison«, in: The Mankind Quarterly, 3 (2007) (in press).

Oesterdiekhoff, Georg W.: *Archaische Kultur und moderne Zivilisation*, Hamburg/Münster/London 2006.

Oesterdiekhoff, Georg W.: *Kulturelle Bedingungen kognitiver Entwicklung: Der strukturgenetische Ansatz in der Soziologie*, Frankfurt/Main 1997.

Oesterdiekhoff, Georg W.: *Kulturelle Evolution des Geistes: Die historische Wechselwirkung von Psyche und Gesellschaft*, Hamburg/Münster/London 2006.

Oesterdiekhoff, Georg W.: *Zivilisation und Strukturgenese: Norbert Elias und Jean Piaget im Vergleich*, Frankfurt/Main 2000.

Piaget, Jean/Inhelder, Bärbel: *Psychologie des Kindes*, Frankfurt/Main 1980 (*The Psychology of the Child*, New York 1969).

Piaget, Jean: *Das moralische Urteil beim Kinde*, Frankfurt/Main 1973 (*The Moral Judgment of the Child*, Harmondsworth 1977)

Piaget, Jean: *Psychologie der Intelligenz*, Stuttgart 1984 (*Psychology of Intelligence*, Totowa, New Jersey 1968).

Poortinga, Ype (Ed.): *Basis Problems in Cross-Cultural Psychology*, Amsterdam 1977.

Post, Albert Hermann: *Bausteine für eine allgemeine Rechtswissenschaft auf vergleichend-ethnologischer Grundlage*, Oldenburg 1880.

Raddings, Christopher: »Evolution of Medieval Mentalities«, in: American Historical Review 83 (1978), 577–597.

Raven, J./Raven, J. C./Court, J. H.: *Manual for Raven's Progressive Matrices and Vocabulary Scale*s Oxford 1993.

Richburg, Keith B.: *Jenseits von Amerika: Eine Konfrontation mit Afrika, dem Land meiner Vorfahren*, Berlin 1999 (*Out of America*, New York 1997).

Schild, Wolfgang: *Alte Gerichtsbarkeit*, Munich 1980.

Schoefthaler, Traugott/Goldschmidt, Dietrich (Eds.): *Soziale Struktur und Vernunft*, Frankfurt/Main 1984.

Schweitzer, Albert: *Selbstzeugnisse*, Stuttgart 1960.

Seagle, William: *Weltgeschichte des Rechts*, Berlin 1967 (*The History of Law*, New York: Tudor Publishing 1946).

Selman, Robert: *Entwicklung des sozialen Verstehens*, Frankfurt/Main 1984 (The Growth of Personal Understanding, San Diego 1980).

Snarey, J. R.: »Cross-Cultural Universality of Social-Moral Development: A Critical Review of Kohlbergian Research«, in: Psychological Bulletin 97 (1985), pp. 202–232.

Staewen, Christoph/Schoenberg, Fritz: *Kulturwandel und Angstentwicklung bei den Yorubas Westafrikas*, Munich 1970.

Staewen, Christoph: *Kulturelle und psychologische Bedingungen der Zusammenarbeit mit Afrikanern*, Munich 1991.

Sueton: *Kaiserbiografien*, Essen 2004.

Tertullian: *Über die Spiele*, Stuttgart 2002.

Tietjen, A./Walker L. J.: »Moral Reasoning and Leadership Among Men in a Papua New-Guinea Society«, in: Developmental Psychology 21.6 (1985), pp. 982–992.

van Dülmen, Richard: *Theater des Schreckens*, Munich 1988.

Volhard, Ewald: *Kannibalismus*, Stuttgart 1939.

Werner, Heinz: *Einführung in die Entwicklungspsychologie*, Leipzig 1959 (*The Comparative Psychology of Mental Development*, New York 1964).

Wiedemann, Thomas: *Kaiser und Gladiatoren: Die Macht der Spiele im antiken Rom*, Darmstadt 2001 (*Emperors and Gladiators*, Florence 1995).

Wrede, Richard: Die *Körperstrafen: Von der Urzeit bis ins 20. Jahrhundert*, Wiesbaden 2004.

III.3 Classical Tradition, Humanity, Occidental Humanism

Hellenic-Roman Civilization and its Claim for Universal Validity[1]

HUBERT CANCIK

> »*universus mundus una civitas communis deorum atque hominum.*«
>
> CICERO, *DE LEGIBUS* 1,26 (ca. 52 ante Christum natum)

> »The whole world is one state common for gods and men.«
>
> CICERO, *ON LAWS* 1,26 (ca. 52 BCE)

1. CLASSICAL TRADITION

1.1 Europe

Once upon a time somebody asked a wise man from India: »What do you think about European civilization«? He answered: »I think it would be a good idea«.[2] Keeping in mind always this ironic warning,

1 This chapter was published earlier in Professor Cancik's collected articles in the book *Europa – Antike – Humanismus: Humanistische Versuche und Vorarbeiten*, ed. by Hildegard Cancik-Lindemaier, Bielefeld 2011, pp. 83–92.

2 Mahatma Gandhi, oral tradition.

may I venture to present to you one component of this good idea – classical tradition and occidental humanism.

According to this tradition Europe was initially not an idea, but a princess from Phoenicia who came over to the West, voluntarily or seduced. Her brother Kadmos, in search of the princess, also came to the West, bringing with him, incidentally, the art of writing. This happened in the year 1518/17 BCE, says ancient chronography.[3] The Greeks, when they wrote our classical literature, always remembered their oriental heritage – alpha, beta, gamma etc. being in form and name a ›Phoenician‹ alphabet. The date and the myth remind us that Greek culture originated and developed at the margins of the Ancient Oriental Cultures. Contacts of long duration in Asia Minor and the Aegeis stimulated what has been called the ›Greek miracle‹. Priamos, king of Troy, for example, was held by the Greeks to be a vassal of Ninos the Assyrian – the first man who built up an empire.[4] The Trojan war, was conceived as the first conflict between West and Orient, dated by the ancients to 1209/08 (Marmor Parium).[5]

Classical Antiquity originated as a derivative culture, on the margins of the late Ancient Orient. It ended after 2000 years with the restoration of the imperium Romanum in the West by Charlemagne and the rise of Islamic states in the East of the Empire, around 800 CE. Within this chronological frame the ancients already have singled out two golden, perfect, high-ranking classical periods: the Attic or Periclean epoch (500 to 300 BCE) and the Augustan epoch, from the late Roman republic to the death of Augustus (80 BCE to 14 CE). The phrase ›classical antiquity‹ therefore, comprehends a historical and a normative notion: It means a special part of Europe's early history and a paradigm of culture and humanity established by the *antiqui*, i.e. by

3 Marmor Parium, epoch 7 (Jacoby, F.: *Die Fragmente der griechischen Historiker*, Leiden 1962, nr. 239).

4 Cancik, H.: »Der troianische Krieg – Seine Bedeutung für das Geschichtsbild der Griechen und Römer«, in: *Troia – Traum und Wirklichkeit: Katalog zur Ausstellung*, Stuttgart 2001, pp. 174–179; Cancik, H.: »Wie die Alten den Troianischen Krieg datiert haben. Homers Epen im Geschichtsbild der Antike«, in: Hofmann, H. (Ed.): *Troia: Von Homer bis heute*, Tübingen 2004, pp. 53–75.

5 Jacoby: *Die Fragmente*, nr.239, ep.24. Eratosthenes dates the Fall of Troy to 1184/83 BCE.

our ancestors who have gone before us (*ante nos*), whom we, the epigones, the *posteri* are following on the way to the future.

1.2 »Homer who was Wiser than All Greeks« (Heraclitus)[6]

a) Upon the basic features of classical antiquity I would not dare lecture. We can, however, catch a glimpse of the beginnings of that cultural process called classical antiquity, if we look on the Homeric poems, our first literary document, written about the 8th century BCE. It is immediately evident that these poems are perfect and, typologically, late. The rhythm is rationalized and standardized to a very high degree. The language is highly artificial, a mixture of several dialects with traces from Mycenaean times. The techniques of composition, characterization, motivation are manifold and efficient. By means of careful chronology and stringent causation Homer construes wide ranging actions, complex processes, multilayered conflicts. It is no surprise that the ancients considered him to have been the first historian. Innumerable speeches, dialogues, discussions, confidential talks, and prayers exhibit hope, sorrow, plans and their failure, reflections on the unpredictability of God or the blindness and frailty of man.

Homer's is an enlightened world: few miracles, less magic. The gods are humans, only stronger, faster, and immortal. They are sitting on mount Olympos, drinking, laughing and looking at the mortals down on earth, with sympathy and care.[7] No surprise that the ancients considered Homer to have been the first theologian.[8]

b) It is a ›transcendent vision‹ of his world that Homer has created in the forge of Hephaestus.[9] The smith-god is fabricating a new shield for Achilleus. He decorates it with eight scenes in gold and silver:

---

6 Heraclitus frg. 56 VS from Hippolytus 9,9. Cf. Heracl. frg. 42 VS from Diogenes Laertius 9,1: to »throw out« Homer from the poets' contests; frg. 57 VS from Hippolytus 9,10: »but the teacher of most of them (is) Hesiodus; they are convinced that he knows best, [...]«.

7 Homer, *Iliad* 3,1–4.

8 Lamberton, R.: *Homer the Theologian: Neoplatonist Allegorical Reading and the Growth of Epic Tradition*, Berkeley, Calif. 1986.

9 Homer, *Iliad* 18, 468–617.

(1) heaven, earth, the heavenly bodies and signs of the zodiac. Small wonder, that the ancients considered Homer to have been the first astronomer.
(2) A town at peace: Homer describes the public space, the place of marriage and lawsuit, the agora, being the centre of public life.
(3) The counterpart is a town at war; here, and only here, some gods are involved.

There follow scenes taken from economic life: agriculture (4), harvesting under control of the king (5), wine-growing with dancing and music (6), cattle- and sheep-breeding (7).

The cycle of pictures is closed by a bright dancing-scene (8), a public celebration of young and beautiful men and women in ostentatious dressing. No scene is particularly dedicated to the gods, nowhere is religion the centre of a scene.[10] Nevertheless, this work of art, namely Achilleus' shield, is meant to represent the totality of life, the whole world covered by heaven, embraced by the ocean, the first ›Weltbild‹ of Western culture. Homer exhibits this work of art in the process of making, as *poíesis* and, perhaps, he hints at his own work. The artist plays with his medium: what is produced from metal, gold and silver gives the impression of sound, movement, liveliness – »as if they were living mortals«.[11] Despite wild beasts (scene 7), war and death, this world is *kalós* – beautiful. There are, in the description of Achilleus' shield, except for the names of the gods, no specific Greek or Trojan traits: the description claims to be universal, to convey the general idea of good life.

c) Homer the poet, the artist is, to the ancient mind, the first geographer, historian, astronomer, philosopher, theologian, rhetorician: in short, he is the quintessence of Greek culture. He is, I would like to add, also the first educationalist. All the arts could be learned from Homer; he is the core of the Greek educational system. Greek children learned the art of reading and speaking, the elements of art and science, wisdom and morals by rehearsing Homer. In addition, Homer introduced the example of an engaged, but unsuccessful teacher –

10 There is a sacrifice in the king's hall and there are gods in the war.

11 Homer, *Iliad* 18, 539: *hos zooí brotoí* – note the antithesis; cf. 18,548: the impression of colour.

Phoenix – and wrote the first educational romance: Telemachos, son of Ulysses, who sets out to search for his father, leaving his home and his mother, tutored by Athene in the guise of Mentor.[12]

d) »Homeros has educated Greece«, says Plato.[13] Greek *paideía*, culture and education, was not limited to native Greeks, however. On the contrary: A Greek, so runs the definition of Isocrates, is not one who descends from Greek parents, but one who participates in Greek education.[14] Therefore, so-called barbarians like Romans, Jews, or Germans could become Greeks. Classical tradition is not restrained, neither by racial nor by national barriers; it becomes human and universal. Thus classical tradition could become the basis for occidental humanism.

2. OCCIDENTAL HUMANISM

2.1 Niethammer – Herder – *studia humaniora*

Occidental humanism is first and fundamentally an educational movement, rooted in classical tradition. So occidental humanism is neither a philosophy nor a religion. It is neither classics (ancient history, classical philology and archeology) nor, more generally, our so-called classical heritage. Rather it is a theory of a pedagogic reform. It was constituted by Friedrich Immanuel Niethammer (1766–1848). Niethammer was first a professor of philosophy in Jena, later a professor of theology in Würzburg and, since 1808, active in the school administration of Bavaria. In this year he published a pamphlet entitled: »*Der Streit des Philanthropinismus und Humanismus in der Theorie des Erziehungsunterrichtes unserer Zeit*« – ›The controversy between Philanthropinism and Humanism in the contemporary theory of educa-

---

12 Homer, *Odyssey*, books 1–4: Telemachia. Cf. Fénelon: *Les aventures de Télémaque*, 1699.

13 Plato, *Republic* 10,606e: (*Hómeros*) *ten Helláda pepaídeuken*. Plato goes on to criticize this.

14 Isocrates, *Panegyricus* (published 380 BCE) 50: to call Greek rather those who share our education than those who share our common nature (i.e. descent).

tion‹. It is in this monograph that Niethammer explains education (»*Bildung*«) as »shaping humankind in the individual«; since reason (»*Vernunft*«) is the essential characteristic of humankind, he demands a »general formation of mind« (»*Vernunftbildung*«) for all men, classes, occupations. This general formation should be accomplished, according to Niethammer, by the consideration of the »ideas« of nature, state, god, necessity and freedom, pity and morals. Only after this period of general formation should children be trained for a special job. For some people, however, Niethammer provided for the general formation of the mind a »*Humanitätsbildung*«, that is, an integral education of all gifts and abilities in order to form the »whole man« (»*den ganzen Menschen*«): this, says Niethammer, »is the ideal of mankind, that we honour by the venerable name of ›humanity‹« (»*Humanität*«). The classical tradition grants the means by which this sublime goal is to be reached: languages, art and literature, mythology and philosophy. As a member of the educational administration Niethammer, elaborated detailed curricula for the classes.

This is occidental humanism at the stage of pedagogic reflections, designed for the higher bourgeoisie, more precisely for its male part, in the German countries, in a moment of an acute political crisis.[15]

2.2 Humanity – *humanitas*

a) It was Immanuel Niethammer (1766–1848) who coined not the word but the concept of »*Humanismus*« in 1808 CE. However, he presupposes a rich discussion on the terms ›human, mankind, humanity, *humanité*‹. The term ›*Humanität*‹ was borrowed from Herder's »Letters for the Promotion of Humanity«, published in 1793/97. Herder, too, enriched the German language by a neologism. With explicit argumentation he connects the French word ›*humanité*‹ with the notions of ›reason, freedom, education, right‹ and deliberately introduces it as a loan-word (›*Humanität*‹) into German, only a few years before Niethammer published his pamphlet.[16] Herder, in his attempt to define

15 The reforms in Prussia, Badenia and other German states after the collapse of Prussia and her allies in the double battle of Jena and Auerstedt (1806); the Prussian residence moves to Königsberg; Napoleon occupies Berlin.

16 Herder, Johann Gottfried: »Briefe zur Beförderung der Humanität (1793/97)«, in: *Johann Gottfried Herder: Werke in 10 Bänden*, vol. 7, ed.

and illustrate ›*Humanität*‹, relies heavily on the classical tradition. He reviews the history of the word in its Latin context and Greek antecedents. He quotes at length Marcus Aurelius the Stoic and Caesar; he rehearses the Stoic catechism of Persius; he lectures, finally, insistently on Homer, in four letters. Some digressions show Herder, the cosmopolitan, evoking »Confucius, the Socrates of the Sineses« (letter 28), for example.

To conclude: the concept of *Humanität* in Herder is deeply rooted in classical tradition. The anthropological and ethnic core of this concept is Stoic: nature and reason are key terms; human weakness is a stimulus for progress; ›education‹ of the individual and the human species is conceived in Stoic terms.[17] With Herder's foundation of humanity we find the common ground of European humanism. The Latin words *homo, humanus, humanitas* live on in the neo-Latin dialects of the Spaniards, French, and Italians. The *studia humaniora/studia humanitatis*[18], i.e. education by classical tradition, is a common practice, always modified according to special needs. The *(h)umanista* had appeared in the Universities of the Italian Renaissance: he lectured on rhetoric, history, and poetry.[19]

This, then is the genealogy of European humanism: (1) classical tradition – (2) *humanitas, studia humaniora, artes liberales* – (3) humanité, Humanität – (4) Humanismus. The basic term is *humanitas*, a word which in Latin, already, has six meanings.

Hans-Dietrich Irmscher, Frankfurt/Main 1991, especially letters nr. 27 to nr. 39.

17 Herder, Johann Gottfried: »Ideen zur Philosophie der Geschichte der Menschheit (1784/91)«, in: *Johann Gottfried Herder: Werke in 10 Bänden*, vol. 6, ed. Martin Bollacher, Frankfurt/Main 1989, 9,1: »Es gibt also eine Erziehung des Menschengeschlechts; eben weil jeder nur durch Erziehung ein Mensch wird und das ganze Geschlecht nicht anders als in dieser Kette der Individuen lebt«.

18 Our first evidence of this expression is to be found in Cicero, who has probably coined it: *pro Murena* 61 (written in 63 BCE) and *pro Archia poeta* 3 (written in 62 BCE); cf. Cicero, *pro Caelio* 24 (written in 56 BCE). Cicero did not (yet) conceive a special education program.

19 Pisa 1490; Bologna 1512.

b) The semantic field around the Latin word *humanitas* is built up by six clearly distinguished components:

(a) *genus humanum* – all *men/human beings* together (in contrast to animals, individuals, nations);
(b) *societas humana* – society of mankind, bound together by the kinship of nature and common experience; family of man; *cosmopolis*;
(c) *condicio humana* – the weakness, frailty, and mortality of man (in contrast to the gods, the ›immortal‹);
(d) *clementia, benevolentia* – gentleness, softness, kindness (in contrast to cruelty, fierceness of wild beasts);
(e) *eruditio, educatio, formatio; paideía* – education;
(f) *cultus* and *urbanitas* – civilized life and urban life-style.

Several elements in this semantic field of *humanitas* are constituted by Stoic philosophy. The anthropology of Stoicism is naturalistic and empirical. Nature and reason, *physis* and *lógos*, are its basic elements. Stoic philosophers stress the equality and original freedom of all human beings. Nature, they claim, has made us all from the same material and to the same goal in life; she has borne us as relatives, given us mutual love and made us sociable, i.e. capable of forming a peaceful society.[20] There is a worldwide state, cosmopolis, and quasi-civil rights for all men in this city; M. Tullius Cicero declares:[21]

»universus mundus una civitas communis deorum atque hominum« –
»The whole world is one state common for gods and men«.

Men are free and equal by Nature. Human rights are rooted – historically and systematically – in the law of Nature. This is the source from which the claim for universal validity arises.

20 Seneca, *epistulae* 95,51–52; Seneca calls this argument the *formula humani officii*.

21 Cicero, *de legibus* 1,26 (ca. 52 BCE).

3. CLAIM FOR UNIVERSAL VALIDITY

3.1 Empirical, Historical, Theoretical

The statements made by Herder, Cicero, Seneca and other stoic, neo-stoic or stoicising authors put forward general principles which include humanity and the claim for universal validity. Some of these statements refer to biology, such as e. g. the laws of self-conservation (*conservatio sui*) and self-love (*amor sui*) which hold true for all living beings. Other statements refer to law and politics. They rely on observation and experience, tradition, research and speculation, or, to say it in Greek: these generalities are empirical (Greek: *empeiría*), historical (Greek: *historía*), theoretical (Greek: *theoría*). They do not convey revelation nor absolute truth, but can be refuted and improved. Their foundation is reason and nature. Reason is natural and naturc is structured by reason. Since all men participate in these constituents, namely *logos* and *physis*, all men are able to understand and accept these statements; this hopeful assumption is called *consensus omnium* – general consent.

I am not sure if this foundation of ethics will convince all analysts of moral language.[22] Through the inspiration of stoicism, however, the European Enlightenment created human rights from the Law of Nature.[23] »That all men are by nature equally free and independent and have certain inherent rights«, thus reads the Virginia Bill of Rights in 1778; this is sincere modern stoicism and has become a universal rule or even positive law.

---

22 For an analysis of the »naturalist fallacy« cf. Hare, R. M.: *The Language of Morals*, Oxford 1952 (German: *Die Sprache der Moral*, Frankfurt/Main 1983, p. 109ff.: »Naturalismus«); Moore, G. E.: *Principia Ethica* (English: 1903), Stuttgart 1970, chap. II: »Naturalistische Ethik«; short remarks upon Stoicism: §27.

23 Forschner, M.: *Über das Handeln im Einklang mit der Natur. Grundlagen ethischer Verständigung*, Darmstadt 1998, chap. III: »Über natürliche Neigungen und den Selbsthaß der Vernunft. Die Stoa als Inspirationsquelle der Aufklärung«.

3.2 Humanity and the Princess

Humanism is neither philosophy nor religion. Its concept of humanity, however, is based on some philosophical, primarily stoic, concepts which do not aspire to being an elaborated, coherent system of anthropology. Humanism, insofar as it is an educational movement and part of a classical tradition, complements universal statements on man and nature, law and society necessarily through particular historical examples, through mythical imagination and edifying quotations from accepted authors. It is just this seemingly arbitrary synthesis of philosophical eclecticism and history, poetry, law and biology which characterizes humanistic designs. A humanist discourse on freedom, therefore, will duly embark on the development of universal concepts in Aristotle's *Politiká* and Zeno's *Prohairesis* (choice, will) but will inevitably come down to Salamis and the battle-cry of a small Greek navy fighting against masses of Persian ships:[24]

»Eleutheroúte patrída, eleutheroúte de
paídas gynaíkas, theón de patroíon éde
thékas te progónon«.
»Liberate the fatherland, liberate
children, wives, the seats of our fathers' gods
and the shrines of the ancestors!«

Salamis, Marathon and Thermopylae are the names of small spots in Greece, but have a highly symbolic value. They evoke strong emotions and, in some people, remembrance of our first tragedy (Aeschylus' *Persians*) and of the father of historiography and ethnography (Herodotus' *Histories*) and of that modern short story with its mutilated title: »*Wanderer, kommst du nach Spa...*«.[25] In the humanistic discourse, these mythico-historical arguments complement in a systematic, but nonphilosophical way, the disquisition on freedom.

---

24 Aeschylus, *Persians* vs. 403–05. The historical commentary to the tragedy is Herodotus.

25 Böll, Heinrich: »Wanderer, kommst du nach Spa...«, (first published in: Frankfurter Hefte 5.11 (1950), pp. 1176–81), see now: Böll, H.: *Wanderer, kommst du nach Spa... Erzählungen*, Munich ^{38}2000. Böll quotes the epitaph for the Greek soldiers in Thermopylae.

To conclude: European humanism is universal and particular. It preserves, like other universal movements (e.g. Judaism, Catholicism, Islam), its particular origin (Jerusalem, Rome, Mecca). European humanism has to deal with the general meaning of the words humanity or human dignity, the foundation of human rights including religious freedom, banning of torture and the death penalty. And simultaneously it has to preserve the memory of Olympia and Troy; the vision of the dance of life and beauty on Achilleus' shield; the name of a Phoenician princess who came from the East to the occidental shores; and it has to preserve the answer of a wise man from India, who, when asked about European civilization, said: »It would be a good idea«.

BIBLIOGRAPHY

Aeschylus: *Persians*.

Böll, Heinrich: »Wanderer, kommst du nach Spa...«, in: *Frankfurter Hefte* 5.11 (1950), pp. 1176–81.

Böll, Heinrich: *Wanderer, kommst du nach Spa... Erzählungen*, Munich 2000.

Cancik, H.: »Der troianische Krieg – Seine Bedeutung für das Geschichtsbild der Griechen und Römer«, in: *Troia – Traum und Wirklichkeit. Katalog zur Ausstellung*, Stuttgart 2001, pp. 174–179.

Cancik, H.: »Wie die Alten den Troianischen Krieg datiert haben. Homers Epen im Geschichtsbild der Antike«, in: Hofmann, H. (Ed.): *Troia. Von Homer bis heute*, Tübingen 2004, pp. 53–75.

Cicereo: *pro Murena*, written in 63 BCE.

Cicero: *de legibus*, ca. 52 BCE.

Cicero: *pro Archia poeta*, written in 62 BCE.

Cicero: *pro Caelio*, written in 56 BCE.

Fénelon: *Les aventures de Télémaque*, 1699.

Forschner, M.: *Über das Handeln im Einklang mit der Natur. Grundlagen ethischer Verständigung*, Darmstadt 1998.

Hare, R. M.: *The Language of Morals*, Oxford 1952 (German: *Die Sprache der Moral*, Frankfurt/Main 1983).

Herder, Johann Gottfried: *Briefe zur Beförderung der Humanität* (1793/97), in: *Johann Gottfried Herder. Werke in 10 Bänden*, vol. 7, ed. Hans-Dietrich Irmscher, Frankfurt/Main 1991.

Herder, Johann Gottfried: *Ideen zur Philosophie der Geschichte der Menschheit* (1784/91), in: *Johann Gottfried Herder. Werke in 10 Bänden*, vol. 6, ed. Martin Bollacher, Frankfurt/Main 1989.

Homer: *Iliad*.

Homer: *Odyssey*.

Isocrates: *Panegyricus*, published 380 BCE.

Jacoby, F.: *Die Fragmente der griechischen Historiker*, Leiden 1962.

Lamberton, R.: *Homer the Theologian. Neoplatonist Allegorical Reading and the Growth of Epic Tradition*, Berkeley, Calif. 1986.

Marmor Parium, epoch 7.

Moore, G. E.: *Principia Ethica* (English: 1903), Stuttgart 1970.

Plato: *Republic*.

Seneca: *epistulae*.

III.4 Humanity as Trans-Individuality

Tang Junyi's (1909-1978) Philosophy of *Renwen* Humanism

STEPHAN SCHMIDT

INTRODUCTION

Among the representatives of so-called »Contemporary New Confucianism« (*dangdai xinrujia*),[1] Tang Junyi was the most unequivocal

1 Within the limited space of this paper I shall not try to outline the philosophical import of this movement. Suffice it to say that modern New Confucians were driven by a sense of the predicament in which traditional Confucian culture found itself after the onslaught of Western civilization in general and Western-style scientific thinking in particular. By engaging in a dialogue with Western philosophy these Chinese thinkers sought to reconstruct their own tradition, thereby giving it a new and modern conceptual outlook. See Bresciani (Bresciani, Umberto: *Reinventing Confucianism: The New Confucian Movement*, Taipei 2001) and Lee Ming-huei (Lee Ming-huei: *Der Konfuzianismus im modernen China*, Leipzig 2001) for brief biographical sketches of the movement's most important figures. Metzger (Metzger, Thomas: *Escape from Predicament: Neo-Confucianism and China's Evolving Political Culture*, New York 1977), Chang Hao (Chang Hao: »New Confucianism and the Intellectual Crisis in Contemporary China«, in: Furth, Charlotte (Ed.): *The Limits of Change – Essays on Conservative Alternatives in Republican China*, Cambridge/MA 1976, pp. 276–302), and some of the essays in Makeham (Makeham, John [Ed.]: *New Confucianism: A Critical Examination*, New York 2003) provide use-

advocate of the idea of Confucian humanism.[2] For him, humanism was the essence or, as he liked to put it, the »spirit« (*jingshen*) of Confucianism and thus of all Chinese culture. Already a brief glance at the titles of some of his writings confirms Tang Junyi's concern with the notions of Chinese culture and humanism and their intricate connection: *The Spiritual Values of Chinese Culture* (1951);[3] *The Reconstruction of the Humanistic Spirit* (1955)[4]; *The Development of China's Humanistic Spirit* (1957).[5] In the present essay I will draw on these and other writings in order to work out Tang Junyi's concept of Confucian humanism. By doing so, my first objective is to raise awareness that the seemingly universal term *humanism* can be spelled out in different ways, among which, of course, I can only present here the one that Tang Junyi claimed as specifically Confucian. Again, I think this is but one out of many possible and actual Confucian *humanisms* or, for that matter, Confucianisms, but hopefully one that can enrich and inspire the discourse on both the multiple facets and the actual rele-

---

ful elaborations of the historical context. Among the many Chinese publications on the subject, I find Zheng Jiadong: *Dangdai xinrujia lunheng* (*A Discussion of Contemporary New Confucianism*), Taipei 1995 particularly insightful.

2 Metzger (»Escape from Predicament«, pp. 29–47 and Metzger, Thomas: *A Cloud Across the Pacific: Essays on the Clash between Chinese and Western Political Theories Today*, Hong Kong 2005, pp. 185–290) provides a good exposition of Tang Junyi's thought, although the latter text in my opinion overemphasizes Tang's epistemological concerns. Below I will try to demonstrate how certain epistemological questions are part of Tang's moral philosophy. Four volumes of essays resulting from an international conference held in Hong Kong in 1988 on the occasion of the tenth anniversary of Tang Junyi's death cover a wide range of issues in his thought. See Huo Daohui: *Tang Junyi sixiang: Guoji huiyi lunwenji* (*Collected Essays from an International Conference on Tang Junyi's Thought*), Hong Kong 1992.

3 Tang Junyi: *Zhongguo wenhua zhi jingshen jiazhi* (*The Spiritual Values of Chinese Culture*), Taipei 1951, reprint 1979.

4 Tang Junyi: *Renwen jingshen zhi chongjian* (*The Reconstruction of the Humanistic Spirit*), Taipei 1955, reprint 2000.

5 Tang Junyi: *Zhongguo renwen jingshen zhi fazhan* (*The Development of China's Humanistic Spirit*), Taipei 1957, reprint 2000.

vance of humanistic thinking. At this stage of the discourse I consider it more helpful to gather different facets from different traditions – even at the cost of some semantic confusion concerning the term in question – rather than trying to find one definition that only purports to comprise them all.[6] In order to mark Tang Junyi's particular brand of Confucian humanism I shall attach to it the prefix *Renwen*, the phonetic transcription of the two Chinese characters usually rendered as »humanism« or »humanistic«. My question, then, is: What precisely does this term imply in Tang's understanding and how does he distinguish it from other variants of humanistic thinking? More specifically, I want to find out on what conception of the human being *Renwen* humanism is built. As we shall see, Tang Junyi develops a challenging notion of what it means to be human(e).[7]

Although he was not a cultural chauvinist, Tang Junyi did believe that there was something unique about the tradition of Confucianism, something that he saw threatened by the apparently unstoppable expansion of modern rationalism and scientism and therefore something that modern Confucians like himself were called upon to preserve for the sake of all humankind. It is for this reason that we encounter in his writings a sense of mission and a certain tone of voice: Tang Junyi analyzes Confucian ideas in a critical way, but with unfailing commitment and a kind of faith that sometimes defies translation into purely academic language. Although presently I am less interested in the nature of Tang's personal spirituality[8] and more in the philosophical import of his thinking, we will encounter a similar difficulty at a later stage of this discussion, when we need to address the question of how

6 Remember that even Immanuel Kant, who tried to define almost every concept he ever used, called it »an important prudential maxim, not to embark at once upon the task of definition […]« (Kant, Immanuel: *Critique of Pure Reason*, transl. by Norman Kemp Smith, London 1933, pp. 261/A 242; translation slightly altered).

7 Following the dictum from the Confucian classic Doctrine of the Mean »To be human is to be humane«, Confucian thinkers to this day tend to conceive human nature in moral terms. Tang Junyi and his fellow New Confucians are certainly no exception to this.

8 On this see his autobiographical text »My Choice between Philosophy and Religion«, published as an appendix in Tang Junyi (Tang: »The Reconstruction of the Humanistic Spirit«, pp. 562–595).

far some of Tang's key doctrines are founded on philosophical argumentation or a kind of religious belief. Until then, however, I will try to reconstruct his ideas *philosophically* and to present them as part of an argument with the humanistic tradition of the West, which Tang Junyi used as a point of reference for his own reconstruction of Confucian humanism. Indeed, since there is in Tang's writings a kind of ongoing competition between Western and Confucian humanism, the second objective of this essay is to show why Tang Junyi thought that the Confucian version was informed by a deeper understanding of human nature.

1. *Renwen* Humanism and its Negatives: A Preliminary Categorization

In the first chapter of his book *The Development of China's Humanistic Spirit*,[9] Tang Junyi approaches his central category of humanism by distinguishing it from four different modes of what for want of a better term I shall call ›other than humanistic‹ thinking. Although this rough categorization leaves many questions unanswered, it does offer a starting point for our inquiry into Tang Junyi's understanding of what humanism is all about.

The four forms of ›other than humanistic‹ thinking are: non-humanistic thinking (*fei renwen sixiang*), super-humanistic thinking (*chao renwen sixiang*), sub-humanistic thinking (*ci renwen sixiang*) and anti-humanistic thinking (*fan renwen sixiang*).[10] With these four negatives Tang Junyi seeks to distinguish Confucian humanism from other traditions in both China and the Western world. What he calls *non-humanistic thinking* is an intellectual effort directed at non-human objects, such as nature. The natural sciences are obvious instances of non-humanistic thinking, which is the only one of the four forms for which Tang Junyi does not present a Chinese example, because he thinks that in traditional China scientific thinking has not emerged. China always had what he calls »concrete culture«,[11] meaning the kind of proto-scientific knowledge required to tame and exploit nature, but Tang Junyi insists that the ancient Chinese have made no attempt »to

9 Tang: »The Development of China's Humanistic Spirit«.

10 See Tang: »The Development of China's Humanistic Spirit«, p. 9.

11 Tang: »The Development of China's Humanistic Spirit«, p. 12.

understand nature for the sake of understanding nature«.[12] Next, *super-humanistic thinking* is directed at spheres beyond the human life-world, as in the case of Platonic metaphysics and the monotheistic religions of the Judeo-Christian West or, in Tang's view, in certain forms of Chinese Daoism and Buddhism. In super-humanistic thinking, reverence of and obedience to a non-human being – usually called God – is ultimately more important than the businesses of the human life-world. Drawing a strict line between what is secular and sacred, immanent and transcendent, profane and holy, super-humanistic thinking's ultimate concern is always the latter realm, not the former. The third form is called *sub-humanistic thinking*, which *is* directed at human affairs, but fails to fully »affirm and respect the existence and value of human nature, human relationships, humanity, human culture and its history«.[13] Curiously short on examples in this text, Tang Junyi elsewhere criticizes Marx, Freud, Pavlov, and others on the grounds of their one-sided view on human nature, which essentially reduces man to an animal and »fails to see the truth of human nature«.[14] Tang Junyi thinks that by analyzing human nature from their particular perspectives, these and other variants of modern scientific inquiry somehow miss the point – we will have to return to the obvious question of what that point is at a later stage of this discussion. Finally, *anti-humanistic thinking* is the direct negation of the value of man's moral nature, as Tang sees it at work in the ancient Chinese school of Legalism. The

12 Tang: »The Development of China's Humanistic Spirit«, p. 13. It is interesting to see how Tang Junyi and his fellow New Confucians often share certain notions of Chinese culture that we have learned to discard as Western stereotypes. Yet they usually qualify or even reverse the judgment that the notion in question entails. That ancient China did not possess science is, from the New Confucian point of view, no mere a flaw, but proof of the superior humanism of Chinese culture. Unlike their Western contemporaries in Greece or Rome, the ancient Chinese never forgot to direct their thinking at human affairs rather than stones or stars. Tang Junyi (Tang: »The Development of China's Humanistic Spirit«, p. 13) presents the ancient Greek philosopher Thales as the prototype of a scientific thinker: Gazing at the stars in an attempt to understand their order, he was so forgetful of even his own affairs that he fell into a pit.

13 Tang: »The Development of China's Humanistic Spirit«, p. 9.

14 Tang: »The Reconstruction of the Humanistic Spirit«, p. 565.

modern Western tradition of anti-humanism, usually associated with Nietzsche and his followers, is not mentioned here. Tang emphasizes that of these four forms of ›other than humanistic‹ thinking only the last one directly contradicts humanism and is therefore incompatible with its spirit. The other three may well be part of an essentially humanistic culture, such as the Chinese one.

Tang Junyi's presentation of the four forms of ›other than humanistic‹ thinking is too short to be of much systematic value – it is also quite obviously tailor-made to present Confucianism as the prime example of humanistic thinking – but it does provide a first orientation for our discussion. From a Western perspective it is particularly interesting to see how Tang Junyi wants to catch the spirit of Confucian humanism by drawing dividing lines in two crucial directions: For him, Confucianism is neither a religion in the sense of Western monotheism, as it is not concerned with a divine realm beyond and above the human life-world; nor is Confucianism secular in the sense of modern Marxism, Psychoanalysis or Behaviorism, as it still insists on – what exactly?

We may get a first hint at the answer from Tang Junyi's ›definition‹ of humanism, which is, in fact, rather a kind of confession of Confucian faith, indeed almost an oath:

»What I call humanistic thinking is the willingness to fully affirm and respect the existence and value of man's moral nature (*renxing*) and the relations between human beings (*renlun*), the way of human beings (*rendao*), the person/human character (*renge*), human culture (*ren zhi wenhua*) and its history, to not slight, much less attack and distort the above and to not analogize human beings with the non-human or sub-human realm of (mere) natural objects.«[15]

The crucial terms employed in this definition are all taken from the canon of Confucian writings and they all include the character for »human being« (*ren*). Furthermore, we encounter in this definition what I have called the specific tone of voice in which Tang Junyi writes about the Confucian tradition. There is a certain aura, the sense of something that *must* be respected and revered, that *must not* be slighted or distorted, not because it is divine, but precisely because it is human. In a different text Tang makes the telling remark: »A perfect

15 Tang: »The Development of China's Humanistic Spirit«, p. 10.

religion needs not only to serve God as though he had personality/a human character (*renge*), but also to serve man as though he had divinity/a divine character (*shenge*)«.[16] This remark may help us to understand why Tang Junyi draws a dividing line not only between Confucianism and Judeo-Christian monotheism, but also between Confucianism and the secularism of modern scientific thought: Confucianism lacks a notion of the divine realm beyond the human life-world, but modern secularism lacks a notion of the quasi-divine realm *within* the human life-world. What we need to understand is the precise nature of this quasi-divine realm, to which Tang Junyi often refers as a specific kind of »transcendence« (*chaoyuexing*).[17] What does it mean to serve man as though he had a divine character? Instead of consulting the seemingly endless debates of scholars in both China and the West on the question whether or not Confucianism is a religion,[18] I shall try in the following subsections to shed some light on this question by inquiring further into the crucial concept of human being (*ren*). Before I do so, however, I wish to remind the reader that Tang Junyi in his above definition defines Confucianism on the level of our *willingness* (*yuanyi*) to look at people in a certain fashion and an effort to not

---

16 Tang: »The Reconstruction of the Humanistic Spirit«, p. 593.

17 For one such instance see Tang: »The Spiritual Values of Chinese Culture«, pp. 125–132.

18 For a stimulating contribution to this debate see Fingarette (Fingarette, Herbert: *Confucius: The Secular as Sacred*, New York 1972) who is explicitly concerned only with the Confucian Analects, but whose formulation »the secular as sacred« is in line with Tang Junyi's view on Confucianism in general. Taylor (Taylor, Rodney L.: *The Religious Dimensions of Confucianism*, Albany 1990) discusses the entire ancient Confucian tradition, trying to prove its essentially religious character. Philosophically challenging is Lee Ming-huei's (Lee Ming-huei: »Cong Kangde de daode zongjiao lun rujia de zongjiaoxing« [»A Discussion of the Religious Character of Confucianism from the Perspective of Kant's ›Moral Religion‹«], in: Harvard Yenching Institute (Ed.): *Rujia chuantong yu qimeng xintai* [*Confucian Tradition and the Mindset of Enlightenment*], Nanjing 2005, pp. 228–269), a recent attempt to determine the religious character of Confucian thinking by applying Kant's concepts of Moralreligion to the Confucian context. Lee is a student of Tang Junyi's friend and collaborator Mou Zongsan (1909–1995).

see them in another fashion, namely as beings analogous to non-human objects. This element of his definition is easily overlooked, but is in fact crucial, as I hope to make evident in the following discussion. Tang Junyi tries to present *Renwen* humanism not so much as a fixed set of particular beliefs, but rather as a kind of attitude that guides human agency.

2. *Renwen* Humanism: Humanity and Responsibility

Modern Confucians often refer to their own tradition as a kind of »moral effort teaching« (*gongfulun*), thereby emphasizing Confucianism's practical and educational concerns. Traditional Confucianism focused on the effort of every individual to cultivate his or her moral nature and to come as close as possible to the ideal of the *Shengren*, the »moral virtuoso« or »perfectly cultivated man«. This effort included a whole range of exercises from the study of classical texts – in which students encountered various examples of the *Shengren* – to different kinds of rites and rituals, ranging from the strict observance of rules of propriety to the exercise of traditional arts and crafts, such as calligraphy, music, archery and so on. Particular emphasis was placed on interpersonal relationships, especially on displays of filial piety and respect, in which traditional Confucians saw the corner stone of a well-ordered and stable society. In short, moral cultivation gave meaning to one's individual life in so far as it contributed to the integrity and order of the community. New Confucians in the 20th century then faced the difficult task of incorporating these traditional values and virtues into a modern system of ethics. The cultural life-world from which the values stemmed had vanished with the collapse of the old imperial order, out of which arose the necessity to provide justifications of a philosophical kind. What could no longer be taken for granted had now to be argued for; but to make their arguments, the New Confucians also had to find a new language for their discourse, a philosophical terminology the validity of which did not depend on the language game of their tradition. This is why New Confucians like Tang Junyi imported a large number of concepts from Western philosophy into their own discourse, often adapting the meaning to their specific needs.[19]

(a) The Hermeneutics of Human Agency: The Importance of Self-Awareness

In Confucian thinking, all human agency is informed by a self-image of the agent that at the same time expresses the guiding interest of his or her actions. For example, as a philosopher attending a conference I am guided by my self-image of an academic philosopher and hence by the concern to present myself as a *good* philosopher to my colleagues. Accordingly, the way I act and speak will reflect this interest. Other self-images and ambitions I may harbor – such as being a good cook or singer – are without relevance in this context and will have no bearing on the way I present myself. Yet what Confucians are concerned with is not so much my self-image as a particular role-player,[20] but the fundamental self-image of me as a human being, in other words, the guiding image of me in *all* particular social roles. Confucians ask for one guiding image that I may accentuate differently depending on the particular role I am playing in a given context, but which I will avoid violating in any context. If necessary, I will refuse to play roles that conflict with this guiding sense of my Self. This, of course, presupposes a degree of consciousness about my self-

---

19 With regard to Tang Junyi's friend and close collaborator Mou Zongsan, I have tried to demonstrate how the different vocabularies of his writings – Kantian, Confucian, Buddhist etc. – lead to a degree of hybridity that makes Mou's arguments look extremely complex, even when he is expressing rather commonplace ideas. See Schmidt, Stephan: »Mou Zongsan, Hegel, and Kant: The Quest for Confucian Modernity«, in: Philosophy East & West 61.2 (2011), pp. 260–302. My objective in that essay as well as the present one is to cut through the different layers of (often) incompatible vocabularies and to get a glimpse of the particular moral vision of modern New Confucianism.

20 Still, they do define and describe the duties of particular social roles. But ever since Confucius introduced the ultimate moral standard of »humanity« (*ren*) into the discourse, the justification of particular duties and virtues had to apply to this guiding sense of what being human(e) is all about. I will have to say more on this further below.

image – my identity, in modern parlance – and the ability to communicate it. In Tang Junyi's writings, Confucianism is largely an effort to clarify this self-image so that we become able to realize and confirm it through our actions.[21] This cognitive component is captured in his key-notion of »self-awareness« (*zi jue*) which in some contexts amounts to something like »epistemological and moral autonomy«,[22] although the use of the term autonomy requires qualification. Through self-awareness we come to the *right* self-image, and it is of some importance to not misconstrue the

---

21 See the concluding chapter of Tang Junyi: *Zhexue gailun* (*Introduction to Philosophy*), Taipei 1961, reprint 1985. The title of this monumental study, *Introduction to Philosophy*, is something of an understatement, since what Tang Junyi attempts to deliver in its two volumes is nothing less than a comprehensive *system* of all philosophy, both East and West. It is not by chance that the concluding chapter focuses on the notion of self-awareness. See pages 544–560 of the second volume.

22 Metzger (Metzger, Thomas: »The Thought of T'ang Chun-i [Tang Junyi]: A Preliminary Response«, in: Huo Daohui: *Tang Junyi sixiang: Guoji huiyi lunwenji* [*Collected Essays from an International Conference on Tang Junyi's Thought*], Hong Kong 1992, pp. 165–198) translates the term as »epistemological autonomy« and says it »refers to adopting ideas only when completely understanding all the reasons why they should be adopted, instead of adopting them unthinkingly and so being controlled by influences external to the self«. In a later text (Metzger: »A Cloud Across the Pacific«; p. 261) he defines *zijue* more broadly as an agent's »full awareness of the key conditions affecting his or her life«. These are good enough approximations to the complex of meaning of *zijue*, although, as I have stated in footnote 2 above, Metzger tends to overstate Tang Junyi's epistemological concerns. For Tang is concerned with epistemology mainly because he sees it as a necessary cognitive component of the modern philosophical »moral effort teaching« (*gongfulun*) he seeks to establish. The connection is aptly captured in his definition of moral life in one of his early works: »What is true moral life? Self-governance/self-control (*ziji zhipei ziji*) in self-awareness.« Tang Junyi: *Daode ziwo zhi jianli* (*Establishing the Moral Self*), Taipei 1944, reprint (1985), p. 37. In another text Tang Junyi writes »a man with moral sincerity can transcend the limits of particular knowledge« (Tang: »The Reconstruction of the Humanistic Spirit«, p. 577).

Confucian understanding of what it is that makes a self-image right. For Tang Junyi is not primarily concerned with *correct* self-image in a theoretical sense, as judged by the question of whether or not the way I *see* myself is in accordance with the way I actually *am*. Confucianism in general is less about the correspondence of images (or propositions) to facts than of facts to norms. The right self-image, therefore, is the one that enables me to do the right thing so that through my actions I *become* the person I am supposed to be. We can see here that the translation of *zi jue* into »autonomy« is precarious, in so far as autonomy in the strict Kantian sense means that an agent *generates* the norms with which his or her actions comply, whereas in Confucianism the norms are given and have their origin in what was traditionally called »Heaven« (*tian*). Furthermore, we see that what New Confucians seek to justify are not the norms and values themselves – which they largely take for granted – but their validity under the radically changed circumstances of modernity. They argue that far from being at odds with modernity, traditional values provide the standards on which a future Confucian modernity can be and has to be modeled – although they at least implicitly admit that a certain amount of reformulating has to be done, before this possibility can one day be seized.

From Confucius' times onward Confucians have tried to determine the self-image that is best suited to guide human agency. As mentioned above, the traditional name for this image is the *Shengren*, and the ultimate value according to which one's moral virtuosity can be judged is »humanity« (*ren*).[23] The character for »humanity« consists of the classifier for »human being« plus the numeral »two« – better than any definition could, these two components convey the meaning of the term: Humanity[24] means that every human being is related to other human beings in a profound way and that the nature of this relation entails moral obligations of an absolute kind. In its application, the term is often akin to the Western

23 Note that this *ren* character is different from the one meaning »human being« (as in *Renwen* humanism), although their pronunciation is the same.

24 One might also venture the translation »fellow-humanness«, but for stylistic reasons I will stick to the term humanity for most of this essay.

concept of *dignity*.[25] Confucian humanism as a tradition is rooted in the belief that all human agency has to be informed by the ultimate value of humanity. Confucian thinking over the centuries largely revolved around the question of which particular acts and deeds do best express the spirit of humanity and should therefore serve as models in the moral education of children and students. The idea behind this, of course, was not that students should just mechanically copy certain forms of behavior, but that they should nurture within their own minds the kind of insight and self-awareness that would enable them to act in the spirit of humanity in any situation they might encounter in their lives.

What we have to understand now is the interesting way in which Tang Junyi is a heir to this tradition, albeit one who seeks to sharpen the tradition's philosophical profile so that it becomes obvious why Confucianism has a message for all humankind. The result of this effort is his challenging notion of *Renwen* humanism.

(b) Moral Subject, Epistemological Subject, and the Other

In his book *The Development of China's Humanistic Spirit* Tang Junyi speaks of »humanism's fundamental belief that a concrete human being is always to be regarded and valued as a subject and never as an object«.[26] At first glance, this is but a more jargon-laden restatement of the maxim to respect other people, but it prepares Tang Junyi's critical distinction between Western humanism und Confucian *Renwen* humanism. What is under debate here is the way we look at both ourselves and others. What is our guiding sense of Self and how does it guide the way we perceive and approach other people? In a somewhat schematic but still illuminating fashion Tang Junyi contrasts two different conceptions of the Self, namely the »moral subject« (*daode zhuti*) as opposed to the »epistemological subject« (*renshi zhuti*).[27] It is important to note

---

25 Tang Junyi (Tang: »The Spiritual Values of Chinese Culture«, p. 183) also sees a connection between Confucian humanity and the Christian notion of *agape*.

26 Tang: »The Development of China's Humanistic Spirit«, p. 61.

27 Note that Tang Junyi is not always faithful to this terminology, but sometimes uses different terms. Still, the distinction in question is crucial for his notion of Renwen humanism and its meaning remains the same regardless

that in the New Confucian discourse both terms serve various functions at the same time: Both can refer to *social roles* which people adopt in different circumstances; solving a mathematical equation, I play the role of an epistemological subject, whereas when I help an elderly woman to safely cross the street, I do so as a moral subject. On a different level, both terms also represent general *cultural types*. To some degree, the moral subject is a modern conceptualization of the traditional Confucian *Shengren*, whereas the epistemological subject represents the Cartesian *Cogito* and hence a typically Western concept of the Self. Since Tang Junyi often develops his ideas by way of a critical dialogue with Western thinkers he does not always bother to clearly distinguish both levels of his terminology. Let us now take a brief look at what the distinction implies.

As epistemological subjects we occupy center stage in our worldview and field of vision. Around us we see nothing but objects with which we deal by applying concepts to them, that is, we name and define them and thereby fix them in their respective positions. The crucial question is: What happens when within this field of vision we encounter the presence of another human being? From the perspective of the epistemological subject, the logical way to deal with other human beings is the like way: We assign them a place in our field of vision and treat them as objects. The obvious problem with this is that the other person will try to do the same with us. The famous analysis of the look in *Being and Nothingness* by Jean-Paul Sartre – a self-proclaimed humanist – can serve to illustrate the kind of confrontational situation that arises when two epistemological subjects meet and try to prevail over the other.[28] Identifying with one such subject and therefore writing in

---

of differences in wording. See Schmidt, Stephan: »Moralsubjekt und Erkenntnissubjekt: Zu einer kategorialen Unterscheidung im modernen Konfuzianismus«, in: polylog: Zeitschrift für Interkulturelles Philosophieren 19 (2008), pp. 61–82.

28 Tang Junyi places Sartre in the camp of Western humanists (see Tang: »The Development of China's Humanistic Spirit«, p. 64), but to my knowledge he does not discuss Sartre's analysis of the look, which I introduce here as a kind of Weberian Idealtyp, in order to exemplify the concept of an epistemological subject. Obviously, Sartre's position is in-

the first person singular Sartre states: »I grasp the Other's look at the very center of my act as the solidification and alienation of my own possibilities«. And: »With the Other's look the situation escapes me. To use an everyday expression which better expresses our thought, *I am no longer master of the situation*«.[29] As long as two subjects try to remain the sole master of the situation, their encounter necessarily assumes the form of a struggle.

> »In fear or in anxious or prudent anticipation, I perceive that these possibilities which I am and which are the condition of my transcendence are given also to another, given as about to be transcended in turn by his own possibilities. The Other as a look is only that – my transcendence transcended«.[30]

It is quite telling that Sartre, without apparent hesitation, assumes that the most fundamental way in which human beings relate to each other is that of a struggle. In his analysis, the Other appears first and foremost as a threat to my subjectivity. As soon as I feel the gaze of another person upon myself, my world begins to come apart. My transcendence – which in Sartre is my freedom to project different possibilities of action – is denied and crossed out by the other person's transcendence, as both possibly claim the same space. There is a potential rivalry between my freedom and that of the other person. Regardless of how the encounter plays out in concrete, underneath every interaction between human beings Sartre locates this confrontation of two conflicting claims to freedom. We may dismiss his model as just another existentialist dramatization of every day life coming to a head, but from a Confucian perspective there is something typical about Sartre's point of view.
Before further pursuing this argument, let us take a look at the Confucian paradigm of interpersonal encounters. In the canonical book of *Mencius* (2A, 6), Mencius argues that all human beings

---

formed by Hegel's dialectic of master and slave in the *Phenomenology of the Spirit.*

29 Sartre, Jean-Paul: *Being and Nothingness: An Essay on Phenomenological Ontology*, transl. by Hazel Barnes, New York 1969, pp. 263, 265.

30 Sartre: »Being and Nothingness«, p. 263.

have a kind of innate moral character that becomes apparent in our responsiveness to the suffering of others. He says:

> »My reason for saying that no man is devoid of a heart sensitive to the suffering of others[31] is this. Suppose a man were, all of a sudden, to see a young child on the verge of falling into a well. He would certainly be moved to compassion, not because he wanted to get in the good graces of the parents, nor because he wished to win the praise of his fellow villagers, nor yet because he disliked the cry of the child«.[32]

On an occasion like this, Mencius claims, we become aware of this inner morality of ours that at other times may be hidden from our own consciousness, yet presents itself forcefully vis-à-vis the potential or actual suffering of a fellow human being. Confucians have traditionally called this inner morality the »heavenly heart« (*tian xin*) or the »original/authentic heart« (*ben xin*), which is original and authentic in that it is spontaneous and uncorrupted by the non-moral motives Mencius has excluded from his thought experiment. Seeing the child about to fall into the well, the man is moved solely by his »heart of compassion« (*ceyin zhi xin*) which Mencius calls »the germ of humanity« (ibid.),[33] i.e. that out of which true humanity can grow. In New Confucian parlance, this is at the same time an instance of self-awareness, namely of the awareness that I have a heart that cannot stand to see others suffer and therefore compels me to act.

In a brief but illuminating fashion, Tang Junyi refers to the thought experiment of the child on the well in his book *The Spiritual Values of Chinese Culture*. What is located in every man's authentic heart, he states, is a fundamental »connecting responsiveness« (*gan*

---

31 A more literal and forceful translation would be »a heart that cannot bear the suffering of others« (bu ren ren zhi xin).

32 I quote from the translation by D.C. Lau (Lau, D. C.: *Mencius – A Bilingual Edition*, Hong Kong 2003, p. 73). Note that Mencius does not claim that the man will necessarily rush forward to save the child. What he does claim, however, is that he will feel the urge to do so, namely a spontaneous response from within his heart, which he is free to not follow, but which he cannot suppress altogether.

33 Here I depart from Lau's translation in which ren is rendered as »benevolence«, not »humanity«.

tong)[34] that transcends individuality by linking all human beings with one another. Philosophically speaking, this link is the condition of the possibility of *com*passion. We can see here that Tang Junyi takes the »fellow-humanness« of *ren* (humanity) literally and seriously. He explicitly denies that compassion comes out of an intellectual procedure by which I put myself in somebody else's shoes, imagining the unpleasantness of a sensation like falling into a deep well and than acting according to some form of the Golden Rule. For Tang Junyi, this is but a secondary operation, which we are free to undergo when we wish to rationalize the primary thing: The conscious responsiveness to the potential or actual suffering of a fellow human being. Tang Junyi speaks of a »mental state in which we transcend all individual desires«[35] and become aware of a fundamental truth of human existence: We are not isolated human beings, but are connected by a trans-individual bond that makes it impossible for us to not feel the Other's suffering when we see it – although, of course, we can still choose to ignore this insight and to act *as if* somebody else's plight was a matter of indifference to us.

Obviously, the contrast between the two paradigms could hardly be bigger. Whereas in Sartre human beings necessarily perceive each other as rivals, because their respective ways of transcending themselves are ultimately at odds, Confucianism insists that the most fundamental relation between humans is that of a compassion transcending individual desires. Whereas in Sartre the Other is an obstacle to the realization of my transcendence, in Confucianism this realization is only possible in the presence of the Other, as it consists in my responsiveness to and responsibility for him or her. Far from being the one who blocks access to my transcendence, the Confucian Other, so to speak, opens the only door through which I can enter transcendence, which therefore is not *mine* at all, but always has to be *ours*. In the next subsection we have to see how Tang Junyi makes an attempt to integrate elements of the Western model into an understanding of moral and epistemological subjectivity that is neither helplessly naïve nor unnecessarily antagonis-

34 For his brief reference to Mencius' thought experiment see Tang: »The Spiritual Values of Chinese Culture«, pp. 142–43.

35 Tang: »The Spiritual Values of Chinese Culture«, p. 142.

tic. He does so by adopting a Buddhist distinction to serve his Confucian needs.

(c) Changing Perspectives: Clinging and Not-Clinging to Individuality

The first thing we have to note is that Tang Junyi is by no means oblivious of the fact that as natural beings we *are* individuals. He is also not one to deny the great benefits reaped by the epistemological subject in its role as the main agent of Western civilization in general and Western modernity in particular. Indeed, it is one Tang's recurrent themes that China has to adopt Western ways of scientific thinking in order to become a truly modern nation herself.[36] And still he is clearly convinced of the primacy of moral subjectivity over epistemological subjectivity. What does this mean?

Of central importance in this context is a distinction of Buddhist origin that comes to play a crucial role in Tang Junyi's thought. It distinguishes two different modes of human existence: one in which human beings mistakenly cling to what is constantly changing and another in which they do not. In Chinese, this complex meaning is comprised in the two brief terms *zhi* and *wu zhi,* which for the sake of brevity I shall translate as »clinging« and »not clinging«, respectively. The Buddhist distinction refers to the unwholesome realm of ignorance that causes sentient beings to cling to what constantly arises and perishes and consequently to suffer from the frustration of unfulfilled desires, over against the wholesome realm of enlightenment and insight into the impermanence of all things. Despite its epistemological and ontological implications, the Buddhist distinction is basically a soteriological one: It is meant to guide sentient beings from the former realm or state to the latter and thus from suffering to salvation.[37]

---

36 The famous Manifesto on the Reappraisal of Chinese Culture written by Tang Junyi and jointly published by him and three fellow New Confucians in 1958 gives testimony to this conviction. For an English translation of the text see Tang Junyi: *Essays on Chinese Philosophy and Culture*, Taipei (no year given), pp. 492–562.

37 On this see Kantor, Hans Rudolf: »Ontological Indeterminacy and its Soteriological Relevance: An Assessment of Mou Zongsan's (1909–1995) In-

As Tang Junyi sees it, Western philosophy clings to the perspective of the epistemological subject to an unhealthy degree, namely to the degree that even ethical reflections take it as their starting point. Western philosophers speak of inter-subjectivity, for instance, but they employ a conceptualization of the subject that necessarily turns one of the subjects involved into an object. We may recall here Tang's definition of *Renwen* humanism, given above, in which he states that human beings should never be analogized to non-human objects. Yet this is precisely what Western ethicists do when they take as a starting point for their reflections a concept of the human being that abstracts from his or her morality. For morality, in Tang Junyi's understanding, is just another word for trans-individuality. For him it makes little sense to first perceive human beings as isolated entities and then to ask how they can act morally.[38] If we are to correctly understand moral agency we have to start with the moral subject, and that is with the addressee of the Other's call for help (respect, assistance, attention, recognition etc.). As moral subjects we are *respons*ible. Responsibility, taken literally, means to look at everything, including ourselves, from the perspective of the Other. And if we do look at ourselves that way, we are to find out that epistemological subjectivity abstracts from this whole dimension of responsibility and thus negates it. Therefore, we must not think of epistemological subjectivity as our natural and necessary state of existence – although to a certain degree it is necessary, as Tang Junyi knows – but as a deficient and inauthentic one in which we temporarily deny our moral subjectivity in order to go about the business of daily life. Put differently, we should *assume* the role of the epistemological subject, but not *cling* to it when dealing with other people, and we should not mistake it for true selfhood or the realization of personal freedom.

At the root of this conceptual and epistemological clinging is what Tang Junyi, following the established terminology of his tradition,

---

terpretation of Zhi Yi's (538–597) Tiantai Buddhism«, in: Philosophy East & West 56.1 (2006), pp. 16–68.

38 See the discussion in Tang Junyi (1951: 147–154) in which the terminology suggests that Tang is having Immanuel Kant in mind, whom he views as a typical example of the individualistic fallacy so common in Western thought. A little later (p. 164–65), Kant's name is explicitly mentioned.

calls »selfish desires« (*si yu*).[39] Selfishness is the exact opposite of responsibility: Looking at everything, including the Other, from the perspective of what I want and how I may subject it (him/her) to my own needs. As Tang Junyi knows, this perspective is *natural* in that it is rooted in our biological constitution as beings with certain undeniable needs and desires, for food, drink, sex etc. It would be naïve to assume that we could be entirely free from these natural desires[40] and therefore wrong to damn them as sin, as the Christian tradition does.[41] Still, Tang Junyi insists that human beings also possess a *moral nature* and are therefore free to not follow every selfish impulse that emanates from their biological constitution.
In the thought experiment of the child on the well it is easy to see what responsibility means: To save the child. It takes no reasoning to glean the moral imperative from the context of this story, but it is also not difficult to imagine situations in which it is less obvious to see what needs to be done, if not because of the complexity of the situation, then because of our accustomed neglect of the Other's call for help. Moral cultivation is the continuous effort to fight this neglect and to adjust our moral antenna so that we hear the call even when it is only a whisper. Through moral cultivation we expand the sphere of our responsibility, which in the Confucian understanding is potentially endless, because of our togetherness with all other people. This togetherness requires us to direct all our love, respect and reverence at our fellow human beings, not for the sake of God or some other divine entity, but for the sake of our humanity or fellow-humanness. *Renwen* humanism, then, is a kind of fellow-humanism – or, to borrow Levinas' words, an *humanisme de l'autre homme*[42] – as it always takes two to realize it. *Renwen* hu-

39 See Tang: »The Spiritual Values of Chinese Culture«, p. 162.

40 Tang: »The Development of China's Humanistic Spirit«, p. 162.

41 In an interesting passage, Tang Junyi (Tang: »The Spiritual Values of Chinese Culture«, p. 163) defends the biblical Adam whose act of eating the forbidden fruit he interprets as the first and necessary step to gain self-awareness.

42 There are, in my view, striking similarities between the ethics of Levinas and New Confucians like Tang Junyi and Mou Zongsan, although they were apparently unaware of one another and came from very different cultural backgrounds. Within the limits of this paper I cannot delve deeper in-

manism is a humanism not of the individual, but of trans-individuality. Cognizant of the fact that as natural beings we are individuals, it insists that as moral beings we are not. The name for our not being individuals is, of course, humanity (*ren*).

3. DISCUSSION

The discussion so far was my attempt to reconstruct Tang Junyi's notion of *Renwen* humanism in as philosophical a fashion as possible. This is to say that wherever I thought it possible to do so without contorting the idea in question, I have left out of the picture certain elements of Tang's thought that connect his ideas to a worldview which I think cannot be adequately pictured in purely philosophical terms. Yet, as a matter of both fairness and completeness, in this final section I shall try to give the reader an impression of what has been left out before.

My claim made above that Confucianism is searching for the *right* self-image rather than the *correct* one may lead us to think of trans-individuality as an educational device, invented to make the students of Confucianism look beyond their own selfish desires and to heed the needs of others. And while this is certainly an important aspect, we cannot ignore that for Tang Junyi there is something more to it. Following Mencius, he takes it to be a fundamental truth about human nature that something in every human's heart simply cannot stand the suffering of others, and that this something consists in a kind of connection between human beings which is not added to their existing individual personality, but is in fact primordial. Of this connection we can become aware through a process of moral cultivation and close introspection, for the connection manifests itself within our very own hearts. This is the story of the child on the well, which Mencius concludes by saying that he who has no heart of compassion »is not human« (*fei ren ye*).[43] Tang Junyi introduces his notion of trans-individuality in an attempt to *explain* this fact of compassion, for he apparently

to this connection, although I do find it worthy of further exploration. For some very preliminary remarks see Schmidt: »Moralsubjekt und Erkenntnissubjekt«, pp. 76–82.

43 Lau: »Mencius«, p. 73.

thinks that on the basis of mere individuality the prefix *com* in compassion is rather hard to account for. Again following Mencius, he does not believe that compassion is something we learn, but thinks that every process of moral learning needs to presuppose this »germ« (*duan*), as Mencius calls it, without which our learning simply will not bear any fruit. The germ has to be there before the process of learning and cultivation can set in.

What Tang Junyi has in mind when he speaks of this process is what he calls a »dialectical development of the moral consciousness« (ibid.) which leads to a kind of Hegelian *Aufhebung* of our selfish desires.[44] Basically, this dialectical development echoes the familiar step-by-step process laid out in the canonical *Great Learning*: An individual's moral effort to first rectify his or her own moral mind and then gradually expand his cultivation to include his or her family, the clan, the country, until finally a state of cosmic harmony is reached. Although Tang Junyi does not always use grand names like cosmic harmony to define the ultimate goal of Confucianism's moral effort teaching, he does so often enough to render any exclusively ›secular‹ interpretation of his thinking incomplete. For instance, in a passage the first half of which I have quoted in footnote 14 above, Tang Junyi states that »a man with moral sincerity can transcend the limits of particular knowledge to attain an exalted and intimate realization of the origin of the universe and human life«.[45] What Tang describes here is maybe not, strictly speaking, a display of divine or otherworldly powers, but it does go beyond the powers of ordinary humans to gain insight into the origin of the universe through an exercise of moral sincerity. What we encounter here is precisely the kind of ›superhuman human being‹ traditional Confucians have called a *Shengren*: The embodiment of moral perfection and the exemplary display of humanity. *This* kind of transcendence does not stop at saving children from falling into wells, but

---

44 Note that Hegel is never far from Tang Junyi's mind, and that Hegelian concepts appear everywhere in his writings, sometimes recognizably carrying Hegel's ideas and sometimes mere vessels for Tang Junyi's own thought.

45 Tang: »The Reconstruction of the Humanistic Spirit«, p. 775. The term rendered as »realization« (*canwu*) makes one think of an elevating and transformative insight into a higher kind of truth.

aims at peace and harmony on the grandest possible scale. Tang Junyi is not shy of stating his conviction that

> »the expansion of the inherent religious spirit of the Chinese people [...] will manage to harmonize all religions, satisfy their essential needs, forever eliminate the mutual contempt in which the followers of different religions hold each other hence nip religious wars in the bud«.[46]

Behind this lies Tang Junyi belief in the Mencian dictum that man is essentially good[47] and in the possibility that everybody can become a *Shengren.*[48] Obviously, the possibility of moral perfection serves an important theoretical function as the foundation from which duties and maxims can be deduced – since one can become morally perfect, one has the duty to pursue this goal. But it is difficult to see how Tang's belief in human goodness and the super-human powers of the *Shengren* can be reconciled with his sober-minded view of the biological constitution of human nature mentioned above.

For these reasons I am inclined to sum up the discussion as follows: We have to recognize that a kind of religious belief in both the potentially unlimited progress of moral cultivation and the equally unlimited healing powers of Confucianism (as the program of such a cultivation) was the driving force of Tang Junyi's thinking. Yet the resulting ambition to present Confucianism as the cure for all maladies of modern humankind was also what ultimately drove him beyond a philosophically viable form of Confucian humanism. The present essay was an preliminary attempt to shoulder the task that in my view results from Tang's daring endeavor: To return to a more modest but also philosophically more consistent form of Confucian thinking and to work out its possible contribution to a revival of humanistic thinking in the modern world.

---

46 Tang: »The Reconstruction of the Humanistic Spirit«, p. 593.

47 Whether or not human nature is essentially good is the topic of a debate between Mencius and his adversary Gaozi in the book Mencius (6, A), see especially Lau: »Mencius«, p. 247.

48 This is yet another Mencian dictum, see Mencius (6, A7), Lau: »Mencius«, p. 248. To be sure, there are more than a few passages in Tang's books that suggest he was trying very hard to believe without really managing to do so. This, too, may be a source for the ambiguity permeating his thinking.

BIBLIOGRAPHY

Bresciani, Umberto: *Reinventing Confucianism: The New Confucian Movement*, Taipei 2001.

Chang Hao: »New Confucianism and the Intellectual Crisis in Contemporary China«, in: Furth, Charlotte (Ed.): *The Limits of Change – Essays on Conservative Alternatives in Republican China*, Cambridge/MA 1976, pp. 276–302.

Fingarette, Herbert: *Confucius: The Secular as Sacred*, New York 1972.

Huo Daohui: *Tang Junyi sixiang: Guoji huiyi lunwenji* (Collected Essays from an International Conference on Tang Junyi's Thought), Hong Kong 1992.

Kant, Immanuel: *Critique of Pure Reason*, transl. by Norman Kemp Smith, London 1933.

Kantor, Hans Rudolf: »Ontological Indeterminacy and its Soteriological Relevance: An Assessment of Mou Zongsan's (1909–1995) Interpretation of Zhi Yi's (538–597) Tiantai Buddhism«, in: Philosophy East & West 56.1 (2006), pp. 16–68.

Lau, D. C.: *Mencius – A Bilingual Edition*, Hong Kong 2003.

Lee Ming-huei: »Cong Kangde de daode zongjiao lun rujia de zongjiaoxing« (»A Discussion of the Religious Character of Confucianism from the Perspective of Kant's ›Moral Religion‹«), in: Harvard Yenching Institute (Ed.): *Rujia chuantong yu qimeng xintai* (Confucian Tradition and the Mindset of Enlightenment), Nanjing 2005, pp. 228–269.

Lee Ming-huei: *Der Konfuzianismus im modernen China*, Leipzig 2001.

Makeham, John (Ed.): *New Confucianism: A Critical Examination*, New York 2003.

Metzger, Thomas: »The Thought of T'ang Chun-i (Tang Junyi): A Preliminary Response«, in: Huo Daohui: *Tang Junyi sixiang: Guoji huiyi lunwenji* (Collected Essays from an International Conference on Tang Junyi's Thought), Hong Kong 1992, pp. 165–198.

Metzger, Thomas: *A Cloud Across the Pacific: Essays on the Clash between Chinese and Western Political Theories Today*, Hong Kong 2005.

Metzger, Thomas: *Escape from Predicament: Neo-Confucianism and China's Evolving Political Culture*, New York 1977.

Sartre, Jean-Paul: *Being and Nothingness: An Essay on Phenomenological Ontology*, transl. by Hazel Barnes, New York 1969.

Schmidt, Stephan: »Moralsubjekt und Erkenntnissubjekt: Zu einer kategorialen Unterscheidung im modernen Konfuzianismus«, in: polylog: Zeitschrift für Interkulturelles Philosophieren 19 (2008), pp. 61–82.

Schmidt, Stephan: »Mou Zongsan, Hegel, and Kant: The Quest for Confucian Modernity«, in: Philosophy East & West 61.2 (2011), pp. 260–302.

Tang Junyi: *Daode ziwo zhi jianli* (Establishing the Moral Self), Taipei 1944, reprint (1985).

Tang Junyi: *Essays on Chinese Philosophy and Culture*, Taipei (no year given).

Tang Junyi: *Renwen jingshen zhi chongjian* (The Reconstruction of the Humanistic Spirit), Taipei 1955, reprint 2000.

Tang Junyi: *Zhexue gailun* (Introduction to Philosophy), Taipei 1961, reprint (1985).

Tang Junyi: *Zhongguo renwen jingshen zhi fazhan* (The Development of China's Humanistic Spirit), Taipei 1957, reprint 2000.

Tang Junyi: *Zhongguo wenhua zhi jingshen jiazhi* (The Spiritual Values of Chinese Culture), Taipei 1951, reprint 1979.

Taylor, Rodney L.: *The Religious Dimensions of Confucianism*, Albany 1990.

Zheng Jiadong: *Dangdai xinrujia lunheng* (A Discussion of Contemporary New Confucianism), Taipei 1995.

Notes on the Contributors

Hubert Cancik, Professor emeritus of Classics at the Eberhard-Karls-Universität, Tübingen (Germany). Born in 1937, University studies in classics, archeology, and languages of the Ancient Near East in Berlin, Münster, Manchester, and Tübingen.

Fields of research: cultural history of antiquity; history of ancient religions; history of classical scholarship.

Some publications: *Römische Religion im Kontext: Gesammelte Aufsätze I*, ed. by Hildegard Cancik-Lindemaier, Tübingen 2008; *Religionsgeschichten: Gesammelte Aufsätze II*, ed. by Hildegard Cancik-Lindemaier, Tübingen 2008; *Franz Overbeck: Werke und Nachlaß*, vol. 3: *Schriften bis 1898 und Rezensionen*, ed. by Hubert Cancik and Hildegard Cancik-Lindemaier, Stuttgart/Weimar 2010; *Europa – Antike – Humanismus: Humanistische Versuche und Vorarbeiten*, ed. by Hildegard Cancik-Lindemaier, Bielefeld 2011. As Editor/Co-Editor: *Handbuch religionswissenschaftlicher Grundbegriffe*, Stuttgart 1988–2001; *Der neue Pauly*, Stuttgart/Weimar 1996–2003.

Georg Essen, Study of Catholic Theology and History in Münster and Freiburg (Ger); 1994 PhD-Thesis (Dr. theol.); 1999 Habilitation (venia legendi for »Dogmatic Theology«) at the Faculty of Catholic Theology Münster (Ger); 2001–2011 Chair of Dogmatic Theology, Faculty of Philosophy, Theology and Religious Studies, Nijmegen (NL); 2006–2011 Chair of Theory of Religion and Culture, Faculty of Philosophy, Theology and Religious Studies, Nijmegen (NL) (additional); 2006–2009 Fellow at the Kulturwissenschaftliches Institut, Essen; 2011 Visiting Scholar at Stanford University; since 2011 Chair of Dogmatic Theology and History of Dogma, Faculty of Catholic Theology, Bochum (Germany).

Fields of Research: Systematic Theology and Philosophy of Religion, especially in the frameworks of modern theology and philosophy. During the last decade the research focus is on Christology, Eschatology and Meta-history, the Doctrine of God in modernity, esp. in the public political culture, Humanism in the era of globalisation.

Recent Publications: *Die Freiheit Jesu: Der neuchalkedonische Enhypostasiebegriff im Horizont neuzeitlicher Subjekt- und Personphilosophie*, Regensburg 2001; *Sinnstiftende Unruhe im System des Rechts: Religion im Beziehungsgeflecht von modernem Verfassungsstaat und säkularer Zivilgesellschaft*, Göttingen 2004; *Geschichtstheologie und Eschatologie im 20. Jahrhundert: Eine Grundlegung*, Münster et al. 2011.

Recently edited: (with M. Striet) *Kant und die moderne Theologie*, Darmstadt 2005; (with N. Jansen) *Dogmatisierungsprozesse in Recht und Religion*, Tübingen 2011; (with Chr. Danz) *Pantheismusstreit – Atheismusstreit – Theismusstreit: Philosophisch-theologische Streitsachen in der religionsphilosophischen Achsenzeit*, Darmstadt 2011.

Bernhard Giesen, Professor of macro-sociology at the University of Konstanz.

Fields of research: Historic-comparative analysis of public opinion and collective identity on a national level; sociological analysis of intellectual discourse rituals; analysis of national rituals of commemoration.

Recent Books: *Kollektive Identität: Die Intellektuellen und die Nation,* vol. 2, Frankfurt/Main 1999; *Triumph and Trauma*, Boulder 2004; *Zwischenlagen: Das Außerordentliche als Grund der sozialen Wirklichkeit*, Weilerswist 2010.

Recently edited: *Cultural Trauma and Collective Identity*, Berkeley 2004 (with J.C. Alexander, R. Eyermann, N. Smelser and P. Sztompka); *Religion and Politics: Cultural Perspectives*, Leiden 2005 (with D. Suber); *Social Performance: Symbolic Action, Cultural Pragmatics and Ritual*, Cambridge 2006 (with J.C. Alexander and J.L. Mast); *Iconic Power: Materiality and Meaning in Social Life*, New York 2011 (with J.C. Alexander and D. Bartmanski).

Oliver Kozlarek, teaches political and social philosophy as well as social theory at the Institute for Philosophical Research at Universidad Michoacana de San Nicolás de Hidalgo in Morelia, Mexico. He has been a visiting fellow at the Kulturwissenschaftliches Institut in Essen at the New School for Social Research and at Stanford University.

Fields of research: theories of modernity and globalization, critical theory, globalization and humanism, Latin American political and social thought.

Recently edited and authored books include: *De la Teoría Crítica a una crítica plural de la modernidad,* Mexico 2007; *Entre Cosmopolitismo y »conciencia del mundo«*, Mexico 2007 (Siglo XXI); *Humanismo en la época de la globalización: Desafíos y horizontes*, Mexico 2009 (with Jörn Rüsen); *Octavio Paz: Humanism and Critique* Bielefeld 2009; and *Moderne als Weltbewusstsein: Ideen für eine humanistische Sozialtheorie in der globalen Moderne*, Bielefeld 2011.

Georg W. Oesterdiekhoff, PD Dr. Dr., has his venia legendi for sociology from the University of Karlsruhe, Germany. He studied sociology, history, and philosophy. He took his doctorates in psychology at the University of Bremen and in sociology at the University of Duisburg, both Germany.

Fields of research: His main interests are social change and sociological theory, especially the reconstruction of the cultural history of mankind by developmental-cognitive approaches. His own approach is called »Structure-Genetic Sociology«, applying developmental psychology as a micro-sociological basis for the explanation of long-term and historical changes.

Books: *Zivilisation und Strukturgenese*, Frankfurt/Main 2000; *Entwicklung der Weltgesellschaft: Von der Steinzeit zur Moderne*, Münster/Hamburg 2005; *Kulturelle Evolution des Geistes: Die historische Wechselwirkung von Psyche und Gesellschaft*, Münster/Hamburg 2006; *Mental Growth of Humankind in History*, Norderstedt 2009; *The Steps of Man Towards Civilization*, Norderstedt 2011.

Jörn Rüsen, Senior Fellow at the Kulturwissenschaftliches Institut (Institute for Advanced Study in the Humanities) at Essen; Professor emeritus for General History and Historical Culture at the University of Witten/Herdecke, head of the research project (2006–2009) on »Humanism in the era of globalisation – an intercultural dialogue on culture, humanity, and values« at the Kulturwissenschaftliches Institut in Essen.

Fields of research: theory and methodology of history, history of historiography, strategies of intercultural comparison, general issues of cultural orientation and intercultural communication in modern societies; humanism in a globalizing world.

Books: *Zerbrechende Zeit*, Cologne 2001; *Geschichte im Kulturprozeß*, Cologne 2002; *Kann Gestern besser werden?*, Berlin 2003; *History: Narration – Interpretation – Orientation*, New York 2005; *New Ways of Historical Thinking* (Chinese), Shanghai 2005; *Kultur macht Sinn,* Cologne 2006.

Edited: *Western Historical Thinking: An Intercultural Debate*, New York, Oxford 2002; *Meaning and Representation in History*, New York 2006; (with Henner Laass) *Humanism in Intercultural Perspective – Experiences and Expectations*, Bielefeld 2009; (with Stefan Reichmuth and Aladdin Sarhan): *Humanism and Muslim Culture: Historical Heritage and Contemporary Challenges*, Göttingen 2012.

Stephan Schmidt, Freelance writer, DFG Fellow at the Institute for Advanced Studies in Humanities and Social Sciences at National Taiwan University in Taipei (until May 2011) with a research project on Modern Confucian Thought.

Fields of Research: Intercultural Philosophy, Moral Philosophy, Hermeneutics, New Confucian Thought.

Books: *Die Herausforderung des Fremden*, Darmstadt 2005; Chun-Chieh Huang, *Konfuzianismus: Kontinuität und Entwicklung*, Bielefeld 2009 (translated and edited).

Volker H. Schmidt, Associate Professor of Sociology at the National University of Singapore.

Fields of research: sociology of justice, social policy (with a special emphasis on health care), social theory, and global modernization (with a special emphasis on East Asia).

Books: *Politik der Organverteilung*, Baden-Baden 1996; *Bedingte Gerechtigkeit*, Frankfurt/Main 2000.

Recently edited: *Modernity at the Beginning of the 21st Century*, Newcastle 2007.

Georg Stauth, Freelance writer, formerly Professor of Sociology, Bielefeld University (1992–1994). Fellowships and Senior Fellowships e.g. in Oxford (St. Antony's College 1988-1990), Singapore (NUS 1990-1992), Adelaide (Flinders Univerity 1985) Geelong/Melbourne

(Deakin University, 1994–1996), University of Mainz (2000–2008) and at the KWI, Institute of Advanced Study in the Humanities, in Essen, 2003–2006 and also at Universities in Egypt (latest Ain Shams Univ. 2010). He serves at the Advisory Board of ›*Theory, Culture and Society*‹ (from 1984 on) and is the joint founder of the ›*Yearbook of the Sociology of Islam*‹ (1998–2008). Recent main Books: *Politics and Cultures of Islamization in Southeast Asia*, Bielefeld 2002; *Ägyptische heilige Orte*, vol. I-III, Bielefeld 2005-2010; *Herausforderung Ägypten*, Bielefeld 2010.

Ernst Wolff, Professor of philosophy at the University of Pretoria and Fellow of the *Kulturwissenschaftliches Institut* (Institute for Advanced Study in the Humanities) in Essen.

Fields of research: Social and political philosophy, philosophy of technology, phenomenological hermeneutics.

Books: *Political Responsibility for a Globalised World*, Bielefeld 2011; *De l'éthique à la justice*, Dordrecht 2007.

Zhang Jie, Professor, is Dean of the School of Foreign Languages and Cultures, Nanjing Normal University.

Fields of research: Western literary criticism and theories and Russian literary studies.

He has published e.g.: *Study of Polytonal Novel Theory*, Guilin 1992; *Exploration into the World*, Guilin 1993; *History of Russian Literary Criticism in the 20th Century*, Nanjing 2000.

Index of Names